MODERN SCIENCE IN THE BIBLE

MODERN
SCIENCE
IN THE BIBLE

Amazing Scientific Truths
Found in Ancient Texts

BEN HOBRINK

HOWARD BOOKS
A DIVISION OF SIMON & SCHUSTER, INC.
New York · Nashville · London · Toronto · Sydney

Howard Books
A Division of Simon & Schuster, Inc.
1230 Avenue of the Americas
New York, NY 10020

First Howard Books hardcover edition February 2011

HOWARD and colophon are trademarks of Simon & Schuster, Inc.

For information about special discounts for bulk purchases, please contact Simon & Schuster Special Sales at 1-866-506-1949 or business@simonandschuster.com.

The Simon & Schuster Speakers Bureau can bring authors to your live event. For more information or to book an event, contact the Simon & Schuster Speakers Bureau at 1-866-248-3049 or visit our website at www.simonspeakers.com.

Designed by Renata Di Biase

Manufactured in the United States of America

10 9 8 7 6 5 4 3 2 1

Library of Congress Cataloging-in-Publication Data
Hobrink, Ben.
Modern science in the Bible : amazing scientific truths found in ancient texts / Ben Hobrink.
    p. cm.
Includes bibliographical references.
1. Bible and science. I. Title.
BS650.H57   2011
220.8'5—dc22   2010025572

ISBN 978-1-4391-0892-5
ISBN 978-1-4391-6694-9 (ebook)

CONTENTS

PREFACE

The Bible is not a textbook written to teach us physics, biology, or astronomy. It is a book that tells us about the relationship between God and mankind. Still there is no other book from antiquity that contains so many scientifically well-founded assertions as the Bible.

Interwoven in the Jewish and Christian religions is an abundance of objective and verifiable facts about history and science. This cannot be said of any other religion. Only in the twentieth century have we discovered how scientifically correct all these facts are. Christians do not have to tie themselves in all sorts of knots in order to defend the credibility of the Bible; they are not left "with their backs to the wall." On the contrary, the only thing one has to do is carefully study the *details* in science and in the Bible. Then in many cases this book is shown to be 3,500 years ahead of science.

The scientific facts in the Bible are only mentioned in passing. This makes sense, because, after all, it is a *spiritual* book, a book that addresses mankind's relationship with God. This makes it all the more striking that so many facts testify to a deep scientific insight. And if even such passing remarks are true and important for our physical well-being, how important must be the essential, spiritual message! This means that you cannot simply put this book aside as a "collection of fairy tales." No, it has something to say that is important for your *eternal* well-being.

To date, hundreds of books have been written about the spiritual significance of the laws in the Bible. And all this significance remains valid. But the book you are now holding seeks to emphasize the scientific *facts* in the Bible.

I have not written this book to prove the existence of God or the inerrancy of the Bible but to share with you my amazement at this remarkable book. The Bible is a book full of facts, that people in antiquity could not possibly have known empirically. I believe that as our scientific knowledge increases, dozens more facts will be discovered that demonstrate that the Bible was actually written by God Himself.

The Bible does not contain reports of scientific research,
nor reports about experimental testing,
but it does indeed contain the corresponding
conclusions and recommendations.

Hence the title
Modern Science in the Bible.

1.

Modern Science
in the Bible?

In my first year as a biology student during a lunch break, the conversation turned to scientific blunders in the Bible. A fellow student poked fun by recounting the biological slip in Leviticus 11:6: "The rabbit, though it chews the cud, does not have a split hoof; it is unclean for you." A rabbit that chews the cud? Ridiculous! Rabbits don't chew the cud. That's only done by ruminants, such as cows, sheep, goats, antelope, deer, giraffes, and camels. They digest their food a second time, but not animals such as hares and rabbits!

I was at a loss for words. I believed what the Bible said was true, but I didn't have an answer, certainly not as a *biology* student. For the rest of the break, they all had a good laugh. Only years later did I find the answer to his taunt.[1] A rabbit does indeed digest its food twice. Not in the way a sheep or a cow does, but through reingestion it regularly eats its own excrement and therefore does ingest its food a second time.

Another instance when a scientific fact from the Bible made a deep impression on me was when I read about the circumcision of Jewish boys.[2] It appears that men who were circumcised as infants don't suffer from penile cancer and have about ten times fewer infections of the urine passages than uncircumcised men.

Even more surprising is the significance of the *day* on which Jewish boys are to be circumcised. In Leviticus 12:3 it states that circumcision must take place precisely on the eighth day of life. Circumcision on the eighth day was so important that it took precedence over all other commandments. Even if the eighth day fell on the Sabbath or a major festival, the baby boy still had to be circumcised. Only in the twentieth century was it revealed that the eighth day specifically is the best day in life on which to perform circumcision. On that day bleeding stops much more quickly than on any other day in a person's life.

The third instance, and what led to the writing of this book, is the account of the construction of Noah's ark (Genesis 6:14–16). The ark has been shown to be the best and *most stable* design of vessel.[3] The dimensions and proportions in length, width, and height are the most ideal for a seagoing vessel not driven by a sail or engine. Large ships are still built in accordance with this design. Compared with Noah's ark, the vessels mentioned in other accounts of the Flood around the world are extremely primitive and unscientific. For example, in the Babylonian account of the Flood (the *Gilgamesh Epic*), the main character, Utanapishtim, survives the Flood in a cube-shaped boat. This happens to be the *least stable* design of vessel. While at sea, it will gradually start to roll over the waves. It's not difficult to distinguish which of the two accounts of the Flood is the more plausible and more scientifically well founded.

Only in our times are we beginning to understand something about the dietary and hygiene laws mentioned in the Bible. Only recently have we become aware of the many scientific facts in the realms of physics, geology, astronomy, shipbuilding, and so forth—facts the writers of the Bible, humanly speaking, could not have known. I believe that as our knowledge expands, we'll discover even more facts in agreement with the claims of the Bible.

SCIENCE IN THE TIME OF MOSES

Babylon and Egypt are the cradle of Western science. Fifteen hundred years before Christ, science in these countries was at a higher level than in any other country in the world. The Babylonians invented the wheel, and they were well versed in astronomy and mathematics. They divided the night sky into constellations and described the courses of the planets. It's thanks to them that a circle has 360 degrees and that our clock is divided into twelve hours and an hour into sixty minutes. The Egyptians were the first to have a solar calendar with 365 days, and they were also very adept in astronomy and mathematics. In the sixteenth century before Christ, they already had comprehensive textbooks about medicine and medical instruments.[4]

The "Holy Books" of 1552 BC are well known among Egyptologists. These books contain the essence of all human wisdom known at the time. In 1872, Professor Georg Ebers got hold of one of these books, which is now known as the Papyrus Ebers. It contains over eight hundred remedies and prescriptions for a variety of ailments (for example, how a fractured bone should be put in splints or how to treat a wound). The anatomical knowledge of the Egyptians was at an amazingly high level. But the cause of any illness or what should be done to cure it was completely unknown. The strangest and most revolting medicines were recommended: the head of the electric eel, cat's dung, guts of the goose, tail of a mouse, the eyes of a pig, milk of a woman, semen of a man.[5] Some simple prescriptions:

Removing embedded splinters:

Worms' blood—cook and crush in oil.
Mole—kill, cook, and drain in oil.
Asses' dung—mix in fresh milk.
Apply to the opening.

Healing an open wound:

Place cow's fat or cow's meat on the wound in order to ripen it.
Crush human excrement in yeast of sweet beer, sefet oil, and
    honey.
Apply as a poultice.[6]

Success was always assured. The splinters could easily be removed after a few days, having become loose by time anyway. The fact that the patient died a few days later from tetanus, because of tetanus bacteria in the asses' dung, didn't detract from the efficacy of the medicine. If any of you readers have ever complained about the treatment of open wounds in hospitals nowadays, you can be thankful you didn't live at the time of the pharaohs ...

An extra-special dressing for beautiful, long hair, made for Queen Schesch:

Heel of an Abyssinian greyhound—1 part
Date blossoms—1 part
Asses' hooves—1 part
Carefully boil in oil and then rub in.[7]

Remedy for dyeing gray hairs:

Hoof of an ass, roasted
Vulva of a bitch
A black tapeworm
And the uauit worm, which is found in dung
The whole cooked in oil and gum and rubbed well into the scalp.[8]

The queen's remedy for hair growth was "top quality" and probably as effective as the best hair growth remedies of our time. The very mention of the latter potion was enough to have the hair cells change their color out of sheer fright.

The fame of the Egyptian doctors spread throughout the world. The Greek poet Homer wrote around 850 BC, "Egypt . . . there every man is a physician, wise above human kind."[9] Despite the ancients' astounding anatomical knowledge, all illnesses were attributed to gods or demons. The therapies were magical formulas and rituals to appease these gods and demons.[10] The Egyptians were well able to *describe* the symptoms of an illness, but their methods to *prevent* or *heal* the ailment didn't get much further than tossing about bones, casting spells, and applying filthy concoctions to the place of the infection. The same applied to the medicine of the Babylonians. This remained the predominant approach to medicine for the next three thousand years.

The most eminent physician of the thirteenth century, Gilbertus Anglicus (Gilbert of England, 1170–1230), wrote that when treating a wounded nerve, it should first be cut across to relieve pain and prevent lockjaw (tetanus) and that a mixture of earthworms and oil beaten together should be applied. Another famous physician, Antonio Scarpa of Italy (1752–1832), stated that the eyes of a young woman dying of smallpox should be burst.[11] In its Proceedings of 1651, the Royal College of Physicians and Surgeons of London described as a medication: swallows' nest, horn of a stag and a unicorn, powder of an Egyptian mummy, excrement, etc.[12]

THE UNIQUENESS OF THE LAWS OF MOSES

During the heyday in Egypt, Moses lived as a prince in Pharaoh's court. Around 1500 BC he studied at the best university in the world and was "educated in all the wisdom of the Egyptians" (Acts 7:22). No doubt he studied the "Holy Books" of 1552 BC, but it's striking that in his writings, *no* mention is made of incantations, demons, or strange and deadly ways of treating diseases.

Moses didn't adopt the teachings of his professors indiscriminately. On the contrary, he gave his people a serious warning to follow only the commands of Yahweh and not the prescriptions of Egypt (see Leviticus 18:1–5). This means that you won't find any medical mistakes in the Pentateuch. Moses had such great faith in God that he put aside all the wisdom of Egypt and simply recorded the instructions of God.

If Moses had followed the counsel of his learned professors, we would find in his writings recommendations such as "crush the heel of an Abyssinian greyhound" or "make a salve of dog's excrement and flies and apply it to the wound." Nothing of the kind. Right at the start of the Bible (see Genesis 1:1), Moses contradicts all the scholars of Egypt. The Egyptians had bizarre views about the origins of the earth: the earth hatched from a winged egg that flew around in space,[13] and mankind emerged from white worms that were found in the slime of the Nile.[14] But Moses was not influenced by this and wrote, "God created the heavens and the earth," and "God created man" (Genesis 1:1, 27). In all his writings, Moses maintained this distance from his teachers.

SOCIAL LAWS AND THE
LANGUAGE OF THE BIBLE

In evaluating the scientific facts in the Bible, we have to bear in mind that there is a great difference between the worldview of the Old Testament and the worldview of our modern day. In Western society, we make a clear distinction between physical life and spiritual life. In the Old Testament, there's no such distinction between a happy life on earth and a happy life in heaven. The rules in the Bible are intended to bring about the health and happiness of the *entire* being—both in heaven and on earth. For God, rules referring to both spheres are equally important. This is the reason why in the books of Moses, the social and spiritual laws are intermingled.

In the Torah,* there are relatively few sacrificial laws (twenty-two chapters) that relate only to spiritual life. Most of the laws are social laws (thirty-two chapters), directed toward daily life. These laws are also referred to as ethical or moral laws. Besides these laws, there are eighteen chapters about the construction of the tabernacle and 115 chapters (including Genesis) about the history of the people of Israel.

Some of the social laws are easily recognizable, such as the rights of slaves and of the weak in society (see Exodus 20–23). But a large number of these social laws aren't readily distinguishable, because they are presented in a religious guise.

---

* The first five books of the Bible were written by Moses. In Greek, they are referred to as the Pentateuch (five books) and in Hebrew as the Torah (instruction). The fact that Moses was indeed the writer of the Torah we will deal with in chapter seven.

	History	Social laws	Tabernacle	Sacrificial laws
Exodus	1–19, 24, 32–34	20–23	25–31, 35–40	
Leviticus		11–15, 17–20, 25	8–10	1–7, 16, 21–24, 26–27
Numbers	1–4, 9–19, 19–34	5, 19, 30, 35–36	7–8	6, 15, 18, 28–29
Deuteronomy	1–4, 6–11, 27–34	5, 13–15, 17–25		12, 16, 26
Number of chapters	65	32	18	22

Global overview of the four books of the Law of Moses. Exodus 1–Numbers 19 was written at the beginning of the journey through the desert, and Numbers 19–Deuteronomy 34 after the journey, about thirty-eight years later.

SOCIAL LAWS IN A RELIGIOUS GUISE

There are at least two reasons why many social laws in the Bible are presented in a religious guise. (By this I mean that the everyday, practical laws are described as if they were strict religious principles.)

First, without the threat of curse and punishment, the Israelites would never have obeyed the laws of God. No scientific argument would have convinced them. It would have sounded like nonsense in their ears, as it would to the peoples who lived after them. In Europe, this was the case until the end of the Middle Ages, and in lesser-developed countries, it continues to be the case today.

Secondly, the Israelites would certainly not have been satisfied serving the invisible God, Yahweh, in a purely "spiritual" way, without rules and symbols. Mankind needs rules and symbols in life. The Israelites were all too eager to make a golden calf and to have idols, for the simple reason that they wanted to have tangible gods like the neighboring peoples (see Exodus 32). Much of the religious packaging in the Bible is a concession on God's part to mankind's need for something tangible in the faith, to be able to make concrete sacrifices. According to many rabbis, God did not command animal sacrifices because they had any value in themselves, but because otherwise the Israelites would have become involved in idolatry and human sacrifice.[15]

What is important to God is not the ceremonies and sacrifices, but the spiritual and physical well-being of mankind.[†] God said to the Israelites, "For in the day that I brought them out of the land of Egypt, I did not speak to your fathers or command them concerning burnt offerings and sacrifices. But this command I gave them, 'Obey my voice . . . that it may be well with you.'" (Jeremiah 7:22–23 RSV). At the beginning of the Israelites' journey through the wilderness, God did not speak about offerings and sacrifices. He just told the people to obey Him, and that to their benefit. But such a simple commandment was not enough for the Israelites. They needed strict rules to keep them in line, in order for them to live healthy lives.

The words of the Lord Jesus also reveal that the religious aspects of the Law were not as important as some people might think. Although the dietary laws of the Old Testament are particularly strict, still Jesus said, "Nothing outside a man can make him 'unclean' by going into him" (Mark 7:15). By this He didn't mean to say that from then on all foodstuffs were healthy. Of course not; it was still best to live in accordance with the dietary laws of the Old Testament. But Jesus meant that the religious aspects of these laws were not nearly as important as the Jews thought. The same applies to the Sabbath rest, the requirement to do no work one day of the week. The purpose of this law is not to teach people blind obedience, but to provide time to rest, time to stop rushing around, and to enjoy life (see Mark 2:27). These and other examples show that the health aspects in the Bible are far more important than some might realize. It wasn't God's intention to keep men and women only spiritually and morally pure. God had a greater goal in mind: the total health of men and women, both spiritual *and* physical.

---

† Many of the offerings and sacrificial laws have also a deeper, spiritual meaning. They are a foreshadowing of the work of Jesus Christ. We will go into this in more detail in chapter seven.

The Language of the Bible

Another point we must bear in mind is that the Bible wasn't written in scientific language or with a scientific goal. Otherwise it would soon be out-of-date and would be incomprehensible to most people. No, the Bible speaks in the language of the everyday and in the language of what we see.

In daily life everyone speaks in an unscientific way. We still say "the sun comes up" or "the sun goes down," although we know that it is not the sun that moves but Earth. When navigating a ship, we still act as if the sun and stars move around the earth. If you set course in this way, you know exactly where you'll end up. And this is what's important, not whether your use of language is scientifically accurate.

An erudite professor is particularly admired if he can explain difficult subjects in everyday language. But if the Bible does so, for many people it suddenly becomes unreliable!

The Bible does not teach us a worldview at all. Its intention is *not* to teach us cosmology or the like. The aim of the Bible is to point us to the life and death of Jesus Christ and to tell us how we can come into contact with God.

The biblical accounts are presented from the perspective of ordinary, everyday people. They explain in everyday language things that are indeed reliable—even things concerning biology, geology, physics, or astronomy. The Bible was written at a specific time; its language may reflect a certain era, but the content and the lessons we can learn from it are valid for all time.

SUMMARY

At the time of Moses, science in Egypt and Babylon was at a higher level than in any other country in the world. And yet the understanding of the prevention and cure of diseases didn't go any further than primitive superstition, incantations, and the application of filthy concoctions. In the Bible, there's nothing of this primitive superstition to be found. Nor are any of the medical and scientific blunders of the Egyptians and Babylonians found within the pages of the Bible.

Although the Bible focuses on the spiritual aspects of our existence, the information it gives proves to be reliable in every area of life. Many people have an incorrect view of the Bible, because they aren't used to thinking in a holistic way (comprising the whole of life); and also because the Bible isn't written in scientific language, but in the sometimes flowery terms of the vernacular.

For some Westerners it may be confusing that in the books of Moses spiritual and social laws are intermingled and many social laws are given a religious guise. Careful investigation reveals that there are two important reasons for this: To start with, at the time, a "religious guise" was the only way to force people to obey. No scientific argument whatsoever would have convinced them. Secondly, it seems that for God, social life is as important as spiritual life. God isn't so much interested in all sorts of ceremonies and sacrifices but is much more interested in the *total well-being of mankind*.

For I know the plans I have for you, . . .
plans to prosper you and not to harm you,
plans to give you hope and a future.

JEREMIAH 29:11

2.

COUNTERING EPIDEMICS

It is hard for us to imagine the primitive living conditions of people from the time of Moses until the late Middle Ages. Today in Western society we have ensconced ourselves in comfortable houses, each with a refrigerator and a stove in the kitchen, a deep freeze and a washing machine in the utility room, a vacuum cleaner and an iron, hot and cold running water, a bathroom with plumbing, and a variety of cleaning agents. We can read hundreds of books and magazines about food and health. Besides this, the authorities safeguard the quality of our food. If something does go wrong, the doctor (generally) can give good advice.

When Moses wrote the laws in Exodus, Leviticus, and Numbers, the Israelites were facing a forty-year journey through the desert, a journey in extremely primitive conditions. There was no water for washing, hardly any firewood to cook with, no refrigerators, no medicine. Temperatures were above 100 degrees, and there were all sorts of creatures on their path and in their tents at night.

When you learn about the living conditions in the land where the Israelites came from (Egypt) and where they were going to (Canaan), you're appalled; you understand much better why Moses wrote all those strict hygiene laws. You see that these laws are scientifically extremely accurate. They are an unsurpassed system of measures for good public health. The laws of Moses were not only valid in his time but retain their efficacy for all centuries and for the whole of humanity.

Later on, we will consider a few examples from the Middle Ages, but let us first see what the situation was like in Canaan, when the Israelites arrived there.

HYGIENE IN CANAAN

Archaeological research has revealed that the average life span of the Canaanites was no more than thirty years, and more than half of the people died before their eighteenth birthday.[1] In Egypt, if anything, the situation was even worse. The archaeologist Strouhal writes about this, "For ordinary people, life expectancy was about twenty to twenty-five years. . . . This was due to the poor hygiene, the wide spread of endemic [regularly occurring] diseases, the occurrence of epidemics, and the inefficacy of most medical treatments."[2]*

Unhygienic conditions in a primitive village.

---

* The quotations of Strouhal are translated from the Dutch edition of his book. The text and page numbers may differ from the English edition, which I have been unable to obtain. The same applies to quotations from Grzimek in chapters three and four.

There were really only a few people who died of old age. Most died prematurely from parasitic diseases, especially from tuberculosis and forms of helminthiasis (worms in the gastrointestinal tract, like schistosoma, trichinae, and pork tapeworm).[3] There were two major threats to the health of the people. First there were the extremely unhygienic living conditions. Secondly there was the major threat of sexually transmitted diseases. But first, let's look at contributing factors that made Canaan more susceptible to these diseases.

CROSSROADS OF THE WORLD

Canaan was at the crossroads of the world, forming a bridge between three continents: Asia to the east, Africa to the south, and Europe to the north. It was a meeting place for the highly developed civilizations from Egypt and Babylon. There was a flourishing trade along various caravan routes, such as the famous King's Highway (along the Jordan) and the Way of the Sea (along the Mediterranean coast, in most Bible translations mentioned as "The way of the land of the Philistines" Numbers 20:17 and Exodus 13:17). Across the sea, Canaan was a trade center for towns all around the Mediterranean, as well as being the connection via the Red Sea between the Mediterranean and the Indian Ocean.

As a result, the Canaanites became fabulously wealthy, with splendid houses and sophisticated art. They were the first to use an alphabet and had a wealth of fine literature.[4] Their prosperity and highly developed culture were very attractive to the Israelites.

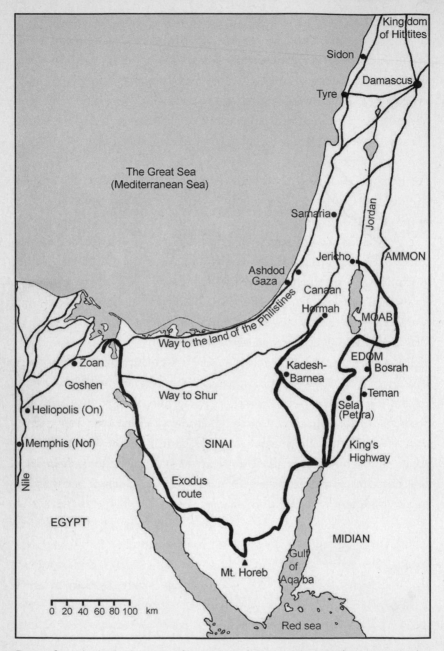

Canaan formed a bridge between Africa, Asia, and Europe. The map shows, among other things: the route the Israelites followed on their exodus from Egypt; the caravan routes along the Mediterranean coast and the Jordan; and a number of important towns, which are mentioned in the following chapters (adapted from the *New Bible Dictionary*[5]).

It can be assumed that the caravans and ships not only provided great riches, but also facilitated the spread of sexually transmitted diseases and epidemics. Throughout the centuries, ports and trading centers have notoriously been a source of immorality and perversity, in which many people have suffered from sexually transmitted diseases.

FREE SEX

The immorality of the Canaanites has become proverbial among archaeologists. Professor Unger wrote, "The erotic aspects of this cult must have sunk to extremely sordid depths of social degradation. . . . Canaanite cultic practice was barbarous and thoroughly licentious. It had a most serious retarding and debilitating effect on every phase of Canaanite culture and community life. . . . The brutality, lust, and abandon of Canaanite mythology was far worse than elsewhere in the Near East at the time . . . and entailed many of the most demoralizing practices of the time, such as sacred prostitution, child sacrifice, and snake worship."[6]

The most popular god was Baal, the god of fertility. He was sometimes depicted in the form of a bull, because of his strong sexual drive. Quite a lot is known about the daily life of the Canaanites and about their worship of Baal. This is because of the clay tablets which have been found since 1929 in the ruins of the town of Ugarit, near the Mediterranean Sea in what is now Syria. The immorality of the Canaanites is illustrated throughout their religious literature, such as the pleasure with which the goddess Anath wades up to her knees in the blood and excrement of her defeated enemies and then washes her hands in it. The blasphemous poems about the eighty-eight times she has sex with Baal in the form of a cow and the sexual escapades of the supreme deity, El, with his two wives/ daughters speak volumes.[7] Things weren't much better among the surrounding peoples. The Hittites were permitted to have sex with a horse or a mule,[8] and other peoples had no restrictions whatsoever in the area of sex.

In the Bible, too, we read about the unbridled lust of the Canaanites and about a sexual orgy in honor of Baal (see Genesis 19:4–9 and Numbers 25). Their excesses were accompanied by perverse rituals.

CHILD SACRIFICE

The extremes of the immorality of the Canaanites are illustrated not only by their sexual perversity, but also by their sacrifice of children.[9] Excavations have revealed that children from three to twelve months old were burned on altars. And during the construction of a house, they were bricked alive into walls or foundations or were buried under the threshold of the house. This was done to invoke blessing and prosperity from the gods. We read about child sacrifices of the Canaanites in Deuteronomy 12:31 and in 2 Kings 3:27. In 2 Kings 16:3, Psalm 106:34–38, and Jeremiah 7:31, we read that these customs were adopted by the Israelites. It's obvious that such perversity and child sacrifice had an influence on all aspects of life. Not many ethical values would have remained intact, such as faithfulness in marriage or to the family. Not many people would have learned to care for the well-being of the weak and the sick in society.

The way of life of the Canaanites represented a serious threat to the public health of the Israelites, both on a physical level and on a spiritual level. From a medical point of view, the greatest threat lay with the parasitic diseases, which plagued the country, especially sexually transmitted diseases and plague. Diseases of this type have the greatest chance of spreading in hot countries where people have a low social status and poor hygiene—precisely the conditions in the country to which the Israelites were going. The fact that these diseases indeed had a devastating effect is revealed by the low life expectancy of around thirty years.

In our eyes, the measures to protect the people of Israel, which Moses took following God's instructions, were extremely strict. But if God hadn't commanded this, countless Israelites would have died in the most appalling conditions due to sexually transmitted diseases and deadly epidemics. Ultimately, with the strict rules, many more lives were spared than were lost in the extermination of the Canaanites.

When we read that the innocent inhabitants of Canaan had to be destroyed, it seems cruel and unjust to us (see Deuteronomy 7:1–2). But on closer inspection, it's clear that the inhabitants were not so innocent at all. Besides all their sins of perversity and corruption, it was *they* who were murdering innocent children—even their own children!

Gonorrhea

The greatest threat to public health were the sexually transmitted diseases, especially gonorrhea.[†] This disease is caused by the bacteria *Neisseria gonorrhoeae* and, after chlamydia, is the most prevalent venereal disease in the world. It's characterized by the constant discharge of an inflammatory substance from the genitals. Until 1946, when penicillin was first produced on a large scale, there was no medicine for this condition. The only thing people could do was wash the genitals regularly.

If the disease is not treated and if women are infected repeatedly with gonorrhea and chlamydia, about 25 percent become infertile.[11] Throughout the world, venereal diseases still account for almost *two thirds* of all infertility.[12] Many newborn babies who pass through the birth canal of an infected woman become blind. For this reason, in many hospitals around the world, a few drops of silver nitrate solution or antibiotic are applied to the eyes of newborns as a preventive measure. Around 1900, about 30 percent of all blindness in the world was a result of venereal diseases.[13] It can be assumed that this was the case throughout the whole of history.[‡]

Through modern treatment with antibiotics, the spread of venereal diseases in Western countries has been greatly reduced. But globally every year there are sixty-two million new cases of gonorrhea.[14] For decades in the United States, more people have been infected with chlamydia and gonorrhea than with all other contagious diseases put together (not counting the common cold).[15] From 1965 to 1977, the time of the hippies and free sex, the incidence of gonorrhea in the United States tripled, reaching one million new cases a year.[16] In 1963, the World Health

---

† We won't deal with other venereal diseases such as syphilis and chlamydia, because they are not clearly described in the Bible. But these two venereal diseases so often occur together with gonorrhea, we can assume that many gonorrhea patients had syphilis and chlamydia as well. Nowadays, up to 45 percent of gonorrhea patients suffer from chlamydia,[10] and until the beginning of the nineteenth century, syphilis was considered to be a serious form of gonorrhea. Some experts think that syphilis was first brought to Europe by sailors who returned from America with Columbus in 1493. But according to others, syphilis already occurred before this time in Europe and the Middle East.

‡ This means that there was an almost 30 percent probability that the mother of the man born blind mentioned in John 9 had a venereal disease. Hence the remark, "Who sinned, this man or his parents, that he was born blind?" was not so strange.

Organization warned that in Europe gonorrhea had "reached almost epidemic proportions" and that "the rising tide of venereal diseases has now become one of Europe's most urgent health problems."[17]

If venereal diseases claim so many victims in modern times, how many people must have been infected with gonorrhea and other venereal diseases in licentious Canaan, where sex was completely free and where no treatment for venereal diseases whatsoever was known?

COUNTERING GONORRHEA IN THE BIBLE

In Leviticus 15:2 it says, "When any man has a bodily discharge, the discharge is unclean." In the Septuagint, the Greek translation of the Old Testament, the word *gonorrhea* is used for this discharge (verses 4–13). In other words, the "discharge" does not refer to an emission of semen or to a wound from which blood or pus flows, but it refers to a venereal disease that causes a constant excretion of fluid from the genitals. This fluid is full of bacteria and is extremely infectious, as is the sperm of the diseased.

Leviticus 15 offers measures to prevent the spread of gonorrhea. Because in those days there was no known method of early diagnosis and no known cure for venereal disease, these preventive measures were the *only* way of averting an epidemic. If we study the details, it becomes apparent that we aren't dealing with primitive or random measures, but a finely tuned insight into bacteriology. Moses describes measures for three groups of people: (a) "healthy" people, (b) people suffering from gonorrhea, and (c) defeated enemies.

MEASURES FOR "HEALTHY" PEOPLE

Emission of Semen

All men were—rightly—considered to be potential carriers of venereal disease. When a man had an emission of semen, he was to wash his body, and he remained unclean until the evening (see v. 16). If during an ejaculation any semen got onto an item of clothing or a piece of leather, the same applied: the item of clothing or leather was to be washed thoroughly and remained unclean until the evening (see v. 17).

Sexual Intercourse

After sexual intercourse, both the man and the woman were to wash their bodies, and they remained unclean until the evening (see v. 18). This means that both objects and persons remained unclean until the evening because of contact with semen. If any bacteria remained after washing (people didn't have such showers and washing machines as we do), they would yet be killed during the course of the day by the aridity and the bright sunlight.

MEASURES FOR PEOPLE SUFFERING FROM GONORRHEA

Discharge

If a man had a bodily discharge, that's to say, was infected with gonorrhea, he was unclean, and so was everything he touched. This was the case even if he hadn't had a seminal discharge or had sexual intercourse with his wife. His bed, chair, saddle, drinking cup, tools, and everything he touched were considered unclean. Everyone who touched him or any of these objects also became unclean, had to wash their bodies and clothes, and remained unclean until the evening. Objects made of leather, wood, or metal had to be thoroughly washed. Objects of clay had to be broken. This was because bacteria cannot be washed out of porous clay (see vv. 4–12, 17).

A number of years ago, a homeopathic doctor warned of the transmission of gonorrhea through contaminated objects: "Great caution and cleanliness are required, because it still occurs that little girls whose mother is suffering from gonorrhea sleep in the same bed, use her flannels and towels and in this way are infected."[18]

Spittle

"If the man with the discharge spits on someone, . . . that person . . . will be unclean" (v. 8). Research has revealed that the mouth of a gonorrhea patient (who often has syphilis and chlamydia as well) may be severely contaminated with infectious bacteria, especially after oral sex.

Danger of Epidemic

During the journey through the desert, no one with gonorrhea was allowed to live in the camp (see Numbers 5:2), or later to attend the major festivals in Jerusalem. His relatives were allowed to live with him, with all the above-mentioned restrictions, but he wasn't allowed to live in the camp or come close to the temple. During the major festivals, hundreds of thousands of people gathered around the temple, which meant close contact was sometimes unavoidable while sleeping or washing. The danger of infection was all the greater because Easterners touch, embrace, and kiss one another much more frequently than Westerners. With syphilis in particular, it's known that in such circumstances epidemics can very easily break out.

MEASURES REGARDING DEFEATED ENEMIES

Peoples in Canaan

When enemies were defeated in the land of Canaan, *all* the men and *all* the women, including their children, were to be killed (see Deuteronomy 20:16). The risk of venereal diseases (remember all those ports and towns on the caravan routes) and the temptation to adopt their way of life were too great.

Peoples Surrounding Canaan

When enemies were defeated just outside Canaan, *all* the men, boys, and the *married* women were to be killed, but young girls were allowed to live (see Numbers 31:17–18). This was because young girls hadn't yet had sexual relations and so weren't infected with gonorrhea or other sexually transmitted diseases.

Peoples at a Very Great Distance

When enemies were defeated "at a very great distance," it was only *all the men* who had to be killed. All the women and children were allowed to live, including the women who had had sexual relations. The probability that they were infected with a venereal disease was much less than among the women in Canaan. The women could be taken away by the soldiers, who were allowed to make them their wives (see Deuteronomy 20:13–15).

THREE UNUSUAL CONDITIONS

But if the Israelite soldiers were to have sexual relations with the women-folk of the enemies they had defeated, of course there was still a danger for public health. Not only concerning gonorrhea and other venereal diseases, but also regarding other contagious diseases. This is why there were three extremely unusual—and scientifically justified—conditions for taking away the women who were captured (see Deuteronomy 21:10–14).

a. *Isolation*—First the woman had to live in isolation outside the main camp of Israel for seven days, just like the soldiers who returned from war (see Numbers 31:19). Seven days was long enough to see whether she had gonorrhea or another illness. The incubation period (the time between infection and outbreak) of gonorrhea, and almost all other contagious diseases, is two to seven days.[19] If the woman was infected, then the same rules applied to her as to other infected persons, which we have read in the previous pages. If she wasn't infected, she was allowed to be taken into the house of her new master, but only when she had fulfilled the next two conditions.

b. *Washing*—After seven days, the woman had to wash herself and all the washable objects that had been taken from her house, such as linen clothing, objects of leather, wood, goat's hair, and so forth. Everything that could be purified by fire, such as gold, silver, copper, and iron had to go through the fire (see Numbers 31:22–23). These were remarkably effective measures. Besides the Israelites, there were no other people on earth who regularly washed themselves. This meant that the bodies, clothing, and utensils of defeated enemies were often reeking with germs.

c. *Cutting hair and nails*—The woman had to shave her head, cut her nails, put aside her clothing (probably burning it), and remain in isolation within the home for a month. The logic: clothes of people who seldom or never wash themselves are full of germs; and hair and nails are the greatest repositories of bacteria on the body, particularly in unhygienic conditions. A doctor writes, "The hair, face, axilla, and groin usually harbor the greatest number of bacteria.... The greatest number of organisms on the hands are found around and under the fingernails."[20] A report by the Dutch Health Council states, "The hair is a source of infection, about which people are too little aware. The fact that nurses have to have short nails for reasons of hygiene goes without saying."[21] The same points can be found in the latest guidelines of the World Health Organization.[22]

How is it possible that the Bible is able to prescribe such detailed and accurate measures—and that 3,500 years ago? These regulations are so good that it's impossible to improve on them without modern resources.

EPIDEMICS IN THE MIDDLE AGES

They were golden times, the Middle Ages. Noble knights with hearts of gold, who fought to defend justice and fair maidens. Tournaments with lances and chain mail on snorting horses in virgin forests. In the evenings, great feasts in splendid castles with ladies who had little else to do than get bored and turn men's heads. A wonderful time, about which many a novel and television series has been written and about which the schoolmaster could recount so appealingly. So was the life of the privileged nobility.

But for the masses, the reality was quite different. In the Middle Ages, most people lived in appalling conditions. In the towns, the situation was a good deal worse than in the villages and in the countryside. It was a big mess, without any hygiene whatsoever. Erasmus once wrote that the floors of the homes were strewn with an ancient collection of "beer, grease, fragments, and everything nasty."[23] People never washed. They relieved themselves right in the unpaved streets. If people did have a toilet (and used it), the full receptacle was usually emptied into the same street where the children played and the rats found their food. Billions of flies gorged themselves on the great stacks of refuse and excrement. The pigs and dogs happily gobbled up everything that turned up under their snouts—rotten food, excrement, dead rats, anything that no longer moved, sometimes even corpses. When the mess got too bad, the people left their village and went to live somewhere else. Or they knocked their village down, set the lot on fire, threw sand over it, and built a new village on top of it.

Because of the unhealthy conditions, many people were sickly and died a premature death. Besides this, millions of people died a miserable death through epidemics that suddenly sprang up and for which there was no remedy. The two worst scourges of the time were leprosy and plague.

Leprosy

Leprosy (also known as Hansen's disease) is caused by the bacteria *Mycobacterium leprae*. The victims don't die of it, but because the patients feel no pain, their bodies are wounded very easily, especially the face and the hands. If the injuries are not treated in a hygienic way, they become infected and the affected part slowly rots away. This creates a terrible stench of rotting flesh.

Leprosy occurs all over the world, but especially in poor countries, where people live in close proximity in unhygienic conditions. The number of lepers in the world has been reduced considerably in the last hundred years, but twenty years ago, still over ten million people were suffering from this terrible disease.[24]

Leprosy was known in India as early as six centuries before Christ. In the fourth century BC, the disease reached southern Europe, and from there it spread all over the Continent. During the sixth and seventh centuries AD, leprosy was common in Europe and became a huge social problem. This reached a terrible climax at the beginning of the fourteenth century. Dr. Rosen, a professor of public health, writes, "Leprosy was the great blight that threw its shadow over the daily life of medieval humanity. Fear of all other diseases taken together can hardly be compared to the terror created by leprosy. Not even the Black Death in the fourteenth century or the appearance of syphilis toward the end of the fifteenth century produced a similar state of fright."[25]

What could doctors do to curb the devastation of leprosy? Some of them thought the disease was caused by eating pepper, garlic, food that was too hot, or by eating the meat of diseased pigs.[26] Others thought it was a punishment from God. Obviously their methods of treatment proved fruitless. In some towns, lepers were made to live in isolation because of the stench and their horrifying appearance. But it never occurred to a single doctor that the disease could have been prevented by applying large-scale protective measures as prescribed in the Bible. Because people didn't know God and His Word, or were too stubborn to obey it, there was unnecessary suffering in the world. Professor Rosen writes, "Leadership was taken by the Church, as the physicians had nothing to offer. The Church took as its guiding principle the concept of contagion embodied in the Old Testament. . . . Once the condition had been established, the patient was to be segregated and excluded from the community. . . . Following the precepts laid down in Leviticus, the Church undertook the task of combating leprosy. . . . It accomplished the first great feat in direct prophylaxis [action to prevent disease], namely methodical eradication of a disease."[27] Another professor of medical history writes, "The laws against leprosy in Leviticus 13 may be regarded as the first model of a sanitary legislation."[28]

Banished from Society

In the Bible, we read about an unknown disease, that in Hebrew is called *zara'ath*. This is usually translated as "leprosy," but it would be better to use the general term "skin disease," as in the New International Version. According to the symptoms described, various infectious diseases might be included under zara'ath, such as syphilis, but also actual leprosy.

The biblical measures to prevent the spread of zara'ath were extremely progressive, particularly if we consider them in the context of actual leprosy: "Command the Israelites to send away from the camp anyone who has an infectious skin disease," and "As long as he has the infection he remains unclean. He must live alone; he must live outside the camp" (Numbers 5:2; Leviticus 13:46). To us it seems obvious that lepers should be "sent away from the camp," but until just over a hundred years ago, there were strong protests about this. Only when lepers were separated from society, if necessary by force, and made to live in leper colonies, was the number of lepers drastically reduced.

In 1856 there were still 2,858 lepers living in Norway, along the North Sea coast, and particularly around the town of Bergen. Initially the lepers simply lived among the general population. They made a living by selling their wares at the market and going from door to door as peddlers. In this way, they unwittingly contributed to the spread of the disease. When the government opened special hospitals for them and isolated them from the population at large, their numbers began to decrease. When in 1891 the lepers were forced to live in *complete* isolation, there was a great protest, and disturbances occurred. But their number continued to decrease drastically. In 1930, even before medication for leprosy was discovered, their number had been reduced to 2 percent of the lepers who had lived in Norway before isolation—a fiftyfold reduction within eighty years.[29]

Remarkable Detail

Leprosy isn't dangerous in Western society, because it can be halted by medication. But many people wrongly think that the disease isn't contagious at all. In the active stage, it certainly is. Infection primarily occurs through inhaling the bacteria, that's to say through breathing them in or swallowing them.[30] As long as the medical staff and patients ensure good hygiene, clean hands, clean clothing, and fresh air, there's not much danger of contagion. A doctor who works among leprosy patients writes: "In the prevention of the transmission of leprosy . . . instruction should always be given to a patient . . . on how to dispose of his nose blowings, and also his sputum, in a hygienic manner."[31]

With this knowledge in mind, we suddenly understand the strange instruction in Leviticus 13:45 about what the leper should do if he encountered healthy citizens: "The person with such an infectious disease must . . . cover the lower part of his face and cry out, 'Unclean! Unclean!'"

The leper had to cover the lower part of his face, that's to say his nostrils and mouth—from which the infectious bacteria issue—just as a surgeon puts a mask over his nose to stop the spread of bacteria. Besides this, the leper had to tear his clothes and leave his hair unkempt, so that he could be recognized at a great distance as a leper and wouldn't accidentally infect someone through the air if he had a cold and happened to cough or sneeze.

Karl Sudhoff, a professor of medical history, writes about his deep admiration for the practical laws in the Bible: "The 13th and 14th . . . chapters of [Leviticus] are weighty official documents in the history of preventative medicine which deserve to be written in letters of radiant gold, which . . . were destined to be the germ of our modern prophylaxis against infectious diseases."[32]

THE BLACK DEATH

Another plague that really made the "dark" Middle Ages dark was the Black Death, or bubonic plague, which is caused by the bacterium *Yersinia (Pasteurella) pestis*. The name Black Death was coined because this disease caused hemorrhages to occur under the skin, visible as black marks. In the Middle Ages, there were various epidemics of the plague, but the worst was in the fourteenth century. The sources of the epidemic were marmots in the Gobi Desert in Mongolia.[§] After the disease broke out at the end of the 1320s, it was transmitted by black rats and the rat flea (*Xenopsylla cheopis*) to people in Mongolia, and the Mongolian hordes ensured a quick spread to the farthest corners of the continent. The food transports of the

---

§ The plague is a contagious disease, which is spread by rodents, such as rats, mice, and marmots. But the plague can also be spread by hares and rabbits, which aren't rodents but lagomorphs, a completely separate order (see also pages 72–73 of this book).[33]

Mongolian army, in particular, were an ideal means of spreading the rats with their fleas all over the world. A second means of transmission were the caravans that traveled from the Far East to Europe with silk and valuable furs. In September 1345, the Black Death reached the town of Kaffa, now Feodosiya, on the Black Sea.

The story goes that in 1343, Italian merchants in Kaffa got into a dispute with the Muslim traders in the city. The Muslims called on the local Mongol leader, Jani Beg, for help; he surrounded the Italian quarter of the city and fired on it with catapults. During the three-year siege, the plague broke out among the Mongols. Jani Beg then gave the order to fire the victims over the wall with catapults. The plague then broke out among the Italians as well, who subsequently fled home in their ships in panic.[34]

It's not completely certain whether the story is true, but it is known that the Italians, and more specifically the rats, mice, and fleas on their ships, brought the plague from Kaffa to Italy. In October 1347, the plague reached the city of Messina on the island of Sicily. In December, the plague reached the south of the Italian peninsula, and in 1348, mainland Europe. It's estimated that between 1348 and 1351 over a quarter of the population of Europe died from the plague. Some accounts even speak of 50 percent. In many towns, nine out of ten inhabitants died.

In other areas, such as China, India, and the Middle East, the same percentage of victims succumbed. In Europe, probably twenty-five million people died, and throughout the world, sixty to seventy-five million: a quarter of the world population.[35] It was the greatest disaster in history ever to strike mankind. People fled out of the towns in panic. Fathers and mothers left behind their children. "Sweeping everything before it, this terrible plague brought panic and confusion in its train and broke down all restrictions of morality, decency, and humanity. Parents, children, and lifelong friends forsook one another, every one striving to save only himself. . . . The dead were hurled pell-mell into huge pits, hastily dug for the purpose, and putrefying bodies lay about everywhere in the houses and streets. . . . The sexton and the physician were cast into the same deep and wide grave; the testator and his heirs and executors were hurled from the same cart into the same hole together."[36]

Doctors could do nothing for the victims. All their purgatives, bloodlettings, and leeches didn't help one little bit. Quacks had the chance of a lifetime. According to a book with health tips from 1743, "In times of plague, one should carry Toad's Powder, or a Toad itself, or a live Spider (kept in a convenient box). In order to make Toad's Powder, take three or four large Toads, seven or eight Spiders, an equal number of Scorpions; put them in a well-sealed pot; leave them in it for a time. Add to it Virgin Wax, and close the Pot well; light a fire, so that it all melts; and make it into a Salve, which is put into a well-sealed silver box, being very well assured that as long as one carries it about one's person, the Plague will have no effect."[37]

Professors at the University of Paris thought that the conjunction (coming together) of Saturn, Jupiter, and Mars on March 20, 1345, had contaminated the air on the earth. Other scholars maintained that the warm winds from the tropics were the cause.[38] Some blamed the Jews. Christian doctors thought it was a punishment from God.

Balavignus

Only in the Jewish ghetto in Strasbourg, France, was the situation different. There a physician by the name of Balavignus had his practice. Because of his knowledge of the Bible, he came to the conclusion that the unhygienic conditions in the city were the cause of the epidemic. In 1348 he ordered that the whole Jewish quarter be cleaned and all refuse burned. He carried out everything that should be done according to the sanitation laws in the book of Leviticus. As a result of these actions, all the rats, with their fleas, left that quarter of town and went to "the heathen," because there was no longer anything to be had for them among the Jews. In the quarter where Balavignus worked, only 5 percent of the number of cases of the plague occurred, compared with the rest of the city. The inhabitants soon noticed the difference, but instead of adopting the hygienic rules of Balavignus, people immediately accused him of being one of the chief suspects in the spread of the plague in Europe.[39]

Balavignus was subjected to the most extreme torture. Mad with pain, he "confessed" that he had helped to poison the wells of the Christians and that he had received the poison from some Jews from the south of France. The poison was said to have been made from human flesh, Christians' hearts, spiders, frogs, lizards, and sacred hosts.[40] The news of Balavignus's confession spread like wildfire throughout Europe. Special messengers were sent from town to town to warn that the Jews had poisoned the air, the wells, and the springs (although the Jews were drinking from the same wells, eating the same food, and, outside Strasbourg, were suffering just as much from the plague as the "Christians").

In the years 1348 and 1349 organized massacres of Jews ensued all over Europe. Tens of thousands were slaughtered and burned. In cities such as Basel, Frankfurt, Strasbourg, and Cologne, the entire Jewish population was wiped out. Robert Gottfried writes, "By 1351, 60 major and 150 smaller Jewish communities had been extirpated, and over 350 massacres had taken place."[41] In subsequent years many Jews fled to Poland and Russia.

Quarantine

After Balavignus, other doctors also noticed that the Jewish sanitation laws were important in countering infectious diseases. One aspect was cleaning up refuse. Another aspect was good personal hygiene, such as regularly washing the body, especially after touching a corpse or impurities, such as discharges of blood or a festering wound.

If a Jew became unclean through an infectious disease, he had to observe a period of purification and isolation. This was based on the rule in Leviticus 13:4–7, which says that the priest should keep an infected patient in isolation for fourteen days and then declare whether or not he was clean. "The priest is to put the infected person in isolation for seven days. . . . He is to keep him in isolation another seven days." And in verse 46, "As long as he has the infection, he remains unclean. He must live alone; he must live outside the camp."

Doctors in Italy noticed that fewer epidemics occurred among the Jews than among the rest of the population and that this was partly due to the isolation of patients. The first doctor to institute an official quarantine was Simon de Covina, in Venice, at the time the most powerful city on earth. In the fourteenth century, Venice, just like the rest of Europe, was threatened with extinction through the many epidemics that struck the city. In 1377 Simon de Covina managed to arrange that all sailors who visited Venice had to be kept in quarantine in the town of Ragusa on Sicily for thirty days. Later this period was extended to forty days. It's from this practice that the medical term *quarantine* comes, which is derived from the Italian word *quaranta*—forty. This biblical practice soon became a government law and was made obligatory for all Italians who had infectious diseases.[42] In modern times, it has been discovered that forty days quarantine is excessively long, and we now tend toward the original two or three weeks, as described in the Bible.

Bubonic plague and leprosy were able to continue rampaging for centuries, because most doctors could not provide any solution. An improvement in conditions only occurred after quarantine and other hygienic measures of Moses were put into practice on a large scale. For example, in Paris, from 1553, victims of the plague were kept in quarantine, their houses were cleaned, the streets where they lived were washed clean, and their cesspits were stopped up.ℭ

David Riesman, a professor of medical history, writes, "These practices not only eliminated the plague as a pandemic menace for the first time in history but also led to general laws against infectious diseases, thereby laying the foundations upon which modern hygiene rests."[44]

COUNTERING EPIDEMICS OF
INTESTINAL DISEASES

In his book *None of These Diseases*, McMillen writes, "Europe brought the devastations of leprosy under control by obeying the biblical injunction to isolate the victims. Other preventable diseases continued to decimate mankind. Intestinal diseases such as cholera, dysentery, and typhoid fever continued to take many lives."[45] This was largely due to the incredibly unhygienic way of life. Until the end of the eighteenth century, facilities were extremely primitive, especially in the large towns. People simply threw their excrement, urine, and rubbish into the unpaved streets. René Dubos informs us, "In New York, it was reported, some houses could be

---

ℭ Over half of the world's lepers live in India, where hygienic measures are still far below par. Between 1892 and 1918 eleven million people died of the plague.[43]

reached only by wading through refuse that had accumulated to a depth of two or three feet. Slaughterhouses in the middle of the city (some next to elementary schools) added blood, dung, and flies."[46] With the rain, the filth got into pools and wells and also seeped into the earth, which meant that even underground springs became poisoned.[47] Clothes and dishes were washed in contaminated water, and often even the drinking water was contaminated. A terrible stench permeated the towns and villages. It was a heyday for rats and flies, which spread all sorts of intestinal diseases. "In English cities, one out of every two children died before the age of five of tuberculosis, typhoid, dysentery, cholera and other pestilences."[48]

In many tropical countries, such abuses still prevail: more than a billion people have no safe drinking water, and 2.6 billion people have no sanitation. Fifty to 80 percent of the cases of illness in these countries are attributed to unsafe drinking water.[49]

India—in the dusk, men relieve themselves on the railway. Seventy percent of the population doesn't have a toilet.[50]

Toilets

This huge waste of human lives could have been prevented in the past (and could be now) if people had taken God's instructions seriously. In a single sentence, the Book of Books indicates the way to avoid deadly epidemics such as typhoid, cholera, and dysentery, and also how to prevent all sorts of infestations by worms such as the pork tapeworm, the roundworm, the hookworm, and schistosoma (bilharzias).** "Designate a place outside the camp where you can go to relieve yourself. As part of your equipment, have something to dig with, and when you relieve yourself, dig a hole and cover up your excrement" (Deuteronomy 23:12–13).

It's remarkable how detailed, precise, and accurate this law of Moses is. The excrement must be dealt with *outside* the camp. The excrement must also be put *in a hole* and then *covered up*. This is completely different from what's done by all those people who, until two hundred years ago, were (and in many countries, still are) relieving themselves outside their houses or perhaps even neatly in the house, but then tipping the contents of the chamber pot into the open sewer in the street or out the nearest window.

These simple instructions appear to be particularly effective. The excrement and germs no longer entered the surface water or wells through rainwater, and they were no longer spread by rats and flies. When these instructions were followed, infectious diseases disappeared like snow before the sun. A professor of medical history writes about this rule of Moses, "Certainly a primitive measure, but an effective one, which indicates advance ideas of sanitation."[52] A doctor writes: "The admonitions of Moses are the groundwork of most of today's sanitary laws . . . and to this day they have been little improved upon."[53]

** The worms mentioned occur mainly in areas where toilets are not used or where human excrement is used as fertilizer on the land. The eggs are transferred from the excrement to plants or into the surface water. The eggs of the *roundworm* (Ascaris) enter the alimentary tract of a person if raw vegetables or unboiled water are consumed. In the alimentary tract they develop into larvae, which force their way through the gut wall and spread through the whole body by way of the blood circulation. The eggs of the *hookworm* (Ancylostoma) and of *schistosoma* develop to larvae in the soil and in surface water respectively, after which the larvae penetrate the skin of their victims and enter the blood circulation. By way of the blood, they spread through the whole body and are even able to contaminate unborn babies in the womb. Serious contamination can result in the death of the victim. Fifty years ago, it is estimated that 644 million people were infected with the roundworm (Ascaris), 457 million with the hookworm (Ancylostoma) and 200 million people with *schistosoma*.[51]

SUMMARY

Few people realize that the principles of toilets, of leper colonies, municipal sanitation, quarantine, and combating epidemics are taken from the Bible.

It seems that the books of the Law of Moses are meant especially for people who live in primitive, unhygienic conditions. Actually, until two centuries ago, *everyone* lived in such conditions. This was also the case in Canaan, where almost everyone met with a premature death due to contagious diseases, especially venereal diseases and the plague. On average, people didn't live beyond the age of thirty.

Throughout the centuries, doctors could provide no assistance in the fight against contagious diseases. Hundreds of millions of people died in the most appalling conditions due to venereal diseases, leprosy, bubonic plague, and an abundance of fatal intestinal diseases. All this misery could have been avoided simply by following the laws of Moses, which show how infection and the spread of disease can be prevented.

In primitive conditions in particular, the laws of Moses are shown to be a totally unsurpassed system of measures, something without par in history. Professors of medical history express their great admiration for these marvelous regulations relating to public health. Outside the Bible, nowhere in antiquity are such effective and systematic regulations found for the prevention and cure of diseases.

If you pay attention to these laws
and are careful to follow them . . .
none of your men or women will be childless.
The Lord will keep you free from every disease.
He will not inflict on you the horrible diseases
you knew in Egypt.

DEUTERONOMY 7:12–15

3.

HYGIENE

Is it possible for people to live their whole lives without washing with soap, not even their hands? Not before eating, not before going to bed, not when they have slaughtered a cow, not when they receive guests on a feast day. Never! Staff of the missionary organization Open Doors have told me that in rural Egypt they still encounter people who have never washed their hands or bodies with soap. Already, we have seen that such conditions existed before Christ and in the Middle Ages. But that they still occur in modern times is something you don't expect. Still, outside the Western world, it's almost unknown that good hygiene is necessary for good health. This makes it even more striking that hygiene measures, which are still followed in modern societies, were established in the Bible as long ago as 3,500 years.

DOCTORS, WASH YOUR HANDS

Until the end of the nineteenth century, even the conditions of hygiene in hospitals were almost as bad as those elsewhere. Doctors went from one patient to another without ever washing their hands. If a patient had to be operated on, he made his own way to the operating theater, took off his own clothes, and climbed onto the operating table. The patient was tied down or held down by a few recuperating patients. If he was lucky, the patient was made drunk or knocked out.[1] The surgeon took off his coat, rolled up his sleeves, took a few instruments, and started to operate. If the medical students had to look at anything in the wound, they stepped forward and shoved their unwashed hands into the opening. After the operation, the surgeon wiped his instruments clean on his trousers. It wasn't surprising that almost half of the patients died of blood poisoning and other infections.[2]

Dr. Roswell Park writes in his book about the history of medicine, "When I began my work, in 1876, as a hospital interne, in one of the largest hospitals in this country, it happened that during my first winter's experience, with but one or two exceptions, every patient operated upon in that hospital, and that by men who were esteemed the peers of anyone in their day, died of blood poisoning. . . . This was in an absolutely new building, . . . whose walls were not reeking with germs, as is the case yet in many of the old and well-established institutions."[3]

SEMMELWEIS AND PUERPERAL FEVER

Around 1840, in Vienna (Austria), there was the renowned "Allgemeines Krankenhaus" (General Hospital), which was associated with the university of the city. In that hospital, 17 percent of all new and expectant mothers died without having undergone any sort of operation. In other hospitals, as many as 25 percent of new mothers died. The doctors put the deaths down to prolonged constipation, delayed lactation, extreme anxiety, dirty linen, poor ventilation, and so forth. They were ignorant of the real cause of death and assumed that the disease was nonpreventable. The bodies of the dead women were taken to the mortuary, where they were later examined by the medical staff. In the mornings, the doctors and their students began their daily tasks by performing autopsies in the morgue and then—without washing their hands—headed off to the maternity wards. There they performed pelvic examinations on the expectant mothers and those in labor.

In 1844, the Hungarian doctor Ignaz Semmelweis (1818–65) was put in charge of one of the maternity wards. Over time, he noticed that the women who had been examined by the doctors were particularly likely to become sick and die. After three years he introduced a rule that the doctors and their students had to wash their hands in a bowl of water after inspecting a corpse, before they were allowed to examine the live patients on the ward.

Remember, prior to the introduction of the rule, 17 percent of the new mothers died. After the institution of hand washing, within three months, fewer than 2 percent died. A tenfold reduction within three months! This was clear evidence that the doctors and students were carrying some infectious particles on their hands from the autopsy room to the live patients on the ward.

But fatalities continued to occur. One day, the doctors and their students came into the maternity ward, having washed their hands, and examined a row of beds with twelve new and expectant mothers. The woman in the first bed had a high fever as a result of an infection of the womb. Eventually, all but one of the other women on the ward contracted the fever and died.

Semmelweis made a crucial association: evidently some mysterious thing was being transferred from the one live patient to the others—with deadly consequences. So the rule about hand washing was extended. Now everybody had to wash their hands after examining *each* patient, before moving to the next. The doctors and their students were angered by this unnecessary and time-consuming measure of constantly having to wash their hands again and again, but the mortality rate dropped still further.

The colleagues and superiors of Semmelweis despised and belittled him and were vehemently opposed to his investigations into the real cause of the misery. Their own theories and reputations were at stake, and they were afraid of being held responsible for the deaths of thousands of young women. Semmelweis's annual contract was not renewed, and in 1850 he was dismissed from the hospital. Later his successor chucked the washbasins out of the ward, and the death rate shot up to the previous level. But still no one was convinced.

For eight months, Semmelweis tried to get back his job in the hospital, but without success. Dejected and depressed, he left Vienna and returned to his hometown of Budapest (Hungary). There he managed to find a job in a hospital, and there, too, the death rate among pregnant women was alarmingly high. Again he ruled that the doctors should wash their hands before examining each patient. In that hospital, too, the mortality was reduced straightaway. Some younger colleagues listened to Semmelweis and applied his rules, but many colleagues and superiors passed him in the hospital without even speaking to him.

In 1861, Dr Semmelweis wrote a well-documented book about his work, but it was much too provocative. Several of his colleagues felt personally attacked and were sarcastic in their response. The strain of the ongoing opposition and the suffering of the women who were dying unnecessarily haunted Semmelweis and proved too much for him. His spirit was broken, and in 1865 he died in a psychiatric institute at the age of forty-seven, never having gained the recognition he so much deserved.[4]*

3,500 YEARS BEFORE SEMMELWEIS

Many centuries before Semmelweis, God told Moses what to do after touching a dead body, "Whoever touches the dead body of anyone will be unclean for seven days.... On the seventh day he is to purify himself. The person being cleansed must wash his clothes and bathe with water, and that evening he will be clean" (Numbers 19:11, 19). Here two extremely effective measures are mentioned for the protection of a patient who is to be examined by a doctor. First, a doctor who has touched a corpse must not touch anyone else for seven days. Second, the doctor must thoroughly wash his hands and his clothes.

SEVEN-DAYS ISOLATION

The strict rule about seven days of isolation discourages doctors (or other medical attendants) from touching a corpse unnecessarily.

After touching a corpse, the doctor had to live outside the camp for seven days (Numbers 5:2), which meant that no infectious disease had the opportunity to spread by means of the doctor.

If the doctor had himself contracted a disease through contact with a patient, he would know within seven days whether he was actually ill or not and whether he would be a danger to other patients whom he wanted to treat.

In practice, almost all acute and deadly bacteria appear to have

---

* The story of Semmelweis is recounted in many books. I have followed the account in the book by S. I. McMillen.

incubation times (the time between infection and the outbreak of the disease) shorter than seven days. This means that infection can (almost) always be detected within a week.[5]

WASHING HANDS AND CLOTHES

A doctor writes, "Personnel who have contact with patient excretions, secretions or blood, whether directly or through contaminated objects, may acquire transient carriage of micro-organisms from such contact."[6] So infection can be transmitted not only by touching the patient, but even by touching objects on which blood or excrement from the patient have been. This means it's of the utmost importance to wash hands and clothes regularly.

A modern medical textbook states, "Routine hand-washing before, between, and after contact with patients is recognized as the most important feature of successful infection control."[7] Another textbook states, "Effective hand hygiene is possibly the most important factor in preventing hospital acquired infection, but compliance is poor."[8] This poor compliance still holds true for many hospitals, even in the United States and other Western countries.[9]

In unhygienic conditions, the clothes of a doctor or attendant are even more quickly contaminated by bacteria than in a modern hospital. But even in our modern hospitals, the following applies: "As the uniforms of the nursing staff can very easily become contaminated with pathogenic micro-organisms, they must be regarded as one of the many ways in which infections can be transmitted from one patient to another. . . . Through the movement of the body, the bacteria on the clothing are dispersed into the air. This contamination of the air is only reduced by a complete change of clothing. This means that it's necessary to change clothes several times a week."[10]

Thirty-five hundred years ago, nursing staff in Israel washed their hands often, and they changed and washed their clothes at least once a week. Quite revolutionary!

Medical instruction on the street in China.

In a primitive society, touching a corpse was much more dangerous than it is now. First, because the hygiene measures were much worse than today's, both for the doctor and the patient. Second, because most people didn't die of old age, but of an infectious disease. Third, most patients were covered in fleas and lice, which had sucked up their infected blood. It's known that fleas and lice want to leave a cold, dead body as quickly as possible and crawl or jump onto another, warm body, such as the doctor in attendance.

HYGIENE IN AND AROUND THE HOME

From the time of Moses, the Jewish people have always had concern about personal hygiene, and, in fact, their hygiene rules were a cause of annoyance and contempt. Who takes a bath every week and puts on clean clothes afterward? Why should you throw your food away if a dead mouse falls on it? Why go to all the trouble of burying your excrement?

The Mosaic laws were anachronisms in their time. They were too far ahead of their time to be obeyed or understood by other peoples. The Israelites were the only ones who, as a *whole nation*, attached importance to good hygiene, such as: (1) bathing and washing clothes, and (2) protecting food and water supplies.†

BATHING AND WASHING CLOTHES

The Israelites had to wash their entire bodies several times a week, preferably in clean, running water. They also had to wash their clothes regularly. This wasn't because of body odor or to look smart, but in order to stay healthy! The following are six occasions on which Israelites had to wash themselves thoroughly (with a reference to further explanation).

1. After seminal discharge and after sexual intercourse (see pages 18–19).

2. After touching someone—or any of his household goods— suffering from gonorrhea (see pages 19, 20).

3. After returning from a war (to prevent venereal diseases and other infectious diseases [see pages 20–21]).

4. After touching a corpse (see pages 38–40).

5. After touching an unclean animal or an animal that had died of natural causes (see page 58).

6. After touching a menstruating woman (to prevent infection through the blood [see Leviticus 15:19–27]).

---

† Egyptian priests also had a number of—nonsensical—hygiene rules, such as washing four times a day and shaving the whole body every three days, including the eyebrows and eyelashes. The priests were circumcised, drank filtered water, and weren't allowed to eat vegetables. There was no sense at all in their complicated purification rituals. Moreover, these rules were only intended for this small, select group of priests. No one cared what ordinary people did.[11]

Regularly washing and cleaning were of vital importance in the fight against a whole range of serious diseases; for example, the itch mite (*Sarcoptes scabiei*), which lives and lays eggs *in* the skin of people who lead an unhygienic life, or dangerous mold. But the most important battle was against fleas and lice. These creatures aren't only extremely annoying, but they can also cause epidemics of fatal diseases, such as the plague and typhus.

Body Lice

In his great encyclopedia of animals, Professor Grzimek writes about the danger of the body louse (*Pediculus humanus humanus*), which can transmit the fatal disease typhus (*Typhus exanthematicus*). He writes,

> Without doubt the creature played an important role in the "pestilences" which claimed such a high toll of human lives in the past. Only when people started to change their underclothes at short intervals was the body louse no longer able to complete its development of about three weeks duration on the host. This is why people take it for granted that they no longer have lice and are not afflicted by epidemics of typhus. However, this situation soon changes in the case of war or some other disaster, as a result of which people aren't able to change their clothes regularly. . . . In the civil war in the Soviet Union alone (1918–1922), ten million people suffered from typhus, of which three million succumbed to the illness. . . . On the withdrawal of Napoleon from Russia, in the winter of 1812–1813, more French soldiers fell victim to typhus than to the pursuing Cossacks.[12]

Soap

The Dutch Royal Institute for the Tropics issues the following advice to people who are going to the tropics and subtropics as a healthy lifestyle in hot countries: "Good skin hygiene can prevent much trouble. It is preferable to wash regularly with not too much soap, after which it is necessary to dry off properly."[13] Medical advice on hand-washing confirms this: "Handwashing . . . friction and water alone are almost as effective as soap and water."[14]

According to experts, it's not really necessary to wash with soap. It's more important to wash *regularly*. This is exactly what Moses told the Israelites to do. This meant that without soap, they weren't much worse off than we are with our exaggerated hygiene. Pathogenic bacteria are easily removed from the hands, even without soap.[15] And if any bacteria did remain on the body after washing, these would soon be killed in the dry heat and the intense sunlight in the desert.

PROTECTION OF FOOD AND WATER SUPPLIES

In our modern society, with cold stores, preservatives, pesticides, and vacuum packs, we can hardly imagine how easily in a primitive society food would rot, go moldy, be devoured by rats, or made inedible by bugs. Imagine there were no good storage places, no electricity, no chemical pesticides. How on earth would it be possible to keep your food supply free of all those molds and pests? In India, 10–30 percent of the grain harvest is lost to rats and mice, and globally about 150 billion kilos [330 billion pounds] of grain every year.[16]

Contamination of Food

Moses describes three important causes of food supplies becoming unsuitable for consumption. It's remarkable that he doesn't write how you should protect your supplies from pests, how you should dry the harvest, how you can conserve it, how you can build silos . . . Such things you can think out yourself. Moses only gives indications for the prevention of diseases of which humanly you cannot discover the cause.

Contamination through Dead Animals

When a dead animal falls into a pot of food, the food and also the pot must be destroyed: "When one of them [a weasel, rat, lizard, gecko, skink, chameleon, etc.] dies and falls on something, that article, whatever its use, will be unclean, whether it is made of wood, cloth, hide or sackcloth. Put it in water; it will be unclean till evening. . . . If one of them falls into a clay pot, everything in it will be unclean, and you must break the pot" (Leviticus 11:29–33).

Imagine that in your house, a rat (with its fleas, trichinae, rabies, typhus, paratyphoid, the plague, and other diseases) is so ill that it dies and falls into a pot of green beans or juicy strawberries. You would throw the lot away and clean the pot, even without Moses' having to force you. But then, in antiquity, people weren't so fussy about food—except for the Israelites. They followed laws about food hygiene that were only understood 3,500 years later. As we know now, bacteria can be removed from utensils of leather, linen, or wood by washing them thoroughly. But a clay pot, pan, or oven is porous and the germs that have forced their way into the pores cannot be removed anymore. Washing and rinsing with water doesn't help a bit.

Contamination through Sick People

"When a person dies in a tent, . . . every open container without a lid fastened on it will be unclean" (Numbers 19:14–15).

Most people who died in the past didn't die of old age, but of contagious diseases, such as the plague and tuberculosis. The bacteria causing these diseases (and various others) are spread in the air through particles of spittle, especially through coughing or sneezing. Imagine that someone in your tent or house has died of one of these deadly diseases. You can be sure that the air in such a room is full of germs. If the deceased person happened to have had a fit of coughing or sneezing, then any container that wasn't covered over would be full of deadly bacteria. This is why in such cases the food had to be destroyed, the container and the clothes washed, and the house cleaned.

Slaughtering a cow in Sudan. What about hygiene?

Contamination through Water

"Any food that could be eaten but has water on it [from such a pot] is unclean"‡ (Leviticus 11:34). What a strange rule! Even if it's only water that gets on it, still food becomes unclean. What's the point of that?

First, the water in most countries isn't clean at all, not even the drinking water, and certainly not if the water has been standing in the house for days or if it has dripped from a leaky roof. Second, the food isn't that clean either. There are countless spores of bacteria and molds on it, but they can only multiply in a damp environment. This, together with subtropical temperatures, produces ideal conditions for the high-speed development of germs. If you were to keep such damp food for a few days and then eat it, you would be lucky if you got away with only terrible diarrhea.

‡ *The words "from such a pot" are added in the NIV, but are not in the original Hebrew. The meaning applies to a general rule for food that has water on it.

Contamination of Water

Not only should *food* be protected from contamination by vermin, mold, and bacteria, but it is also vitally important that the drinking water be protected. A leaflet by the water company in my hometown says, "Eighty percent of the diseases in developing countries are attributed to unsafe drinking water. It's estimated that 3.5 million children die annually of dehydration and diarrhea as a result of the lack of sanitary provisions and safe drinking water."[17]

Moses writes, "Any liquid that could be drunk from it [the contaminated pot] is unclean. Anything that one of their carcasses [of animals that move about on the ground] falls on becomes unclean" (Leviticus 11:34–35). We have seen above that in the first part of verse 34, Moses writes that all food on which water has been spilt becomes unclean. In the second part of verse 34, it is stated that also *liquid* on which water has been spilt becomes unclean. For example, if you have a delicious pot of juice into which water from a leaking roof has been dripping, you must throw the whole lot away.

In verse 35 it is repeated that anything (water, food, or cooking utensils) on which an unclean dead animal falls is unclean. As mentioned previously, water in most countries is not very clean, and "animals that move about on the ground," such as rats and mice, are covered in lice, bacteria, viruses, and mold. This is even worse if these animals are so sick that they drop down dead and fall into a pot. The whole content of the pot must immediately be thrown away.

"A spring, however, or a cistern for collecting water remains clean, but anyone who touches one of these carcasses is unclean" (Leviticus 11:36). In the King James Version it says, "a pit, wherein there is *plenty* of water." In other words, if a dead animal falls into a spring where the water is constantly being renewed, or into a cistern in which there's a lot of water, it cannot do as much harm as in a small water container in the home. Water in a spring or a cistern is much colder than water in a house or a tent, particularly in the Middle East. In cold water, germs cannot multiply nearly as fast as in a jug of warm water. Of course, the dead animal had to be removed from the spring or cistern as soon as possible. And the person who removed the filthy creature had to wash himself and his clothes and was unclean until the evening (see Leviticus 11:25).

Refuse Disposal

In chapter 2, we have already read about the importance of good waste disposal. We saw that in the Jewish quarter of Strasbourg, there were twenty times fewer occurrences of the plague than in the rest of the city because Balavignus had his quarter cleaned. We also saw that burying excrement resulted in a reduction in the most serious epidemics, such as cholera, typhoid, and dysentery. Everything must be done to prevent rats, mice, and flies from being able to multiply. As well as the plague, rats and mice also transmit paratyphoid, rabies, typhoid, typhus, trichinosis, foot-and-mouth disease, Weil's disease, and numerous other diseases.[18] Flies transmit diseases including typhoid, cholera, dysentery, tuberculosis, trachoma, and polio.[19]

Thanks to refuse collection, a good drainage system, and good personal hygiene, in Western countries the plague of rats has been vastly reduced, and the summer plague of flies considerably limited, and so also the spread of the diseases mentioned.

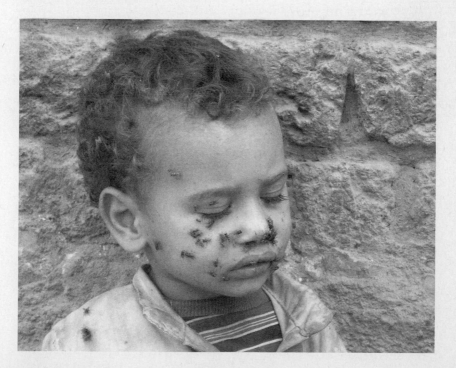

A child covered in flies in an Egyptian village.

Burying Dead Animals

In Leviticus 11, it says that Israelites would be unclean for a day if they touched the carcass of an unclean animal. This applied to unclean land animals, unclean aquatic animals, and unclean animals that "move along the ground." An Israelite wouldn't touch such dead animals for love or money. And if he happened to bump into such a dead animal, for example at night in the dark (see Leviticus 5:2; Deuteronomy 23:10–11 RSV), he had to wash himself and his clothes the next day and remain in isolation until the end of the day.§

This was a wonderful scientific rule, which was completely unknown to other peoples at the time. Particularly in primitive societies, unclean animals are swarming with parasites, especially if they died of natural causes. If you touch their carcasses, you will certainly be infected with parasites. Consider for example the fleas on a rat that is infected with the plague. If an animal like that dies and the body cools off, the fleas look for another host as soon as possible. Whoever picks up the rat is in for it! The only way to get rid of the fleas and other parasites is to wash yourself and your clothes thoroughly immediately after contact.

PENILE CANCER AND THE VALUE OF CIRCUMCISION

A man is born with a superfluous quantity of skin at the end of his penis, which is known as the foreskin. If this isn't removed, the top part of the penis is difficult to clean, especially in the first years of life. With over 50 percent of one-year-old boys, the foreskin cannot be pushed over the glans, and with boys of three years of age, this inability still affects 10 percent. Even when they are older and the foreskin can be pushed over the glans, most boys still don't wash themselves in this place.[20] Through this lack of hygiene, there develops a damp environment in which a large number of bacteria grow. These live on dead skin cells and sebaceous matter, a fatty substance which is excreted through small glands in the skin. The

---

§ In many Bible translations is written "nocturnal emission," but this is an *interpretation* by the translators. The original Hebrew says "accident at night."

bacteria, the skin cells, and the sebaceous matter together form a stinking mass called smegma. This is an ideal feeding ground for the smegma bacillus (*Mycobacterium smegmatis*) and other pathogenic bacteria. In primitive conditions, if people don't wash often and cannot shower extensively as we do, it gets very messy down there.

CIRCUMCISION

With circumcision, the foreskin is cut away, which means that the top part of the penis can be much more effectively cleaned. In most European countries, circumcision is an unknown phenomenon. It is primarily performed as a religious ritual among Jews and Muslims, and among other people, mainly for medical reasons. It is estimated that in Europe about 10 to 15 percent of men are circumcised. In the United States in 1979 it was still 85 percent. Now this has dropped to about 60 percent.[21] The large number of circumcisions in the United States has nothing to do with religious convictions, but is done for reasons of hygiene. Scientists have discovered that circumcised boys are less likely to contract penile cancer and disorders of the urinary passages.

PENILE CANCER

Among peoples whose men are not circumcised and where hygiene leaves much to be desired, as in India, China, and Latin America, the number of cases of penile cancer is particularly high. There, on average, penile cancer constitutes 10 to 20 percent of all cancerous tumors among men.[22] In Brazil, where hardly anyone is circumcised, the number of cases of penile cancer is seventy times as high as in Israel, where almost all men are circumcised.[23] A doctor in a developing country wrote so graphically, "The specific irritant seems to be the pent-up smegma, caked and disintegrated."[24]

Research has revealed that among men who were circumcised as *babies*, virtually no penile cancer occurs, regardless of whether they live in hygienic or unhygienic conditions. Research in 1975 showed that globally only nine cases were known of penile cancer among men who were circumcised immediately after birth.[25] It's remarkable that among

Muslims—who aren't circumcised until they are between three and twelve years old—more cases of penile cancer occur than among men who are circumcised eight days after birth. With them, the smegma bacterium (or some other agent) was already able to pursue its carcinogenic activities for a few years before the circumcision was performed.

In the United States and other Western countries, circumcision is actually not of much value anymore. The standard of hygiene is high, and the prevalence of penile cancer is only 0.2 percent of all cancers in men.[26] According to opponents, this is too small a number to justify routine circumcision of male babies.

However, Edgar J. Schoen, chairman of the Task Force on Circumcision of the American Academy of Pediatrics, writes in response to these opponents: "I am amazed at the claim . . . that no link exists between circumcision and penile cancer. In an incredible example of selective medical amnesia, the authors ignore evidence that has accumulated in the past 64 years. . . . Since 1935, about 50,000 cases of penile cancer have been reported in the United States, only 10 of which occurred in men who had been circumcised as newborn infants—overwhelming evidence."[27]

In unhygienic conditions, circumcision is the best possible way to prevent penile cancer, but it also fights several other diseases of the male sexual organ: (1) In the first year of life, boys who are circumcised as newborns have ten times fewer infections of the urethra than uncircumcised boys, and as adults they contract fewer sexually transmitted diseases[28]; (2) In 2006, researchers with the World Health Organization (WHO) reported that circumcision reduces female-to-male contamination of HIV—the AIDS virus—by 60 percent.[29] Following further research, the WHO now recommends "that male circumcision be recognized as an additional important intervention to reduce the risk of heterosexually acquired HIV infection in men."[30]

THE EIGHTH DAY

It's remarkable that circumcision in the Bible had to take place specifically on the eighth day after birth: "Every male among you who is eight days old must be circumcised" (Genesis 17:12; see also Leviticus 12:3). Why was this rule so strict for the Israelites that it took precedence over all other commandments? Even if the eighth day fell on the Sabbath, on a major festival, or on the Day of Atonement, the baby boy still had to be circumcised.

Scientific research has provided an answer to this. The famous pediatrician L. E. Holt writes that in the first four days of life, babies are extremely susceptible to hemorrhaging: "Hemorrhages at this time ... are sometimes extensive; they may produce serious damage of internal organs, especially of the brain, and cause death from shock or exsanguination."[31] From Holt's reports, it's clear that circumcision can best take place on the *eighth* day.

The fact that babies can so easily bleed to death in the first days of life is because the important agents of coagulation, prothrombin and vitamin K, are not present in sufficient quantities. The quantity of prothrombin the baby has in the first days is left over from the mother and is about one third of normal. And vitamin K is almost entirely absent. This is because the body of the baby didn't receive any vitamin K from the mother and hasn't yet been able to produce it itself. Vitamin K is produced by bacteria in our intestines, but because a baby is born sterile, it takes a few days before the bacteria start to work effectively and sufficient vitamin K is produced.

Through the lack of vitamin K, the prothrombin present cannot work properly. So even when there is some prothrombin, it *cannot be used* for coagulation. This means that any operation or injury between the second and fifth day will put the baby in grave danger. For this reason, in many hospitals mothers are given an extra dose of vitamin K just before the birth or babies are injected with one milligram of vitamin K immediately after birth. After a few days, the bacteria start to proliferate and sufficient vitamin K is produced, which means that the prothrombin present can begin to work. Moreover, the liver begins to produce new prothrombin.

And now it gets interesting.

From the third day, the quantity of available (usable) prothrombin shoots up and on the eighth day reaches the higher than normal level of 110 percent. After this, the quantity drops to normal and remains for the whole of life at the standard level of 100 percent.[32] So on the eighth day, a baby has more available prothrombin than on any other day of its life! This means that on the eighth day, hemorrhaging stops more quickly than at any other moment in its existence. In other words, the perfect day for a circumcision is the *eighth* day.

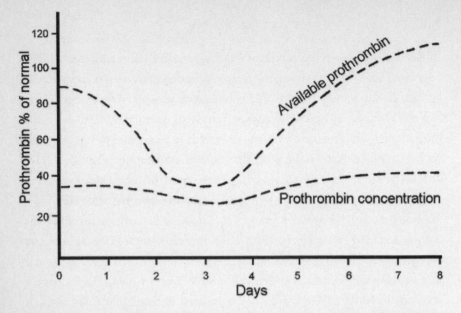

Prothrombin is necessary for coagulation of the blood. On the eighth day after birth, the available (usable) prothrombin is 110 percent of normal. After this it is permanently reduced to 100 percent (Holt, *Holt's Pediatrics*, 42).

An additional reason for performing circumcision as early as possible is that young children are much less troubled by this operation than adults. It appears that children under three weeks only experience pain and discomfort at the moment of the circumcision itself, and not anymore afterward. Children between four weeks and three months suffer from subsequent discomfort for up to two days. Children of three months to a year experience discomfort for three to four days, and adults for more than a week.[33] Moreover, older boys sometimes suffer slight trauma after the circumcision, because they experience the intervention as an assault on their bodies.

After years of research, it has been discovered why circumcision is important and on which day it is safest to perform it. But already four thousand years before modern science made this discovery, God, the Creator of prothrombin and vitamin K, had instituted circumcision and stated on which day it should best take place (see Genesis 17:12). (*With acknowledgment to S. I. McMillen.*)[34]

SUMMARY

In developing countries, conditions of hygiene are still particularly poor, but until 150 years ago, conditions in Western countries weren't much better. This is why it is so striking that as many as 3,500 years ago, the Bible prescribed good and extremely effective measures of hygiene, both for personal cleanliness and for public health (e.g., regularly changing and washing your clothing and washing yourself thoroughly when you have been in contact with a corpse or with someone with an infectious disease).

The protective measures relating to food and water supplies indicate a superhuman knowledge of bacteriology. Equally striking is the hygienic value of circumcision. Men who were circumcised as infants don't suffer from penile cancer and contract far fewer infections of the urethra and other diseases of the male organ than uncircumcised men. The peremptory demand that circumcision be performed on the eighth day testifies to inexplicable scientific insight. The eighth day is the *only* day in life on which the coagulation of the blood is 110 percent of the norm.

In the first chapters, we have been impressed by all the exceedingly sagacious rules in the Bible. A professor of medical history has the following to say about this: "Jewish medicine . . . brought the essential basis of all social hygiene. . . . There arose for the first time the concept of sanitary legislation."[35]

In the next chapter, we will deal with the laws of Moses that refer to healthy eating and which help us to live a long and healthy life. These are laws we have only begun to understand to some extent in the past decades.

They are not just idle words for you—
they are your life.
By them you will live long in the land
you are . . . to possess.

DEUTERONOMY 32:47

4.

NUTRITION

When I was in inland China, I was impressed by many delicacies of the famous Chinese cuisine: dogs, snakes, squids, beetles, ants, crisps made from chicken entrails, medicines made from Tibetan bears' claws and tiger scrotums. I didn't eat much of these delicacies—unless I unwittingly consumed them in the restaurants along the road, where dozens of skinned dogs were for sale. I couldn't resist taking home a tried and trusted Chinese medicine: a bottle of mouse fetuses in alcohol. I wasn't able to discover what it's for; perhaps I should drink some more of it first.

A tried and trusted Chinese medicine: mouse fetuses in alcohol.

A few years ago, a friend who has been living in China for years was offered a very special delicacy. During an important dinner with a high government official, she was served a portion of monkeys' brains—of live monkeys, it must be understood. Before the ceremony, the vocal chords of the monkey are severed . . . and then his head is tied under a table in which there's a hole. Above the table, the skull is carefully opened up and the meal can begin. Our friend declined the delicacy, although this was a tremendous insult to the high-ranking official.

A missionary from Laos told how, when he visited villagers, he was sometimes given a handful of roasted "nuts" to nibble. On closer inspection, they appeared to be roasted beetles. Every now and then one was still moving when he put a handful into his mouth. But a hefty bite soon put an end to the problem and the beetle.

Why is it that Westerners have so little appreciation for such delicacies? Why do they limit themselves to eating a few large mammals, some fish, and occasionally a bird or a shellfish, while in the Third World people eat just about everything that moves?

In antiquity, too, people ate everything that moved, except for a few species of plants and animals that were forbidden locally because of religious taboos. In certain temples in Egypt the priests didn't eat pigs, cows, sheep, fish, or doves, and in some, even vegetables. In other temples, these were allowed. The taboos depended on which god was being worshipped and which animals were regarded as reincarnations of the deity. No one cared in the least what the ordinary people ate. With them, pork was always very popular.[1] There was neither rhyme nor reason to the dietary laws of Egypt or any other country.

The claim that the dietary laws of Moses were adopted from the surrounding peoples is utter nonsense. They were completely independent prescriptions. If you study the *details* of these laws, you see a world of difference between the rules of Israel and those of other peoples. Then it's clear that only the rules of Israel are well founded according to the modern science of nutrition. They are the only ones to make a sensible classification of all edible animals in the Middle East. The author must have had supernatural insight into the laws of public health and ecology (the science of the relationship of plants and animals with one another and with their environments). If we look at these rules through the eyes of a physician or an inspector of public health, a world of insight opens up to us.

BIOLOGICALLY PERFECT LAWS

Before we deal with the different groups of animals, we want to draw attention to two important characteristics of the Hebrew dietary laws.

1. The dietary laws weren't written with religious motives, but with biological motives.

2. The dietary laws weren't written by people with a special knowledge, but rather because this knowledge was lacking.

BIOLOGICAL MOTIVES

In Genesis 9:3, God says to Noah, "Everything that lives and moves will be food to you." This means that it was permitted to eat all animals. But in the laws of Moses, God goes back on this decision and says that only *clean* animals may be eaten (see Leviticus 11). This again seems to be contradicted by the Lord Jesus, who said, "Nothing outside a man can make him 'unclean'" (Mark 7:15). This means that everything may be eaten; unclean animals cannot make a man unclean (see also Romans 14:14, 20, and 1 Corinthians 10:25).

Now what? Is God so whimsical that He goes back on a decision twice? No, *in principle* all animals may be eaten, but for your health it's better only to eat clean animals.

God told Noah that he could eat all animals; but for burnt offerings, he was only to use clean animals (see Genesis 8:20). The fact that God preferred clean animals for burnt offerings was probably enough for Noah to limit himself to clean animals when eating meat. The same applies to us with the laws of Moses: we are allowed to eat everything, but it's healthier to limit ourselves to clean animals.

There have been endless discussions about the meaning of the dietary laws. In the first century, the Jewish philosopher Philo wrote that the laws were established to prevent excessive revelry and to raise us up to an elevated morality. Man must not be a "predator," but a "ruminant," who chews the Word of God again and again.[2] According to others, the laws were written to keep the Israelites isolated from the neighboring peoples.[3] Some theologians say that certain animals are seen as unclean in connection with primitive superstition,[4] or because of an instinctive aversion to certain species of animals.[5] There are rabbis who say that the meat of unclean animals has a negative influence on the men and women's character.[6] Others, including the famous Maimonides (AD 1135–1204), say that all these laws refer only to presenting pure sacrifices in the temple. But Maimonides was also one of the few who suggested that the sanitation laws in the Bible might be related to hygiene and a healthy diet.[7]

Some modern writers point to economic motives: hyraxes and hares are forbidden for consumption because hunting such animals is a waste of time and is done at the expense of breeding productive animals. Pigs are forbidden because they are humans' competitors with regard to food; both are omnivores and so eat more or less the same types of food.[8]

Most of these explanations are partly true, but none provides a satisfactory explanation for all aspects of the dietary laws. Only if you look at the laws from the viewpoint of nutrition do you see how perfectly they fit together, and then all the details fall into place.

In my opinion, the dietary laws weren't written because of religious or ethical motives. The *sacrificial* laws were written with this goal, but not the *dietary* laws. With the *sacrificial* laws, only four (!) species of animals are mentioned: cattle, sheep, goats, and doves, while in the *dietary* laws, dozens of species of animals are described among mammals, birds, fish, and insects. The main motive behind the sacrificial laws must have been religious, but with dietary laws, the main motive was biological. They were rules to guarantee good health, both for humans and for nature (i.e., a healthy biological balance in nature).

Meat market in China. Note the tasty goats' heads in the foreground.

LACK OF HUMAN KNOWLEDGE

It's remarkable that nowhere in the Bible do you find a prohibition about eating certain types of plants. This is in contrast to the dietary laws of Egypt and other countries.

First, this is an indication that the dietary laws weren't adopted from other countries. If this were the case, then in the laws of Moses you would also find recommendations about the consumption of plants.

Second, it's an indication that the laws aren't written because of human knowledge about food. Otherwise they would contain many more rules, which can be discovered experimentally. For example, which plants are and are not harmful. In the Bible, you don't find descriptions of this kind. The Bible is primarily concerned with facts people could not have known. For example, why after eating pork do you only die years later, and why had you better not put storks, vultures, or frogs on the menu?

In brief: the Bible contains especially those hygiene and dietary laws the importance of which primitive mankind could never have discovered empirically.

Only in our time are we starting to understand something about these laws and do we keep voluntarily to the rules that were established by Moses. There's no one forcing us to do so, but still we eat almost exclusively cows, sheep, birds, and fish, and occasionally a rabbit or some shellfish. The great exception to this rule is the pig, but this is a tricky business, as we will see below.

Public Health in a Primitive Society

When reading the dietary laws, just as with the hygiene laws, we must be aware of the terribly unhygienic conditions in a primitive society. Generally speaking, everyone had pigs and rats (with accompanying fleas and lice) living around and *in* the house. The people lived and slept in the same room as the animals.[9] When there was a celebration, the animals were slaughtered and gobbled up. There was no Food Inspection Department. Hands weren't washed properly, and no one had ever heard of the hygienic processing of meat. Such circumstances can still be seen in primitive societies today.

Summers in the land of the Israelites would regularly see temperatures above 100 degrees. At that temperature, hygienically processed meat of healthy animals spoils within a day, not to mention the meat of sick animals slaughtered in unhygienic conditions. This was why the Israelites always had to eat meat within a day. If meat was well roasted or boiled on the first day, it was still permitted to be eaten the next day, but anything left after that had to be burned (see Leviticus 7:15–17; 22:30). If you didn't do this, you ran a great risk of serious food poisoning.

Actually, even in my country, the Netherlands, with its high-tech food industry, walk-in freezers, and superclean households, every year there are over a million cases of food poisoning.[10] The journal of the Netherlands Nutrition Center indicates three main causes of this: contaminated fresh foodstuffs, in particular of animal origin; domestic animals in the kitchen; and unwashed hands when preparing food.[11] These are precisely the points we have mentioned above, points that really were of vital importance in a primitive society.

Unregistered meat market in China. The hygiene leaves a lot to be desired.

STRICT LAWS

In general terms, we can identify six characteristics of a primitive society that explain why the dietary laws of Moses are so strict:

1. There are many sick animals, because there's no knowledge of how to treat illnesses in animals.

2. Meat goes bad very quickly at high temperatures and in unhygienic conditions.*

3. Meat of sick animals spoils even more quickly for two reasons: because there are already many germs in it to start with, and because the germs can develop in it much more quickly than in the meat of healthy animals.[12]

---

* This is why in the tropics, the dead are always buried on the day of decease.

4. Meat is usually not heated sufficiently to kill all the germs, such as bacteria, and worms (e.g., trichinae and tapeworms). This is because it's difficult to gather enough firewood and because the food is heated over an open fire, which means that much of the heat is lost.

5. Without chemical pesticides, the country is crawling with vermin such as rats, mice, locusts, and harmful insects that spread all kinds of deadly diseases and eat the crops. That's why biological pest control in these societies is much more essential than in the West.

6. There are no microscopes or laboratory technologies to detect germs. Simple preventative measures are the *only* possibility to stop people from becoming sick.

CONCLUSION

With the above-mentioned remarks in mind, two main reasons can be advanced as to why certain animals may or may not be eaten.

1. *Public health*—The meat of some animals is far more dangerous for consumption than the meat of other animals (e.g., the meat of pigs and rats may contain deadly germs; the meat of mollusks can spoil extremely quickly).

2. *Biological balance*—Some species of animals are very useful for the balance in nature and therefore must not be eaten, because they eat sick animals and carrion or because they attack pests. (Pests are animals that occur in large numbers and can cause very great damage, such as locusts, rats, and mice.)

General Rule:
All animals that are not dangerous for the health and are less important for the biological balance in nature may be eaten.

WHICH ANIMALS MAY BE EATEN?

We will deal with the animals according to the classification in Leviticus 11. In this chapter, four groups of animals are described, which are found in the Middle East.

Group of Animals	Permitted for Consumption
1. Large land animals	All ruminants (except the camel)
2. Birds	All birds (except birds of prey and carrion birds)
3. Small land animals (including insects)	All locusts and grasshoppers
4. Aquatic animals	All fish with fins and scales

LARGE LAND ANIMALS

Permitted

"You may eat any animal that has a split hoof completely divided and that chews the cud" (Leviticus 11:3). Animals that chew the cud and have split hooves are known as ruminants. The scientific name is *Ruminantia*: cattle, sheep, goats, deer, antelope, and giraffe.[13] The ruminants are herbivores, which means they only eat grass and leaves. When they have filled their stomachs, they find a quiet spot, bring the food from their stomachs back up into their mouths, and then chew it again.

Prohibited

All carnivores, such as lions, bears, dogs, foxes, and cats, were forbidden for consumption; likewise all omnivores, such as pigs and rats. In addition to these, a few herbivores were prohibited: horses, camels, hyraxes, rabbits, and hares (see Leviticus 11:4–7; 26–27). In other words, all animals that did not chew the cud and did not have split hooves were forbidden.

WHY PROHIBIT NONRUMINANTS?

Public Health

For public health regulations in a primitive society it is essential to indicate with a few general rules which animals are dangerous for consumption and which are not.

In ancient times such rules were even more important, because at that time there were no technical tools to discover dangerous germs. Without its being apparent, *any* animal might be harboring a deadly disease.

It is amazing that without scientific research, Moses established exactly the right rule to exclude all dangerous animals from consumption. We see this if we turn for advice to the official meat inspection department in our modern society.

In a textbook on the inspection of slaughtered animals, it says, "The majority of zooparasites which are significant in the examination of meat are detectable through the normal senses. . . . Others can only be identified with a microscope, such as the majority of protozoa [single-celled animals], certain blood filariae [small larvae of pathogen parasites in the blood vessels], and the trichinae."[14]

According to the textbook, still the presence of most parasites is easy to detect with the naked eye, even the microscopic ones, like protozoa and filariae, and also the bacteria and viruses, because *they change the appearance of the meat.*[15] This can also be seen from the illustration at left. Moreover, the great majority of all protozoa, filariae, bacteria, and viruses are *not* dangerous for human consumption, because they are not

After slaughter, (almost) all diseases of animals can be detected with the naked eye, such as this tuberculosis of the liver of a pig.

transmittable to humans, i.e., they are simply excreted when consumed.[16] Their greatest drawback is that they do reduce the quality of the meat.

Ultimately, only the trichinae are life-threatening parasites, because they are transmittable to humans and there is no way whatsoever to detect their presence without a microscope.

Trichinae are worms that are too small to detect with the naked eye (1.4 to 4 mm long and less than 1/16 mm thick). Trichinae cause serious and sometimes fatal diseases, especially if the consumer repeatedly eats meat severely infected with them. Since without a microscope it's impossible to establish whether there are trichinae in meat, it's advisable in primitive conditions to prohibit the consumption of all animals susceptible to trichinae.

This measure is all the more important if the meat isn't sufficiently heated when boiled or roasted. In order to kill trichinae, the temperature, even in the middle of the meat, must be at least 167 degrees. This means the danger of infection is great in impoverished areas where ovens are substandard or if firewood is scarce.

Due to a lack of wood, meat is often boiled or roasted for too short a time.

Scientific research has revealed that trichinae occur in animals such as pigs, wild boars, dogs, wolves, hyenas, jackals, foxes, lions, leopards, bears, cats, badgers, mink, martens, polecats, nutria, hedgehogs, rodents (rats and mice), and also in horses, hippopotamuses, and camels.[17] All but the last three species mentioned are carnivores and omnivores. These are exactly the animals that were not to be eaten by the Israelites!

Only the meat of ruminants is free of the dangerous trichinae.

Experiments have revealed that the meat of cows and sheep cannot even be *artificially* contaminated with trichinae.[18] So to start with, the ruminants don't eat food in which trichinae occur, and, second, if they were to eat trichinae, these would simply be excreted.

Conclusion

All parasites in meat that are dangerous to humans when consumed can be detected with the naked eye, except trichinae. Therefore the general rule in a primitive society is:

Do not eat animals in which trichinae occur. Eat only ruminants.

BIOLOGICAL BALANCE

Predators and omnivores aren't only prohibited because of the danger of trichinae and other dangerous parasites. There's another important reason. Predators are "nature's health police": they have the extremely important task of disposing of weak, sick, and dead animals. The renowned Professor Grzimek writes, "Predators deserve our protection, because they play an extremely important role in maintaining the balance in nature. They prevent too great an increase in diseases and plagues of harmful animals."[19]

This means that the predators weren't to be eaten, on the one hand because they were dangerous because of the trichinae, and on the other hand because they were indispensable for maintaining the health of nature. We will go into this latter point in more detail with birds.

Environmental Awareness

There's perhaps an additional reason why only ruminants were permitted for consumption. Keeping ruminants on a large scale is the least damaging for the environment. Ruminants deal with natural sources of food in a particularly efficient way. They can live on fallow land and in mountainous areas. They live on grass, straw, hay, stubble, and leaves—plants indigestible for humans. They provide healthy meat and good, supple clothing; they provide milk and can pull a plow. Camels and horses could do the same as cattle, but to a much lesser extent; and they are less cost effective as sources of food, because they produce much less meat for the same quantity of grass or leaves they consume.

FOUR EXCEPTIONS

Four species of animals that are prohibited for consumption are especially mentioned in the Bible: camels, hyraxes, rabbits, and pigs (see Leviticus 11:4–8).

According to some researchers, pigs weren't to be eaten because they have such remarkably dirty eating habits. But why then was it also prohibited to eat rabbits and camels, although they have decent eating habits, while chickens and goats gobble up the strangest and most filthy things and are yet allowed to be placed on our menu?

Others maintain that pigs were forbidden because this prohibition was adopted from the Egyptians. But as already mentioned, throughout the centuries, pork was particularly popular in Egypt.[20] It was only forbidden for priests in certain cities and at certain periods. The archaeologist Albright writes about this: "The common explanation for the Biblical legislation concerning pork—that it was not eaten because it was sacred among pagan people—is sheer nonsense. The pig was sacred in certain places and periods, but large and small cattle were even more generally sacred, so that it is quite irrational to single out the economically and religiously much less important pig."[21]

If there's no ethical or religious reason to be found for the prohibition of the animals mentioned, what then is the reason?

Free-range pigs in a large town in China.

The Pig

"The pig . . . is unclean for you. You must not eat their meat" (Leviticus 11:7–8). Why did Moses call the pig unclean? How could he know that eating pork at that time was really perilous?

From time immemorial, pigs have been kept as domestic animals. They are real omnivores—eating everything. They scour around the farm or along the roads, where there's rubbish and excrement and the ditches are used as drains, rooting around in the earth, the manure, and the mud, eating up everything they come across: domestic refuse, tree roots, and insects; young, sick, and dead animals (including rats that have died of deadly diseases, such as the plague). Everything is polished off—creating ideal conditions for the pig to contract deadly diseases, including those from the pork tapeworm and the dreaded trichinae, for which there is no treatment. There are more than forty diseases that can be transmitted by pigs.

The Pork Tapeworm

The most significant species of tapeworms that can live in the intestines of humans are the pork tapeworm (*Taenia solium*) from pigs and the beef tapeworm (*Taenia saginata*) from cattle. Both these worms enter the intestines when half-cooked or raw meat, which contains larvae of the tapeworm, is eaten. The larvae, which are over one centimeter long, grow in the intestines into adult tapeworms of three or ten meters long respectively.

The danger isn't that a tapeworm enters the body through the larvae in pork or beef; this is only unpleasant, not fatal. The danger is in the *eggs* of the pork tapeworm. Of the other tapeworms, only the larvae can live in our intestines, but with the pork tapeworm, the eggs can too. Through a lack of hygiene, people can infect themselves with the eggs through contact with feces or by eating vegetables on which human excrement has been used as manure.

If you ingest the eggs, little larvae hatch in your intestines, which drill through the gut wall and spread around the body through the bloodstream. In this way, cysts containing the tapeworm larvae can form all around the body, especially in the eyes and in the nervous system. If a large number of cysts develops in the important organs, such as the brain, the heart, or the liver, the host human becomes seriously ill, and with repeated infection, this results in death. It takes ten to twenty years before this slowly progressing illness becomes fatal. This process is accelerated and aggravated if you repeatedly eat severely contaminated pork.

People, in primitive societies in particular, who eat pork not adequately boiled or roasted and don't wash their hands and buttocks properly and don't bury their excrement—but even use it as manure on the vegetable plot—suffer from this deadly tapeworm.[22]

Trichinae

Trichinae (*Trichinella spiralis*) live in the intestinal tract of carnivores and omnivores, of which the pig is the most important representative for meat consumption. The female trichinae penetrate the gut wall of the animal and produce young (larvae), which enter the bloodstream and are spread throughout the body. The larvae form cysts in the muscle tissue and can remain alive there for as long as twenty years. A scavenging pig can very easily become infected with trichinae when it eats other animals, such as dead rats.

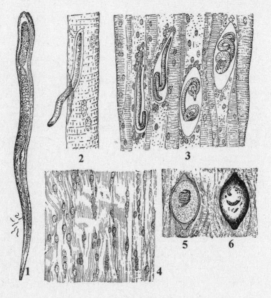

Trichinae: 1. Intestinal trichina that produces young; 2. a young trichina pushes into a muscle; 3. young trichinae; 4. muscle with trichinae in cysts; 5. living; 6. dead trichinae in cysts (enlarged).

If meat of an infected pig is consumed by humans, the calcified cysts dissolve and the larvae are released. The cycle now repeats itself: the adult trichinae drill through the wall of the intestines and produce larvae, which enter the bloodstream and are transported around the body. The larvae form cysts in the muscles and cause symptoms of poisoning: fever, rheumatoid pains, anemia, difficulty in breathing and, with severe infection, death.

Trichinae are especially dangerous with repeated infection, that's to say, when severely infected and undercooked pork is consumed on more than one occasion. Until fifty years ago, there was no remedy whatsoever for this deadly disease. In modern societies trichinae and pork tapeworm have only been conquered by careful and systematic checking and thoroughly cooking the meat.[23]

In the United States, where the checking of pork for trichinae is not obligatory, at least 4 percent of the population is infected with trichinosis.[24] According to some people, it's as many as 20 percent.[25] Fortunately the infection is usually not very severe, because the meat is adequately heated with modern cooking equipment and most trichinae are killed. But still countless people are going about with vague complaints and discomfort, thinking they occasionally have a slight attack of the flu.[26]

Liver Fluke

During one of my lectures, the question arose as to why beef is not prohibited, although a cow can be infected with the dangerous liver fluke (*Fasciola hepatica*). The answer is fourfold:

1. The liver fluke lives primarily in the *bile ducts* of cows, sheep, goats, pigs, deer, horses, and hares. When the animal is slaughtered, the bile ducts must be removed together with the gall bladder. (In Leviticus 3:4, 10, and 15, the "covering of the liver" refers to the gall bladder.) So there's no danger that the liver fluke will be eaten accidentally.

2. If there happen to be liver flukes in other organs, such as the liver, the spleen, or the heart, the liver fluke is easy to detect with the naked eye on inspection of the meat. The worm is on average 9 mm thick and 30 mm long (that's to say, 200,000 times the volume of a trichina).

3. Tests have shown that humans aren't infected with liver flukes by eating animal meat, but by eating plants (most commonly, *watercress*) that are infected with liver-fluke larvae.

4. Infection with liver fluke is not life-threatening, unlike a severe infection of trichinae.[27]

The Rabbit

"The rabbit, though it chews the cud, does not have a split hoof; it is unclean for you" (Leviticus 11:6). An important reason for prohibiting the consumption of rabbits and hares is that they may be infected with the plague, just like rodents.[28] So it might be very dangerous to eat or touch these animals. A second reason is that rabbits and hares may be infected with a bacillus (*Bacterium tularense*) that is similar to the plague bacillus and causes the disease tularemia in humans. When slaughtering and skinning an infected rabbit, the bacteria force their way into the body through small wounds and cause infections. In the United States, annually many dozens of people become infected in this way, especially in rural areas and among hunters.[29]

If the infection isn't treated, serious symptoms can arise, and if an infected rabbit is eaten, there's a considerable risk of the infection resulting in death.[30] That untreated tularemia can constitute a serious threat to public health became apparent during the siege of Stalingrad in 1942. Through an unknown cause, tularemia broke out, and thousands of soldiers died of this disease.[31]

Scientific Blunder?

It's interesting to have a closer look at the often cited "scientific blunder" about the rabbit that *chews the cud* (see Leviticus 11:6). The rabbit isn't a ruminant. It does not belong to the scientific classification of the *Ruminantia*, such as cows, sheep, goats, deer, giraffes, and antelopes. It does not bring back its food from the stomach, through the esophagus into the mouth, to chew it again.

But this doesn't necessarily mean that Moses made a scientific blunder! The rabbit does indeed occasionally ingest its food twice. Rabbits and hares have a peculiar habit, which was first described in 1882 in a French journal for veterinary surgeons. Very early in the morning—besides their normal dry pellets—they excrete soft, amorphous balls that contain four to five times as many vitamins (especially vitamin B) as their ordinary droppings. These balls (caecotrophs) are formed in the blind gut (caecum) and are of vital importance to rabbits and hares, particularly in times of food shortage.[32] Immediately after the balls have been excreted, they are eaten and digested for a second time in a special section of the stomach. When digested the second time, the vitamins and other nutrients are released, which were inaccessible when they were first digested. This process has the same function as the rumination of the true ruminants. Grzimek writes, "In a certain sense, this double digestion is reminiscent of the rumination of artiodactyls [even-toed hoofed animals]."[33]

Five pages previously, Grzimek writes that rabbits and hares are not rodents, but that they form a separate group, the lagomorphs, and, "According to the composition of the blood fluid, the lagomorphs are closer to some hoofed mammals than to rodents."[34]

It's not a biblical blunder that the rabbit was counted among the animals that reingest their food, but a scientific wonder. The Bible does not say that the rabbit belongs to the suborder of *Ruminantia*; that would have been a slip. But it does say it ingests its food again, and that's correct.

The Hyrax

"The hyrax chews the cud but does not have split hooves; so it is unclean" (Leviticus 11:5 NLT). Hyraxes are the size of rabbits and live in colonies in crevices and holes in rocks. They often eat in groups, consuming buds, leaves, herbs, and grass.

The same prohibition applies to the hyrax as to rabbits and hares. Anyone who doesn't know better might have a good laugh at the "scientific blunder" that the hyrax reingests its food. But in the great encyclopedia of animals by Grzimek, it says, "Hyraxes do reingest their food," and "Anyone who sees these marmot-like animals will find it hard to believe that they belong to the order of ungulates [hoofed animals]. . . . For the layman, it seems well-nigh incredible that these small, rodent-like inhabitants of rocks and trees are distant relatives of the elephant."

Three pages later, Grzimek writes, "Unique among all mammals is its intestinal tract: it is namely so that hyraxes have two blind guts . . . the function of the second blind gut is not yet clear."[35] It's not known why hyraxes must not be eaten, but we will perhaps discover this when our knowledge about hyraxes has further increased.

The Camel

The camel is also mentioned as an unclean animal. In the Bible, this refers to the single-humped Arab dromedary (*Camelus dromedarius*). Camels are now no longer included in the suborder of *Ruminantia*, but in a separate suborder of *Tylopoda*, which also chew their food twice. Their hoofs are not split, as with ruminants, but "somewhat split at the front," as Grzimek puts it.[36]

I haven't found much information about the camel. The only remarkable fact was that at a youth camp in Germany, a group of youths became infected with trichinosis because they had eaten camel meat, bought when they were on vacation in Egypt. Evidently the camel can also be infected by trichinae. This would be reason enough to prohibit it for consumption.

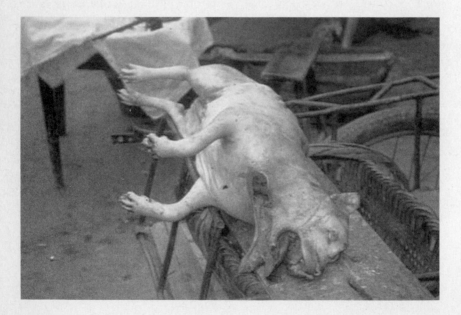

A delicacy in China.

Birds

Almost all peoples in the world have types of bird they regard as sacred or as the reincarnation of a certain deity and which therefore must not be eaten. Israel was the only country in which not a single bird (or other animal) was regarded as sacred. All birds could be eaten if there was no objection to this from a biological point of view. Research has revealed that birds are not susceptible to trichinae.[37] So you might expect that only reasons relating to biological balance would remain.

Biological Balance

In Leviticus 11:13–19, an extensive list is given of types of birds prohibited for consumption.† This list gives an overview of all "protected" birds that were found in Canaan. These were mainly birds important for the biological balance in nature. They ensured that sick and dead animals and even domestic refuse were disposed of and harmful types of animals, such as rats, mice, and locusts, didn't get the upper hand. All other types of bird could be eaten, including songbirds, doves, plovers, fowl, and ducks.

---

† It's not possible to know exactly which type of bird is intended by each Hebrew word. This is why in the lists in Leviticus 11 and Deuteronomy 14, in different translations of the Bible, sometimes different names of birds are given. However, they are always birds of prey. The same uncertainty applies to some of the small predators in Leviticus 11:29–30.

Family	Main food
Permitted for Consumption	
Divers, mergansers	Fish
Petrels, albatrosses	Fish
Pelicans, cormorants	Fish
Terns	Fish
Gulls	Fish, worms
Kingfishers	Fish, insects
Geese, swans	Grass, foliage
Ducks	Grass, aquatic plants, fish
Fowl, pheasants, partridges	Grass, seed
Cranes, rails, bustards	Grass, seed, aquatic plants
Doves	Seed, fruit, young foliage
Cuckoos	Plants, insects
Nightjars, swifts	Insects
Rollers	Beetles and other insects
Woodpeckers	Ants, beetle larvae
Songbirds	Insects, seeds
Prohibited for Consumption	
Crows	Omnivores
Vultures, kites	Carrion
Birds of prey, owls	Mice, rats, small mammals
Storks, ibises, herons, bitterns	Frogs, fish, mice, locusts
Bee-eaters	Insects, locusts
Hoopoes	Caterpillars, worms
Ostriches	Grass, foliage, seeds, small animals

Families of birds found in Israel, with their main sources of food. Some were protected and so prohibited for consumption (see Leviticus 11:13–19). Table and explanation adapted from Hüttermann.[38]

Explanation of the Table

The protected species of birds can be divided into six groups:

1. *Crows*—In the Bible, "any kind of raven" is protected (Leviticus 11:15). These are the crows (*corvidae*), such as the raven, carrion crow, rook, and jackdaw. These birds form a separate group within the large classification of "songbirds." They are truly omnivores that like to eat rubbish and relish the meat the large carrion birds leave on carcasses.

2. *Vultures and kites*—In all tropical countries, carrion birds are protected by law, because they are extremely important in keeping the environment clean. They are indispensable in disposing of carrion. Grzimek writes,

   "Many small towns in tropical America, and also the slums of many large towns, would hardly be able to dispose of their rubbish without the clearance activities of these birds."[39]

3. *Birds of prey and owls*—In antiquity, birds of this kind weren't protected in any country whatsoever, except in Israel. This was unique! For only a few decades have we known how important the protection of these birds is. Birds of prey and owls feed on harmful animals such as rats and mice, and what's also important: "Birds of prey are of extraordinary importance in maintaining the biological balance. They dispose of carrion and live mainly on sick and weak animals."[40] This is why nowadays all birds of prey are protected throughout Europe.

4. *Storks, herons, ibises, and bitterns*—These birds not only catch fish—if all they caught were fish, these species would certainly not have been protected—but also lots of mice and locusts. The stork especially eats lots of locusts. In some African languages, the stork is even called "locust bird" or "locust eater." Of the fish, it eats predominantly sick and dead specimens. In areas with

infestations of mice, storks are found in large numbers.[41] Their task as "feathered cats" is extremely important in agricultural areas where infestations of mice occur.

5. *Bee eaters and hoopoes*—These birds are protected because of their destruction of locusts and other insects. Moreover, it's known that the hoopoe often looks for food on rubbish tips, which is an "unclean" activity.

6. *Ostriches*—These are birds whose protection has no known (yet) reason. Perhaps the protection has something to do with the fact that they are omnivores.

Damage Caused by Pests

Rats and mice—In the Netherlands, with our splendid brick houses and concrete storage silos, where we have an abundance of chemical pesticides and a national rat-control department, every year rats still cause damage to the tune of $50 million.[42] In the United States, the damage to food products by rats and mice is estimated at $900 million per year[43] and the *total* damage by rats alone, at $19 billion per year.[44] In India, 10 to 30 percent of the grain harvest is lost to rats and mice (according to some researchers, even up to 45 percent) and globally at least 150 million tons of grain every year.[45] That is enough to feed over one billion (!) people annually.[46] Besides this, the rat is the primary carrier of fatal diseases such as the plague, typhus, and trichinosis as well as rabies, foot-and-mouth disease, Weil's disease, typhoid, paratyphoid, and many other diseases.[47] Biologists say, "Rats and mice are the most destructive vertebrates on earth," and "The rat is an unmitigated nuisance and pest. There is nothing that can be said in its favor."[48]

Locusts—Locusts can cause great famines. In Morocco in 1962, within five days a swarm of locusts ate 7 million kilos (15.4 million pounds) of oranges. This is more than the annual consumption of oranges in the whole of France. During a serious plague in Turkey, 7.25 million kilos of locust eggs were collected, which corresponds to more than 300 billion locusts. Occasionally there are swarms with a surface area of about fifty square miles and a depth of eighty feet. In 1889, a swarm crossed the Red

Sea with a surface area of as much as 1,900 square miles, estimated to consist of 43 billion tons (!) of locusts. In 1955, an equally large swarm attacked southern Morocco. And to think that some types of locusts can eat their own weight in food in a day![49]

As with rats and mice, the damage by insects is staggering. Even in a modern country like the United States, with its high-tech pest-control techniques, the annual loss of stored food due to insects ranges from two to six billion dollars.[50] Globally about 500 million tons of stored food (grain, tubers, roots, fruit, vegetables) is lost due to insects and mites, adding to a loss of about 26 billion dollars each year.[51] As already mentioned, pest control, as well as the immediate removal of carrion and rubbish, are of exceptional importance for a primitive society. The usefulness of birds as a "natural waste disposal service" can hardly be overestimated.

BATS

Through ignorance, scornful remarks are still made about the fact that in the Bible the bat is included in the list of "unclean birds" (see Leviticus 11:13–19). But this isn't at all such a strange remark. It doesn't say that the bat belongs to the scientific class of "birds" (Aves), but that it's a "flier." The Hebrew word used for "bird" in verse 13 means "flier" or "winged creature." The same word is used in verses 20–23 for flying insects.

In the Bible, the bat is an unclean, that is, protected, species, because it's one of the best insect exterminators and therefore extremely important for the balance in nature. In our times, people have even tried to eradicate the malaria mosquito with bats.[52] Moreover, bats may transmit all sorts of dangerous diseases, such as the deadly rabies. Altogether, reasons enough to prohibit them for consumption.

SMALL LAND ANIMALS AND INSECTS

Small land animals and insects are the "creepy-crawlies": the scurrying mice, slimy toads, filthy bugs, and scary spiders. Animals that many skittish people run away from or jump on a chair to escape. The Bible calls them "animals that move along the ground." There are two types: creepy-crawlies without wings and creepy-crawlies with wings.

Creepy-Crawlies without Wings

"Of the animals that move about on the ground, these are unclean for you:
the weasel, the rat, any kind of great lizard, the gecko, the monitor lizard,
the wall lizard, the skink and the chameleon. . . . You are not to eat any
creature that moves about on the ground, whether it moves on its belly or
walks on all fours or on many feet; it is detestable" (Leviticus 11:29–30,
42).‡ This group also includes worms, spiders, centipedes, snakes, polecats, and others.

The eating of any of these small animals was strictly forbidden. Their
carcasses were not even to be touched. The prohibition is very strict, and
not a single exception is mentioned. It says five times that they are detestable to eat. For Westerners, it sounds strange that such strict rules had to be
issued to prevent the Israelites from eating these filthy creatures. But in the
times of Moses, the Canaanites ate a lot of snakes, lizards, rats, and mice.[53]

Why Prohibited?

We won't deal with the various small land animals individually. But with
these small creatures, too, public health and biological balance play important roles.

1. Public Health

    Rats are the main cause of harmful diseases, such as the plague,
    typhus, and trichinosis. Letting these animals into the house or
    consuming them was a sure way of becoming infected and dying
    prematurely. We also know that many "creepy-crawlies" are car-
    riers of trichinae (e.g., the mouse, hamster, hedgehog, marten,
    polecat, and other small carnivores), which is reason enough for
    such creatures not to be eaten.

---

‡ The meaning of some Hebrew words is not clear, so that among the various Bible
translations, different species may be mentioned.

2. Biological Balance

The small carnivores were also prohibited because they are the best exterminators of pests such as rats, mice, and locusts. On the previous pages, we have read about the damage the rat family and locusts can cause. This aspect cannot be emphasized enough for a time in which there were not yet any chemical pesticides.

Exterminators of Pests

Small predators marten, fox, badger) prefer to eat mice and rats.

Insect eaters (mole, hedgehog) are extremely good exterminators of insect larvae. For this reason, the hedgehog is a protected species in the Netherlands.[54] Moreover, the hedgehog is a formidable mouse catcher.

Reptiles (lizard, chameleon) like to eat insects. Lizards especially can play a considerable role in the control of plagues of locusts. Snakes are important mouse and rat catchers, while other reptiles, such as the monitor lizard, eat all sorts of food, including insects, rats, and dead animals.

Amphibians (frog, toad, salamander) are important exterminators of mosquito larvae. In the tropics and subtropics, they play an important role in the control of malaria mosquitoes and other insects. If too many frogs are caught for consumption, the number of mosquitoes increases and malaria can spread. Frogs and toads also serve as reserve food supplies for large wading birds, such as the stork. A stork prefers to eat locusts, but if there are no locusts or other insects left, it will try to bridge the period of famine with frogs and toads.

Creepy-Crawlies with Wings

"All flying insects that walk on all fours are to be detestable to you. There are, however, some winged creatures that walk on all fours that you may eat: those that have jointed legs for hopping on the ground" (Leviticus 11:20–21). In other words, all insects are prohibited except locusts.§

---

§ The fact that it says here that insects walk on "all fours," instead of on six legs, is because the front two legs were considered to be hands. So the other four were the "back legs" on which they walked.

Why Is It Okay to Eat Locusts?

1. Locusts eat grass and leaves. So they don't eat dangerous food, as far as germs and parasites are concerned.

2. Locusts consist of between 50 and 75 percent protein. This is more than other adult insects and three times as much as the meat of land animals.

3. The intestines of locusts are stuffed with vegetable matter and therefore rich in vitamins.

AQUATIC ANIMALS

Permitted

Of all the creatures in the seas, lakes, rivers, and marshes, only actual fish with fins and scales were permitted for consumption: "Of all the creatures living in the water of the seas and the streams, you may eat any that have fins and scales" (Leviticus 11:9). Examples of these are herring, cod, mackerel, tuna, and salmon. According to the modern science of nutrition, the permitted fish are still the safest source of food from the water. Fish with fins and scales are generally free-swimming and are found primarily in healthy, flowing water.

A seaman who had sailed every ocean and the inland seas of the Middle East told me about the principle the sailors had on board when they cast a line for fun and fished up all sorts of unknown creatures: "Everything that has fins and scales is safe to eat; the rest may be dangerous."

Prohibited

All aquatic animals without fins and scales were prohibited (see Leviticus 11:10–12), such as the shark, eel, squid, mussel, lobster, snail, and also aquatic mammals such as seals and dolphins. Aquatic mammals were of little importance to a primitive society, but probably they weren't to be eaten because they might be infected with trichinae[55] and because they are useful in the dispatch of sick, weak, and dead aquatic animals.

General Rule

Among the prohibited aquatic animals and land animals, there may well be species that could be eaten without any problem. But in a general book of law, such as that of Moses, not all species can be dealt with individually. That would result in an unworkably thick book.

A good legislator will try to establish as concisely as possible a number of generally applicable rules that are of importance to the whole of society. So also with food; there had to be rules that were easy for the layperson to remember and apply. If there are then a number of (aquatic) animals wrongly excluded from consumption, this just has to be tolerated.

Why Prohibited?

Public Health

One reason why "scaleless" aquatic animals such as shellfish, crabs, lobsters, and prawns pose a threat to public health is that their meat spoils *particularly* quickly. In the tropics, it happens within a few hours, more quickly than the meat of any other animal. This was why until recently it was forbidden in the Netherlands (and other Western countries) to sell mussels in the hot summer months.[56] Because cooling technology has now been perfected, it's permitted to supply mussels all year round, but only if the cooling chain is not broken.[57]

A second reason is that shellfish such as mussels grow best in shallow water rich in nutrients (and waste). They are immobile "filterers": they pump water past their gills and filter out the nutrients, which are transported to the mouth by means of small hairs. The more nutrients there are in the water, the better they grow. This is why the cultivation of mussels near human settlements is often a great success. But with the nutritious water, the filters also absorb the germs present, forming an ideal breeding ground. For this reason, in the vicinity of mussel farms, the authorities constantly check the water for germs. And it's also the reason why in the Netherlands these shellfish may not be cultivated in wastewater or in the vicinity of settlements or outlets of drains.[58]

Third, scaleless aquatic animals such as snails are often host to all sorts of pathogenic worms like the schistosoma, which causes bilharzias. See also chapter 2, page 32.[59]

Biological Balance

In modern times, mainly marine shellfish such as mussels and oysters are raised for consumption. In Old Testament times, this consumption was less important. At that time people mainly ate shellfish that lived in freshwater, such as the freshwater mussels.

Imagine if, at that time, freshwater mussels had been allowed to be eaten without restriction, while there were no methods of artificially breeding these creatures. Soon there would not have been many mussels left, and the filtering, and with it the cleaning of the water, would have been greatly reduced. The number of germs would have increased, and people would have become sick.

Grzimek writes, "Freshwater mussels play an important role in nature because they purify the water by their filtering activities. Measurements have shown that per hour, more than forty liters of water pass through the filtration organs of one single mussel. If the mussels in a body of water were to be destroyed, this would mean a disruption of the biological balance, which ultimately would lead to a threat to the life of man himself. It's indeed becoming more and more clear how dependent man is on pure, healthy water."[60]

BAN ON CARRION, BLOOD, AND FAT

Carrion

"Do not eat anything you find already dead (literally: that died of itself). You may give it to an alien living in any of your towns, and he may eat it, or you may sell it to a foreigner"℃ and, "Do not eat the meat of an animal torn by wild beasts; throw it to the dogs" (Deuteronomy 14:21; Exodus 22:31)."

These two rules are evidence of a profound insight into pathology. There is a great difference between animals that have been slaughtered properly according to the rules and animals that have been torn apart or have died of themselves. A slaughtered and approved animal in Israel was by definition in perfect health. An animal that had "died of itself" or had been torn apart in the open field was by definition unhealthy and swarming with germs. This is still the same today.

In nature, animals hardly ever die of old age, but of serious diseases, such as tuberculosis or a form of helminthiasis. Or they are torn apart by predators, because they are too weak or too sick to defend themselves or run away. If you eat the meat of such animals, without cooking it extra long and well, you can be sure of contracting some dangerous disease, particularly if the animal has already been dead for a number of days. This advice—not to eat any animals that died of natural causes or have been torn apart—is so good that it's still followed in all civilized countries. If any butcher in a developed country were to sell meat from such an animal in his shop, he would be given a hefty fine.

Blood

Blood is indispensable in the bodies of higher species of animals. It ensures the supply of water, oxygen, and nutrients and the removal of carbon dioxide and waste matter. Besides this, the temperature of the body is regulated through the blood, and germs are killed. Any cell in the body that does not receive blood dies in a very short time.

Doctors had to learn this lesson by trial and error, as did the personal physician of American president George Washington in 1799. When the president had a bad cold, his doctor thought he would soon have him on his feet again by means of bloodletting. For this, a cut is made in the arm

---

℃ Selling carrion to foreigners was permitted because they didn't take any notice of the peculiar dietary laws of Israel anyway.

** In emergencies, such as during a famine or war, it was permitted to eat carrion of clean animals. But carrion of an unclean animal was absolutely forbidden at all times (Leviticus 11:8, 11 in contrast to Leviticus 11:39–40).

through which the blood can flow away and "the balance of the vital juices is restored," after which the cold will cease. Because the president's cold persisted, so much blood was drawn off him that he died in the arms of his physician. Blood really is the soul, the vitality of all higher organisms.

In Leviticus it says, "The life of a creature is in the blood. . . . Therefore, . . . 'none of you may eat blood.' . . . Any[one] who hunts any animal or bird that may be eaten must drain out the blood and cover it with earth" (17:11–13).

Why on earth were the Israelites not allowed to eat blood? What's wrong with a nice bit of half-cooked black pudding or a dish of uncooked cow's blood, such as the Masai in East Africa regularly polish off? And why did the blood specifically have to be buried? Of course there are also religious motives for forbidding the consumption of blood; for example, the fact that primitive peoples use blood for occult practices, as "food for the evil spirits." But there was more to it than this.

Dangerous to Eat

In unhygienic conditions, animals' blood can be really swimming with germs, especially single-celled organisms (protozoa and bacteria), blood filariae (tiny larvae in the blood that are spread by mosquitoes), and the larvae of trichinae. It's true that, when eaten, most of the germs are killed in the human's aggressive gastric juices, but by no means all. If these organisms get into a person's intestines and multiply, they can cause serious illnesses. The larvae can drill through the gut wall, get into the blood circulation, and spread through the human body.

Dangerous to Keep

Blood is an ideal breeding ground for germs. In a warm tropical or subtropical climate and in unhygienic conditions, the germs develop at top speed to quantities dangerous for human consumption.

In the future, probably more facts will be discovered that reveal why eating blood is bad for the health. Recent research has shown that eating meat rich in blood increases the risk of uterine cancer[61] and several other cancers.

Three women with meat to feed their families. From left to right: pieces of meat dried in a tree, a small deer, a goat's head.

FAT

In antiquity, people were convinced that the fat of animals was healthy. It was a sign of abundance. This makes it all the more remarkable that God, who promised the people of Israel a life of abundance (see Deuteronomy 28:11–13), prohibited the consumption of animal fat. This goes against all sense of logic. "'This is a lasting ordinance for the generations to come, wherever you live: You must not eat any fat or any blood. . . . Do not eat any of the fat of cattle, sheep or goats. The fat of an animal found dead or torn by wild animals may be used for any other purpose, but you must not eat it'" (Leviticus 3:17; 7:23–24).

The Israelites were allowed to eat "fatty meat," meat with fat between the muscles, but not the loose fat under the skin or around the organs. This sort of fat could be used for all sorts of purposes, but not for consumption. So it wasn't even to be used for baking or frying.

Nowadays, it's pretty much taken for granted that animal fat is extremely bad for the health. Books about nutrition and leaflets about heart and vascular diseases all caution against fat in the diet, for the following reasons:

1. Animal fat consists of saturated fatty acids. These are the most significant culprits in the development of heart and vascular diseases, but also of cancer and obesity.

2. In warm tropical or subtropical conditions, animal fat very quickly becomes rancid. And rancid fats contain substances that increase the risk of cancer.[62]

3. Animal fat is a storage place for waste materials and for poisons such as herbicides, chemicals, and antibiotics. When the fat is consumed, all these substances enter the human body.

Heart and Vascular Diseases

For years heart disease and stroke have been the first and third leading causes of death in the United States. Annually about 870,000 people in the United States die of these diseases—35 percent of all deaths.[63] The same is true for most Western countries. The majority of these deaths are caused by consumption of unhealthy food, particularly *animal* fats (frying and basting fats, greasy gravy, biscuits, cakes, snacks). If we weren't to eat any animal fat in the Western world, annually millions fewer people would die an early death of heart and vascular diseases.

It's remarkable that the Israelites weren't allowed to eat the hard, saturated fat of land animals but yet were allowed to eat the oily fat of fish. This reveals an incredibly deep insight into the science of nutrition. The subcutaneous fat of land animals is the most unhealthy food there is, while the fat of fish is precisely the opposite! It's particularly *good* for the health. The oilier, the better.

The fat of fish contains unsaturated, omega-3 fatty acids, which not only combat the increase in cholesterol in the blood, but even *reduce* the cholesterol level. It also contains other essential fatty acids important for the development of the brain and other organs. Consumption of two (oily) fish dishes a week can reduce the risk of heart and vascular disease by 30 percent[64] and has an advantageous effect on an endless list of other illnesses, including rheumatism, diabetes, and cancer. Eskimos seldom die of heart or vascular diseases, because they eat so much fish.[65]

Another remarkable fact is that in countries where not animal fat but vegetable oils (especially olive oil) are the most important sources of fat, as in the countries around the Mediterranean Sea, considerably fewer cases of heart and vascular diseases occur than in northern Europe and America.[66] So if you must eat a lot of fat, eat unsaturated oily fat from fish or use vegetable oils.

Cancer

In the United States cancer is the second leading cause of death. Annually about 556,000 people die of cancer—23 percent of all deaths.[67] The same applies to most Western countries. Scientists estimate that 30 percent of these are caused by unhealthy diet.[68] According to some researchers, the percentage is even twice as high.[69] The greatest culprits are—just as with heart and vascular diseases—the animal fats.

Research has proved that eating a lot of fresh fruit and raw vegetables is very important in avoiding cancer.[70] In all sorts of cancer-prevention leaflets, fresh fruit and vegetables are strongly recommended.

It's telling that right at the start of the Bible, God recommends the same thing—yes, almost gives a command, "I give you every seed-bearing plant on the face of the whole earth and every tree that has fruit with seed in it. They will be yours for food" (Genesis 1:29).

Only after the Fall and after the Flood was it permitted for humans to eat meat (see Genesis 9:3), but the Israelites were only allowed this under strict conditions, as we have read on the previous pages.

"Of the animals you *may* eat . . ." If you must eat meat, that's allowed, but the original plan of the Creator was that mankind would eat mainly grain, fruit, and vegetables. (Leviticus 11:3, 9, 21).

MODERN DIET BOOKS

We can cite dozens more examples showing that eating according to biblical norms is the healthiest for mankind. We will suffice with three recommendations by a nutrition expert.[71††]

Eat Food Created for Consumption

Avoid everything not intended as food. Vegetable products were originally intended as food, but not animal products. They were only permitted later (as we just noted) after the original creation was destroyed by the Flood and many healthy plants became extinct. Eat as little as possible of animals and only products of clean animals. Instead eat as much fresh fruit and as many raw vegetables as possible.

Eat Food as It Was Created

When possible, eat *fresh* fruit and *raw* vegetables. Eat as few refined (white) products as possible, such as refined flour, fat, oil, sugar—because there are no healthy vitamins or minerals in them. Also eat as little food as possible to which chemicals have been added or processed food, such as bread, in which the germ from the grain has been removed to make the bread have a longer shelf life. In this way, twenty vitamins and minerals essential for good health have been removed from the bread.

Do Not Let Any Type of Food or
Drink Become Your God

Even the good food God gives us can become bad if we misuse it or if it demands all our attention. People can become addicted to foodstuffs such as caffeine, fat, sugar, and salt, but also to good and healthy food, and eat too much of it.

---

†† Nutrition expert Russell is a diabetic and writes on page 26 of his book, "Millions of people would recover [from diabetes] if they were to eat in accordance with the three basic principles which the Bible gives."

SUMMARY

The dietary laws in the Bible are intended to make the living conditions in a primitive society as healthy as possible. Two aspects in this play important roles: public health and the biological balance of nature. The only animals permitted for consumption were those that didn't represent a threat to public health and weren't important for the balance of nature. This applied not only to all land animals, large and small, but also to aquatic animals, birds, and insects.

In primitive societies, preventative measures are particularly important, because there was no other way in which to curb the development of pests and germs. Beasts and birds of prey play an exceptionally important role in biological control. Most likely it was mainly for this reason they were not to be eaten. An additional reason is that the meat of beasts of prey may contain numerous germs, which can be fatal when ingested, particularly if the meat isn't cooked thoroughly.

The regulations about the consumption of meat reveal an amazingly profound insight into the science of nutrition. This also applies to the rules about eating carrion, blood, and fat. But the most amazing thing is that even "modern diseases," such as heart and vascular diseases and cancer, cannot be prevented or countered in any better way than by following the prescriptions of Moses. The best guarantee still for a long and healthy life is to follow the dietary rules of the Bible.

WILL THE LAWS OF MOSES EVER BE EQUALED?

How long will it be before people rate the regulations of the Bible at their true value? How long will it be before we realize that the Bible wasn't written on the basis of the human knowledge that was current at the time, but rather to counter the *lack* of such knowledge?

Tens of millions of people have lived in misery and squalor and died unnecessarily prematurely because no importance was attached to the simple and specific hygiene and dietary measures in the Bible. This even applies to our times. Still millions of people are dying unnecessarily in excruciating pain and distress. And who can say what harmful effects of the food we presently eat will be discovered in the future? What about all the foodstuffs that are refined or processed in order to give them a longer shelf life, or genetically modified to give a greater yield, or full of coloring agents and flavorings? These are all additives not originally intended as foodstuffs and that are therefore potentially bad for the health.

Tens of other dietary laws and rules might be mentioned that reveal the progressiveness of the Bible. But including these would make this book too long. We are going to consider other interesting facts of physics and astronomy next.

> Do not let this Book of the Law depart from your mouth;
> meditate on it day and night,
> so that you may be careful to do everything written in it.
> Then you will be prosperous and successful.
>
> JOSHUA 1:8

5.

NATURAL SCIENCES

Utanapishtim spoke to Gilgamesh:
"I will reveal to you, O Gilgamesh, a secret.
In the city of Shuruppak, the gods had gathered.
Their hearts moved them to inflict a flood."

The god Ea, the wise, betrayed their plan,
And said, "O man of Shuruppak, build a boat!
Make all living beings go up into the boat.
The boat which you are to build,
Its measures shall equal each other,
Its length must correspond to its width."

On the fifth day, I laid out the exterior.
Its walls were 120 cubit [60 meters] high,
The width of its deck was equally 120 cubits.
Six decks high I raised it.

Whatever I had I put aboard it,
I had all my family and relatives board the ship,
The domesticated animals and the wild.
I boarded the ship and closed the door.

For six days and seven nights,
The flood and the storm overwhelmed the land.
When the seventh day arrived,
The storm and the flood ceased their war.

On Mount Nisir the ship grounded.
When the seventh day dawned, I sent forth a dove.
The dove flew away, then came back,
No resting place appeared for it, so it returned.

Then I sent forth a raven.
The raven went off and saw the waters receding.
It ate, it flew about, it did not return.
Then I sent out everything to the four winds.

I offered incense on the highest peak of the mountain.
Seven and seven cult vessels I put in place,
And into their bowls I poured reeds, cedar and myrtle."

This is an abbreviated rendition of the Flood story from the great *Epic of Gilgamesh* of the Babylonians.[1] The epic tells about the adventures of King Gilgamesh from the city of Uruk (Erech in Genesis 10:10), who is seeking eternal life. In his wanderings, he encounters Utanapishtim, who tells him how he had built a boat to survive the great Flood.

This *Epic of Gilgamesh* was discovered in 1853 during excavations in the ruins of Nineveh, together with over twenty thousand other clay tablets from the library of King Assurbanipal (668–626 BC).

Clay tablet with part of the *Epic of Gilgamesh.*

At first sight, the story of Utanapishtim resembles the account of Noah and the Flood in the Bible (Genesis 6–8), but there are a few important differences. With Utanapishtim, the boat had the form of a cube, it rained for a week, and the flood lasted for two weeks—an impossibly short time. With Noah, the boat had the form of a large cargo ship, it rained for forty days, and the Flood lasted a whole year.

UTANAPISHTIM'S ARK

Utanapishtim said that he built a boat in the form of a cube (60 x 60 x 60 meters) and that with it he withstood the harsh storms. We would like to take Utanapishtim at his word, but it seems that he was a real landlubber, who knew little of shipbuilding. As it happens, it is impossible to survive a flood in a cube, for all the following reasons:

1. A cube is the *least seaworthy ship*. If you load a cube to the gunnels (six decks) with food and animals, as Utanapishtim did, it will slowly roll over in the water and capsize at the slightest movement of the waves.

2. If only the bottom half of the cube is used for cargo, it is still terribly unstable and catches the wind unnecessarily, which means that it constantly tilts and will very soon be blown upside down.

3. As the length and breadth of the cube are equal, the pressure and tractive force of the water and wind are equal in all directions, making the cube constantly spin around, stopping only if it tips over.

4. The construction of a cube is much weaker than that of a long, flat boat. Through the effects of the wind and waves, it would soon be pulled out of joint and sink, especially in severe weather.

NOAH'S ARK

PERFECT DESIGN

God said, "Make yourself an ark of gopher wood. . . . This is how you are to make it: the length of the ark three hundred cubits, its breadth fifty cubits, and its height thirty cubits" (Genesis 6:14–15 RSV). The cubit was between 45 and 60 cm long. If we set the cubit at 50 cm (1.64 feet), this means that the ark was 492 feet long, 82 feet wide, and 49 feet high.

Shape

The proportions Noah used for his vessel, the length six times the breadth (6:1), were completely unknown for a cargo ship at the time.* The Phoenicians, pioneers in the area of shipbuilding, and other peoples had sailing ships that were about two or three times as long as they were wide. In later centuries, sailing ships were built with a proportion of 4:1, but this extra length was to make room for oarsmen, who had to row if there was insufficient wind.

Until the sixteenth century, the seafaring sailing ships of the Netherlands and other European countries were about twice as long as they were wide. (This calculation is based on the length of the keel in relationship to the width of the ship.) The total length of the ship was greater, but this fact is not relevant because a large part stuck out at the front and the back above water. The stability was not improved by this. The sleekest models were about three times as long as they were wide.[2]

Until . . . in 1594, a Dutch merchant, Pieter Jansz Liorne from the town of Hoorn, commissioned a ship that was four times as long as it was wide and with a much flatter bottom than the usual ships. Pieter Jansz was inspired in this by the account of Noah's ark. His design was an overwhelming success. The ship could transport a third more cargo without a larger crew being necessary. His ships sailed much more easily and were faster than the ships of his competitors.

---

* Centuries later, the Greeks and the Romans had warships with the proportion of 7:1. But this extreme length was to make room for as many oarsmen as possible in order to be able to move quickly and to sink the enemy with battering rams.[3]

The other shipbuilders, who had first mocked the innovation of Pieter Jansz, hurried to build their new ships in the same proportions. In the next eight years, eighty such vessels—the "fluitschip"—were launched in Hoorn. This was the first mass-produced sailing ship.[4]

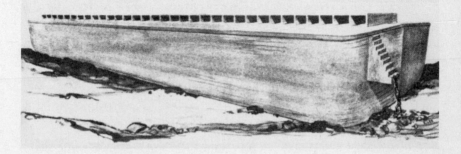

Noah's ark, the most seaworthy design of vessel.

It took shipbuilders thousands of years to determine the ideal proportions for a seaworthy and stable cargo ship. According to current insight, the best proportion for a ship not propelled by an engine or by sail is 6:1. Modern maritime ships have proportions of over 8:1, but they have powerful engines and are built for speed. With the ark, this was not necessary.

Stability

In Genesis 7:20, it says that the water covered the mountains to a depth of fifteen cubits (6.9 meters), probably in order to indicate that the ark could float around freely everywhere. From this, it might be concluded that the draft (how deep it sits in the water) of the fully laden ark was about fifteen cubits. This means that the ark, which was thirty cubits high, was almost half submerged. This is precisely the safest and most stable draft a vessel can have.

Suppose that Noah's vessel was half submerged in water and was pushed over so much by the wind and waves that the roof touched the water—then it would be tilted 31° (see the illustration on the next page). Because the vessel is half in the water, the surface of the water corresponds to the diagonal (L–Q). The weight of the vessel presses down from the center of gravity of the vessel (arrow G_v–W). The water causes upward pressure or buoyancy (arrow G_w–B) from the center of gravity of the part under water (triangle LNQ). The two forces are equal, but they are not in the same line. They are opposite in direction and reinforce each other to right the vessel.

Technically speaking: the upthrust and downthrust combination is equal to their force times the distance. As long as the upthrust B is not aligned with the downthrust W and is at the side under the water, the ship will try to right itself to the original position. In other words, as long as the intersection M (where the arrow G_w–B transects the metacenter plane of the vessel) is above G, the ship is stable and will right itself to its original position.

Noah's ark would have to tip over almost 90° before M coincides with G. This means that it would only capsize at 90°. At any angle less than 90°, the vessel rights itself again. With Utanapishtim's ark, M and G coincide and the vessel will capsize at the slightest movement of the waves. (Adapted from Morris.)

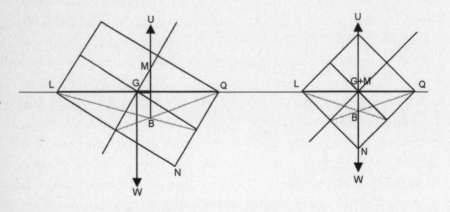

Noah's ark   Utanapishtim's ark

Cross section of Noah's and Utanapishtim's arks.
W = weight of ark acting through center of gravity of vessel (G).
U = buoyancy of ark acting through center of gravity of displaced water (B).
See the text for further explanation.

Unsinkable

Apart from calculations, the great stability of the ark is also revealed by experiments with scale models. At the Scripps Institute of Oceanography in La Jolla, California, experiments were conducted with a scale model, which was used in a Hollywood film in 1976: *In Search of Noah's Ark*. The waves in the wave tank of the institute were in proportion far greater to the scale model than could ever occur in a real ocean. It was shown to be impossible for the ark to be capsized by the waves.[5]

Actually, the danger for a vessel on the open sea is *not* that it capsizes because of the waves, but that its cargo shifts or that it fills up with water when the waves break over it. Both of these were impossible with Noah's ark, because the animals were in rooms (Genesis 6:14), and there was a roof over the entire length.

Another advantage of Noah's ark was that it did not have an engine or sail. In a nautical textbook it says that a ship with its engine turned off gets much less water over it than a ship that is being propelled forward. "Many ships have achieved very good results in bad weather on the high seas by letting the ship find its own course with the engine turned off. Usually the wind will come in, much more from the stern than from the side. The ship will roll terribly but not take on much water."[6]

The biblical account of the Flood describes a vessel with ideal measurements for seaworthiness: not too big to build, not too small to transport all the animals required, half submerged in the water so that the wind had little effect on it, and impossible to capsize. The story of Utanapishtim and all other flood stories around the world use the most unrealistic measurements in describing vessels: sometimes an ark of a kilometer long, sometimes a raft of tree trunks, sometimes a single, hollowed-out tree trunk, and sometimes a boat of reeds. Noah's ark is the *only* design of vessel in all the stories of the Flood that satisfies the requirements of the science of modern shipbuilding.

Was the Ark Big Enough?

According to estimates, a few million species of animals have lived on the earth. The question is, then, how could all these animals survive for a year in a wooden box 492 feet long? My tutor, Professor Lever of the VU

University of Amsterdam, calculated that there must have been at least 2.5 million animals in the ark, including at least 210,000 birds.[7] These are indeed immensely large numbers. But if Lever had paid more attention to the details of the account of the Flood, he would have reached very different conclusions.

The Contents of the Ark

The ark was about 492 feet long, 82 feet wide, and 49 feet high. The volume was therefore about 1,976,856 cubic feet divided over three decks. It was made of gopher wood, probably an extremely suitable type of wood, stronger and tougher than any type of wood we know nowadays.[†] Suppose that Noah needed about a quarter of the room available for all the beams and planks, for example 476,856 cubic feet, then there would be 1,500,000 cubic feet of living and working space left for Noah and his animals.

Noah must have had some extensive discussions with his sons and made a lot of calculations regarding how the living quarters could best be divided up. They will have used the space as efficiently as possible, for example by building many compartments one on top of another and storing the food above the compartments or in unused corners. So the useful space Noah had at his disposal was indeed the 1,500,000 cubic feet mentioned. This is the same amount as 562 standard (American) railroad cars, which can each transport 240 sheep. So the ark could have transported more than 134,000 animals of the size of a sheep (calculated after Morris).[8]

How Many Animals Were There in the Ark?

How many animals were really in the ark? In Genesis it says, "You are to bring into the ark two of all living creatures, male and female, *to keep them alive* with you. Two of every kind of bird, of every kind of animal and of every kind of creature that moves along the *ground*" (Genesis 6:19–20).

These verses reveal that it referred to:

---

† Some Bible translations use the term cypress or cedar wood, a softwood from a coniferous tree. This is completely unjustified, because the meaning of the Hebrew word *gopher* is unknown.

1. Animals that had to be kept alive: those in danger of drowning.

2. Animals that moved on or above the ground: that is, mammals, birds, and reptiles.

In other words, there were no aquatic animals, such as fish or shellfish. Neither were there any animals that would be able to survive the flood through their eggs or larvae, such as many insects and amphibians. And even no animals that could survive the flood on floating plants and trees, such as most insects and invertebrates.

According to estimates, there are about two million different species of organisms living on the earth. This includes about a million species of insects and half a million other species of animals, the majority of them mollusks, worms, and single-celled organisms; plus 400,000 species of plants. Of all the species of animals, the majority live in water and so could survive the Flood on their own.

Of the vertebrates, there are about 40,000 species: 4,000 mammals, 9,000 birds, 5,000 reptiles, 2,000 amphibians, and 20,000 fish.[9] Of these animals, too, the majority could survive the Flood on their own; consider for example the fish, sea snakes, amphibians, dolphins, and whales.

There were fewer than 20,000 species of true land animals and birds that had to be saved in the ark, plus an unknown number of (very small) invertebrates. But did all these *species* of animals really have to go into the ark?

Of Every Kind

The Bible says that of all land animals and birds "of every kind," one pair had to be taken into the ark. So it does not say that a pair of every *species* had to go into the ark, but of every group that was of a certain "kind." We find the same words in the account of Creation, where God creates the plants and animals "according to their kinds" (Genesis 1). In Hebrew, this word means "related to." Thus it was not necessary for two million separate species of animals to go into the ark, but only a small number of kinds—"basic types." In the ark there was, for example, the basic type of "dog," from which all canines later developed, such as the wolf, jackal, dingo, coyote, but also the four hundred breeds of dog, from the Pekinese to the Great Dane. A lot of research will have to be done to find the precise borders of a basic type, but usually these borders correspond with what is known in biology as the genus (plural genera) or sometimes with the "family."[‡] The basic type of dog comprises the whole family of canines (Canidae), and the basic type of camel, the whole family of camels (Camelidae). Biologists distinguish about 700 families of vertebrate animals and about 8,000 genera. Of these, a male and female of each had to be taken into the ark. This means that there was a minimum of 1,400 animals and a maximum of 16,000 animals in Noah's ark.

According to John Woodmorappe and others, the land animals (mammals, birds, and reptiles) average the size of a rat.[10] This means that the equivalent of 1,400 to 16,000 "rats" had to go in the ark. Suppose each "rat" had a cage of, on average, 1.6 x 1.6 x 1 foot (standard space for laboratory rats),[§] then the 16,000 animals could be housed in a space of 40,960 cubic feet. That is less than 3 percent of the space present in the ark. So there was 97 percent of the room left, that is, 1,460,000 cubic feet, to work and to store food and water.

Another calculation: there are about 20,000 species of land animals. Suppose that these *species* really had to go into the ark and that they were on average the size of a sheep. This would mean that about 40,000 sheep had to be able to get in the ark—of each species a male and a female. This number of sheep fits into 167 American train cars. As already indicated, the usable space in the ark was equivalent to 562 train cars, and so there would still be 395 cars left for transporting food. An impressive and comprehensive discussion about all the physical and biological considerations relating to the ark is found in the book *Noah's Ark: A Feasibility Study*.[11]

---

‡ A genus is the smallest category of plants and animals that can normally be recognized without scientific study.

§ *We should remember that the ark was only a temporary confinement of animals in an emergency situation, not necessarily a luxury accommodation. The primary purpose was to survive, in reasonable health, a disastrous flood for a year.

210,000 Birds in the Ark?

How did Professor Lever get the idea that there must have been 210,000 birds in the ark? Lever read, "Take with you seven of every kind of clean animal, a male and its mate, . . . and also seven of every kind of bird, male and female" (Genesis 7:2–3). As, according to Lever, there exist 15,000 species of birds on the earth, and of each species seven pairs were to go into the ark, there must have been 15,000 x 2 x 7 = 210,000 birds in the ark.℃

But what does the Bible really say?

1. It does not say that Noah had to take seven pairs of every *species* of bird into the ark, but as we have already shown, of every *basic type*.

2. Of all animals (clean and unclean), one pair were to come of their own accord to the ark. Regarding the clean animals and birds in our text, it does not say that they would come of their own accord. There it says, "Take with you . . . ," that is to say, catch and take (Genesis 7:2–3). Besides the animals that came of their own accord to the ark, Noah had to catch a number of clean animals and birds in the vicinity and take them into the ark; not from all over the world, but from the *vicinity*.

3. From the context, we can conclude that it did not refer to all the birds in the vicinity where Noah lived, but to the *clean* birds, which, after the Flood, had to be sacrificed to God together with the *clean* land animals (see Genesis 7:2 and 8:20). So this was only a very limited number of animals, as we have been able to see in the list of clean land animals and clean birds in chapter 4 on pages 63 and 76.

℃ The distinction between species is not always quite clear. Some biologists split one species into two species, while others prefer to refer to two subspecies. Grzimek, for example, comes to far fewer species than Lever: "Nowadays there are about 8,700 species of bird alive, which represents almost twenty percent of all vertebrates."[12]

4. According to some Bible commentators, it does not say that Noah had to catch seven pairs, but seven *individuals*. In Genesis 7:15 in the New Living Translation it says they came "two by two." You can imagine a long line of males and females next to each other. In the same way, it says in Genesis 7:2 "seven of every kind" (NIV) or "by sevens," (NASB and KJV), which means they are arriving in groups of seven, not in groups of fourteen.

So besides the animals that came of their own accord to the ark, there were probably also seven individuals of each clean basic type from the vicinity where Noah lived. Even if we assume that there were seven *pairs* of *all* the basic types in Noah's neighborhood, then it would still be only a very limited number.

Conclusion: The statements in the Bible about the design and size of the ark and about the number of animals that were in it are scientifically justified. There was more than enough space in the ark.

A GLOBAL FLOOD

In 1929, newspaper headlines screamed, "Proof of the Flood Found!" The archaeologist C. L. Woolley had discovered under the ruins of the city of Ur of the Chaldees, halfway between Baghdad and the Persian Gulf, a layer of river sediment three meters thick. Woolley was convinced that he had found proof of the Flood. "There could be no doubt that the flood of which we had thus found the only possible evidence was the Flood of Sumerian history and legend, the Flood on which is based the story of Noah."[13]

Since that time, archaeological textbooks point to this layer of sediment as proof of a so-called flood (which, according to the writers, was of course not global, because nobody believes anything like that). Unwittingly we are put on the wrong foot by this.

What are the facts?

Woolley found a layer of sediment in only two of the five pits he dug at Ur. So the flood did not engulf the whole town, but only a part. Three other layers of sediment in the nearby area were hundreds of years younger than the sediment at Ur. Some 3.7 miles away, in the town of Tel Obeid, no trace whatsoever of a flood was to be found. In other towns in Mesopotamia, too, thick layers of sediment have never been found.[14] In other words, Woolley's flood was a local flooding and had nothing to do with the Flood in the Bible.**

With a truly *global* flood, such as that described in Genesis 7 and 8, you would expect something quite different than here and there a layer of silt three meters thick. Then you would expect to find thick layers (also called strata) of sediment in large parts of the world, not a few meters thick, but tens to hundreds of meters thick. And that is exactly what is found all over the world.

THE GRAND CANYON

The Grand Canyon in Arizona is a gigantic gorge about 220 miles long, 4–12 miles wide, and 1 mile deep. In the canyon deposits of sediment are found above one another in perfectly horizontal, intact layers totaling 1 mile thick. Between the layers there is no trace of erosion to be seen, which is what would be the case if the strata were formed (tens of) millions of years after one another. The only explanation for such a perfect, undisturbed stratification is a rapid deposit by water, while the total dimensions of the strata point to a flood of gigantic proportions.

How the Grand Canyon (not the strata, but the gorge itself) originated is subject to discussion. It was probably formed a few hundreds of years after the Flood, when a huge natural dam broke and two enormous, high-altitude lakes—which were left by the Flood—emptied, causing water to gush down, carving the canyon. What is notable in this process—the forming of the canyon—is the destructive force a large quantity of fast-moving water can have (see also chapter 6, page 185). In a short time, about 2,400 cubic miles of rock were washed away and deposited in the Gulf of California. (To have an impression of how much 2,400 cubic miles is: all the rivers of the world together contain only 300 cubic miles

---

** Time and again we read in the media about "the" discovery of the Flood. These are all descriptions of regional floods, such as in the book Noah's Flood, about the bursting of the Bosporus between the Mediterranean Sea and the Black Sea.[15]

of water.[16]) Two books that describe the forming of the Grand Canyon in detail are *Grand Canyon: Monument to Catastrophe* and *In the Beginning.*[17]

The vast horizontal layers of the Grand Canyon are proof of a worldwide Flood.

Around the globe there are many indications that the flood was worldwide:

+ Seventy-five percent of all strata in the world were shaped by water.

+ On average, there is one mile of sediment on the continents that was laid down by water. That is five times as much as on the seabed nowadays. So there must have been a huge quantity of water above the continents.[18]

+ Of these sediments, more than half were laid down by *seawater*. This means that there were times when the continents were totally flooded by the sea.

+ In many places there are strata of tens to hundreds of meters thick, which are forcefully curved and folded, without any sign of cracking or of broken-off rocks, scree, or grit. Something like this is only possible if the *entire* formation of strata was still relatively soft and flexible when it was curved, and if it was covered with water. Soft strata do not have fractures and do not form scree, while the water reduces the weight and works as a lubricant, which means the layers bend and slide over one another more easily.[19]

Folds in the strata like this can only develop if they are relatively soft when they are formed.

Incidentally, it is remarkable that modern geologists increasingly assume great, global catastrophes, especially since the publication of the book by father and son Alvarez in 1980 about the impact of a big comet, from which the dinosaurs are said to have become extinct.[20] Prior to that time, you were laughed at if you believed that the surface of the earth was formed by sudden, global catastrophes. The findings of modern geology are coming ever closer to the Flood model. . . . The only thing that differs is the timetable.

Three Hundred Stories of the Flood

Another indication that the Flood was indeed a world-encompassing catastrophe is the existence of 250–300 accounts of the flood all around the world.[21] These stories are found among the most remote tribes in China, India, the mountains of the Himalayas, Scandinavia, Peru, and North America, and even among the indigenous peoples of Hawaii, New Zealand, and the Polynesian archipelago. It is not by chance that all these stories are similar; they all tell about the same event. They all contain the first three points mentioned below, and some of the following points.[22]

1. The complete destruction of every living thing by means of water.

2. An ark (or something similar) as a means of escape.

3. The preservation of a select few.

4. The cause of the flood is the disobedience of man.

5. One man is warned in advance and so saves himself and his family and/or friends.

6. Animals (usually a bird) play a part as fellow inhabitants of the ark and sometimes to provide information about the situation after the flood.

7. The ark finally comes to rest on a mountain.

8. The survivors worship the deity and receive his favor.

The evolution theory has no good explanation for the existence of all these tales of a Flood. Because, according to that theory, humans spread around the world from prehistoric times and the various peoples did not have any contact with one another in their earliest history. So they could never have adopted stories from one another.

How can these stories all be basically the same? This is only possible if two conditions are fulfilled:

1. The Flood took place in human history, so that the stories could be passed on.

2. The Flood was world-encompassing. If there were only regional floods, stories of the Flood would not occur all over the world, but only among the peoples who lived in or near the regions affected.

From unexpected quarters, more and more books are appearing about the fact that in "recent" times, a flood did indeed occur. Mr. and Mrs. Tollmann, for example, demonstrate with dozens of proofs that the world was hit by a tremendous comet about ten thousand years ago, which caused an incredibly huge earthquake, worldwide volcanic eruptions, a heat storm, a tsunami kilometers high, rainfall lasting for weeks, extremely heavy snowfall at the poles, and so forth. Because of the huge increase in dust in the atmosphere, there was darkness for months, which meant that a cold period of many years developed (an ice age), which lasted until long after the Flood. The remarkable thing about the book is that it doesn't come from Christian quarters. The Tollmanns are not Christians and only assume scientific facts.[23]

CHINESE CHARACTERS

A very interesting indication of a global Flood comes from a completely unexpected quarter, namely ancient Chinese characters. According to linguists, the Chinese developed their script as long ago as 2,500 years before Christ, and it is possible to discern from the characters how the ancient Chinese thought.

Many characters are constructed from simple basic characters (known as "radicals"). There are 214 of these radicals, which every Chinese person knows by heart, at least if he or she can read and write. If we dissect the characters to their simplest forms, we come to some surprising conclusions.

The character for "boat," for example, is constructed from three characters: vessel + eight + mouth (in the meaning of "people," mouths which have to be fed).

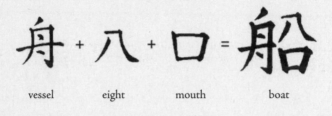

vessel   eight   mouth   boat

In other words, when the Chinese for the first time wrote down the character for "boat," they thought of a well-known vessel from history, in which there were eight people: Noah with his wife and three sons and their wives (see Genesis 7:13). A coincidence?

The character for a great flood looks like this:

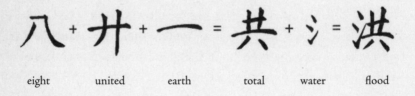

eight   united   earth   total   water   flood

In this, we see two striking words. First the word "total," which is composed of the words: eight + united + earth. Eight people on earth united together formed the total (the total population). If the character "water" is added, you get a completely different word, namely "flood" (also meaning "extensive"). So the idea was: an extensive flood is something that covers the whole earth with water, with eight people surviving.

The character for "covet" is also telling:

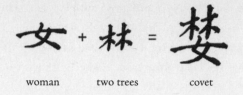

woman   two trees   covet

When the very first designer of the characters had to think of something for the word "covet," he chose the character for a woman near two trees (see Genesis 3:6). A coincidence again?

Another remarkable character is the character for "west."

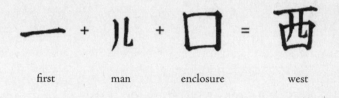

first   man   enclosure   west

Why does the character for "west" consist of the character for a man in an enclosure (= garden)? Could it be that it was referring to a special man in a special garden, which for the Chinese lay to the west . . . the Garden of Eden?

If you put the character for "woman" together with the character for "west," you get the word "necessary" (a second meaning is "to want"). Adam in the Garden of Eden, which was in the west, thought it was necessary for him to be given a wife (see Genesis 2:20).

first   man   enclosure   west   woman   necessary

There are dozens of such characters the Chinese devised at the beginning of their existence. For example, "joy" (= God with the first man in a garden), "forbid" (God who speaks near two trees), and so forth.[24]

To know more about how to analyze Chinese characters, go to: www. zhongwen.com.

It is indeed quite remarkable that in this way the realm of thought of the most ancient Chinese is incorporated in the characters of their script. Quite remarkable that the story of Noah can even be found in distant China! How would this ever be possible if there had never been a global flood and if the Chinese had not descended from Noah in historical time?

THE ORIGINAL STORY

The biblical stories about the Flood are not fabrications that have been adopted from the surrounding peoples. Neither are the stories of the Sumerians and the Babylonians older than the stories of Israel. They are all descriptions of the same, true events, of which various versions are in circulation. They all have a common source: the persons who experienced it as eyewitnesses and passed it on: Noah and his sons.

There are two important indications that the biblical accounts of Creation and the Flood are completely authentic and not adopted from the Sumerians or Babylonians, as is often claimed. First, only the accounts in the Bible are scientifically well founded, as we have seen on the previous pages and as we will see in chapter 6.

Second, many Hebrew words and expressions that are used in the account of the Creation (Genesis 1 and 2) and the account of the Flood (Genesis 7 and 8) are completely different from the words in the ancient Sumerian and Babylonian stories. Some of the old Babylonian words and expressions do occur in other chapters of Genesis, but specifically *not* in the accounts of the Creation and the Flood.[25] This means that the biblical accounts developed independently of—and even prior to—the Sumerian and Babylonian stories. For the accounts of the Creation and the Flood, Moses probably used clay tablets dated from the time of Noah.

There are dozens of other interesting, scientific remarks in the Bible in the area of the natural sciences. Let us consider a few about the earth, astronomy, and the theory of probability.

THE EARTH

WATER ECONOMY OF THE EARTH

The Hydrologic Cycle

In the book of Ecclesiastes in the Bible, it says, "All streams flow into the sea, yet the sea is never full. To the place the streams come from, there they return again" (1:7). These are two interesting remarks.

First, Ecclesiastes claims that the sea does not get full from all the rivers that flow into it. This is remarkable, because in total about 24 cubic miles of water flows into the sea every day. That is 1,100,000,000,000 gallons an hour. And yet the sea does not become full.[††]

Second, Ecclesiastes says that the water in a river returns to the source from which it rose. How could the writer of Ecclesiastes know that water indeed returns to the source from which it came, that there is recycling of water (a hydrologic cycle) on Earth? Only in the seventeenth century, with the work of Pierre Perrault and Edme Mariotte, was it possible to provide watertight proof that there is a hydrologic cycle.[27]

When rainwater falls on the earth, the water flows along streams into a river or seeps underground to a spring. From the spring the water wells up and subsequently flows along streams and rivers to the sea. There it evaporates through the heat of the sun, after which it condenses in the cold air and becomes clouds, which drop rain, snow, or hail on the earth. That water again flows along the springs and rivers into the sea. In this way, precipitation and evaporation balance out precisely, so that the sea always stays just as full.

In the book of Job, there is a remarkable description of how evaporation works: "He draws up the drops of water [water vapor NLT], they distill rain from the mist; which the clouds pour down" (36:27–28 NASB).

[††] It is estimated that every day over 1,000 km^3 of water evaporates globally (850 km^3 from the sea and 150 km^3 from the land). This evaporated water condenses in the air and forms precipitation, of which 750 km^3 falls on the sea and 250 km^3 on the land. This means that 100 km^3 more water falls on the land than that evaporates from it. These 100 km^3 are drained away by the rivers into the sea. (The figures are rounded off and may differ according to other researchers, because they are estimations.)[26]

In modern terms: the water rises through evaporation, after which mists develop, which are concentrated into clouds that become increasingly heavy, until rain falls from them.

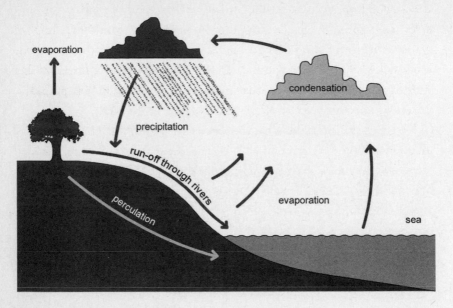

Hydrologic cycle—recycling of water.

The prophet Amos adds a detail: "He . . . who calls for the waters of the sea and pours them out over the face of the land . . ." (5:8). Research has revealed that about 85 percent of all precipitation is derived from the evaporation of seawater. How could Amos have known that?

The prophet Isaiah gives another detail: "As the rain and the snow come down from heaven, and do not return to it without watering the earth and making it bud and flourish . . ." (55:10). According to Isaiah, the water will return to the air again, but only after it has watered the earth. It is remarkable that the three statements above are in complete agreement with the description of the hydrologic cycle in geology textbooks.[28]

The Weight of the Clouds

In Job 26:8 it says, "He wraps up the waters in his clouds, yet the clouds do not burst under their weight." This is an interesting remark if you consider that a small, fluffy cloud can contain as much as 2 million pounds of water, as heavy as two hundred elephants.[29] In one single thunderstorm, more than 1,000,000,000 pounds of water can fall on the earth. With a hurricane, even 12,000 times as much: 12,000,000,000,000 pounds.[30] How is it possible that this all remains hanging in the air?!

Together with Job, we have to admit that we still do not understand everything about all those terribly heavy clouds, which float in the sky: "Do you know how the clouds hang poised?" (Job 37:16), or as the King James Version puts it, "Dost thou know the *balancings* of the clouds?" Job certainly wouldn't have understood anything about it. And most of us will never have even thought about it. Meteorologists nowadays know an awful lot more about the hanging and balancing of the clouds than Job did. But despite their research, they can still not give a "watertight" description of everything that happens in a cloud. They can *describe* broadly speaking how a cloud develops and works, but to really *fathom* it is something quite different! The question to Job is still just as relevant as it was four thousand years ago.

The Weight of the Wind

In Job 28:25 it says that God "gave to the winds its weight, and meted out the waters by measure" (RSV).[‡‡] It is not by chance that Job writes about the *weight* of the wind and the *measure* of the water. Without modern instruments you cannot determine a measure of air; you can only determine its weight. Air is a gas, which flies about in all directions. You cannot pour it into a bucket to measure its volume.

But the remark is interesting for a second reason. Only for just over 360 years have we known that air does indeed have weight. It was

---

‡‡ Almost all translations of the Bible (in many languages) use the word weight here. The New International Version is one of the few translations that uses the word force in this instance, whereas elsewhere in that translation, the same Hebrew word is translated as weight.

Torricelli, a pupil of Galileo, who first demonstrated in 1643 that air has weight and exerts a pressure. It was he who invented the barometer to determine that pressure.

That wind (air) does indeed have weight is shown by the fact that an average storm cloud weighs 22,000,000,000,000 pounds. In a big storm, there are a large number of such clouds, which in exceptional cases may weigh together about one thousand times more.[31] If a superheavy storm like that would move at gale force 8 (that is about 45 mph), this natural force would represent the incredible quantity of energy of 2×10^{18} joules (unit of energy). This is the same amount of energy as 1,100 billion pounds of dynamite. This is five million times as much as the Germans used in the Second World War to flatten a large part of Rotterdam.[32] It is equal to the energy of 40,000 atom bombs falling on Hiroshima.[§§]

The Paths of the Seas

In ancient times, very little was known about the seas and the oceans. Only in the nineteenth century were comprehensive charts made of the world's seas, for example by the oceanographer M. F. Maury (1806–73). He is known as the "father of oceanography." Maury wrote various books about the currents of water and wind in all the oceans of the world. This idea is said to have come to him when he was sick in bed and his son read to him from the Bible. When the boy read Psalm 8:8, "all that swim the paths of the seas," the words "paths of the seas" struck him. Maury said, "If God said there are paths in the sea, I am going to find them when I get out of this bed."[33] A further motivation for him to study the seas and the oceans was Psalm 107:23–24, "Others went out on the sea in ships; they were merchants on the mighty waters. They saw the works of the Lord, his wonderful deeds in the deep."

---

§§ As indicated above, the clouds in a super big storm weigh $1000 \times 10^{13} = 10^{16}$ kg. Wind-force 8 is about 72 km an hour, that is 20 meters a second. The kinetic energy of a mass is $1/2mv^2$. The kinetic energy of the storm is therefore: $1/2 \times 10^{16} \times 20^2 = 10^{16} \times 200 = 2 \times 1018$ joules. If 1 kiloton of dynamite, or TNT (trinitrotoluol), explodes, 4×10^{12} joules of energy are released. The energy that was released from the bomb on Hiroshima was equal to 13 kilotons of TNT, that is: $13 \times 4 \times 10^{12} = 5 \times 10^{13}$ joules. (1 kiloton is a thousand tons, is 10^6 kilograms.) From the calculation above ($2 \times 10^{18} : 5 \times 10^{13} = 0.4 \times 10^5$), it follows that the energy of the storm is as great as 40,000 atom bombs like that dropped on Hiroshima.

Maury posited that the interaction of wind and water gave rise to special currents that created something like "paths" in the sea, which enabled ships to progress more quickly. Using ships' logs, he studied the wind and water currents in the oceans. He observed the ships' fastest routes and mapped them out across the ocean. In this way he identified various major ocean currents.

As a result, shipping saved millions of dollars a year, and the number of accidents was reduced. Since ships have been propelled by engines, it has no longer been necessary to follow these ocean currents, but heavy and slow-moving cargoes still follow these routes. In international shipping agreements, account is still taken of these routes.[34]

In Goshen, Virginia, there is a monument in honor of Maury with the inscription, "Matthew Fontaine Maury, pathfinder of the seas, the genius who first snatched from ocean and atmosphere the secret of their laws. . . . Every mariner for countless ages, as he takes his chart to shape his course across the seas, will think of thee. His inspiration Holy Writ, Psalm 8:8[⊄⊄] and 107:23–24. Ecclesiastes Chapter 1:8. A tribute by his Native State, Virginia, 1923."[35]

The Earth—Spherical and Unattached in Space

Hindus used to believe that the earth was carried by an elephant standing on the back of a giant turtle, which was swimming around in a cosmic sea. The ancient Greeks thought that the giant Atlas bore the world on his shoulders. Some scholars in the early Middle Ages thought the earth was flat and stood on pillars. The Bible has said for three thousand years now that the earth is spherical and hangs unattached in space:

+ "He sits enthroned above the circle of the earth" (Isaiah 40:22). The Hebrew word translated "circle" can also mean clod or lump, that is, something spherical. Old Dutch and German translations of the Bible (Statenvertaling and Luther Bible) have translated it that way.

⊄⊄ In some Bible translations this verse is numbered Psalm 8:9.

+ "He has described a circle upon the face of the waters at the boundary between light and darkness" (Job 26:10 RSV). The boundary between light and darkness—day and night—can only be a circle if the earth is a sphere.

+ "He suspends the earth over nothing" (Job 26:7). This means that the earth hangs unattached in space. This is suspiciously like science of our day!

+ "On that day . . . in the field . . . on that night . . . in one bed" (Luke 17:31, 34). Jesus says that His return will be as sudden as a flash of lightning (Luke 17:24). All His followers will be changed "in a flash,*** in the twinkling of an eye" (1 Corinthians 15:52). He says that *at the moment* of His return, some people will be working in the field during *the day* and others will be in bed *at night*. It is only possible that it is both day and night at the same time if the earth is spherical.

Hence, in the Bible it is said on several occasions that the earth is a sphere and hangs unattached in space.

The Flat-Earth Myth

Atheist thinkers would like to convince us that Christianity is the cause of backwardness in the field of science: Under the influence of the Church, the stupid people in the Middle Ages believed that the earth was flat and that you could topple off it. When Columbus began his journey round the world, he was afraid that he would sail over the edge and would fall off the earth.

This story is complete nonsense.

First of all, the Bible does not teach anything about a flat earth.†††

*** The Greek word here is *atomo*, which means "indivisible"—an indivisible moment of time. It is interesting that according to modern quantum mechanics, an "indivisible moment" does indeed exist, the Planck time: 10^{-43} second. Shorter time does not exist.

††† The texts that are often cited regarding "the four corners of the earth" (Revelation 7:1 and 20:8) refer to the four compass points. This has nothing to do with a flat and square earth—not any more than that Ezekiel 7:2 means that the land of Israel is square.

Second, at the time of Columbus (1492) not a single educated European believed in a flat earth. Anaximander and Pythagoras in the sixth century before Christ already came up with the idea that the earth must be spherical, and Aristotle (384–322 BC) even gave advanced proofs of this. Around 230 BC, Eratosthenes calculated fairly accurately the circumference of the earth. As most of the Church Fathers from the thirteenth century on read the books of the Greek thinkers, they all believed in the spherical shape of the earth. The two most prominent defenders of a flat earth were scholars from *before* the Middle Ages: Lactantius in the third century and Cosmas Indicopleustes in the sixth century.[36] But at the time of Columbus, the spherical shape of the earth was in no way under discussion among scientists.

The reason the myth about the flat earth arose was that "enlightened thinkers" after the Renaissance wanted so much to depict the Church as backward and narrow-minded. The best known books about this are by J. W. Draper (1875) and A. D. White (1896, 1960),[37] who were vehemently opposed to Christianity. Writings of this kind provided atheists and proponents of the theory of evolution with a splendid pretext for depicting the Christian Church as being old-fashioned and unscientific, as in the book *Scientists Confront Creationism*.[38] A large number of writers have exposed the incorrectness and dishonesty of this reasoning.[39]

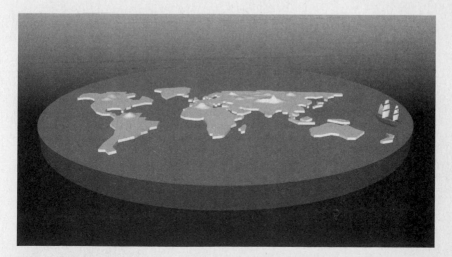

Scholars in the Middle Ages did not believe at all that the earth was flat. This myth was concocted only 130 years ago.

Galileo Galilei

The same applies to the story about Galileo Galilei (1564–1642), who is said to have opposed the "backward church" and proved that the earth moves around the sun and not the other way round.

Rubbish.

Galileo was not opposed to the Roman Catholic Church, but to the (Roman Catholic) scholars who believed unconditionally in the claims of contemporary science. At that time, Greek thinking dominated all aspects of science, and so it did with the scholars and the leaders of the Roman Catholic Church. Following Plato and Aristotle, the scholars thought that the earth stood unmoving in the center of the universe and that the sun and the stars turned around it. This worldview was not founded on a view of the Bible, but on the view of generally accepted science. The fact that the Bible was referred to in the discussions with Galileo is obvious, because at that time many scholars derived their authority from being a member of the Roman Catholic Church.

The historian Santillana wrote in 1958, "It has been known for a long time that a major part of the Church intellectuals were on the side of Galileo, while the clearest opposition to him came from secular circles."[40] The problems for Galileo only started when he mocked the pope, with whom he was initially on good terms, because the pope also believed in the accepted theory of Aristotle.[41]

In Galileo we do not see the triumph of science over the Christian faith, but the triumph of a scientist who dared to shed light on the wrong thinking of prevalent science.

Christian Faith Stimulates Science

The Christian faith has never restrained science. On the contrary, it has provided the greatest possible impetus! Only in countries where the Christian faith has pervaded has systematic scientific investigation been developed. Other religions have never been interested in scientific research. On the contrary, they were often dead set against it, because the natural world around was regarded as divine. They considered it sacrilege if nature was examined and dissected.[42] Associated with this is the fact that all ancient religions (except Islam) are associated with faith in numerous gods, spirits, and magical forces, which counteract one another in mysterious and capricious ways.

Only the Christian faith sees the cosmos as an ordered system, which was created by a rational God and therefore can be investigated and dissected in a rational way. Nature is governed by laws that can be described by mathematical formulas.

Professor Rodney Stark writes, "Science arose only once in history—in medieval Europe. It could only arise in a culture dominated by belief in a conscious, rational, all-powerful Creator." And, "Science was not the work of Western secularists or even deists; it was entirely the work of devout believers in an active, conscious, creator God."[43] Another scientist writes: "Neither the Egyptian, nor the Mesopotamian, nor the Chinese, nor the Islamic civilizations produced natural science in the sense meant here. Modern science blossomed in a unique soil: the Christian way of thinking."[44]

ASTRONOMY

In the Bible, we do not read anything about a certain "scientific worldview" or about modern astronomy. Neither is the Bible written in scientific language, but in the evocative language of the everyday, and from the perspective of the simple person—what you see with the naked eye. We must not try to ascribe to the Bible a modern worldview. Nevertheless, considered with our modern knowledge, there are a number of remarkable facts in the Bible. We will mention two.

THE PLEIADES AND THE ORION

Two constellations that are mentioned in the Bible are the Orion and the Pleiades (Seven Sisters). In Job 38:31, the difference between these two constellations is indicated. "Can you bind the beautiful Pleiades? Can you loose the cords of the Orion?" With the Pleiades, reference is made to binding, and with the Orion to loosening. Is this use of words coincidental?

In our eyes, the stars of the Orion seem to make up a nice group, but they are completely isolated stars, which are at different distances from the earth. They do not belong together; they are not linked with one another. They are "loose."

The stars of the Pleiades do belong together. They are relatively close together and move through space as a group. They are "bound." Astronomers discovered this by taking photos of that part of the sky through their telescopes. When they later made more photos of the same groups of stars, they saw that the Pleiades had moved as a group and that the stars of the Orion each had its own course.

The Winkler Prins encyclopedia of astronomy writes, "The Pleiades is a star cluster . . . and consists of over 3,000 stars, which are situated in the middle of reflection nebulae."[45] An astronomical encyclopedia gives more details, "The masses of nebula seem as if pulled out of shape and drawn into festoons by the attraction of neighboring stars."[46] The stars of the Pleiades seem to be bound together by threads. This is a unique occurrence in astronomy.

It is rather striking that when referring to the Pleiades, the Bible uses the verb "to bind," as if the stars were linked together with threads—something that cannot be observed with the naked eye—and that in the next sentence it maintains precisely the opposite about the Orion.

The Pleiades (Seven Sisters). The threadlike streamers between the stars are clearly visible.

The stars of the Orion seem to make up a nice group, but are completely isolated stars.

Abraham and the Number of Stars

Abraham was more than a hundred years old when God tested him to see if his love for God was greater than his love for his son Isaac. Would Abraham be willing to give up the chance of descendants—which was particularly important for an Easterner—if God were to ask this of him? When it was indeed shown that Abraham was willing to do this, God made a promise to him, "I will . . . make your descendants as numerous as the stars in the sky and as the sand on the seashore" (Genesis 22:17). Of course, old Abraham was very pleased that he would have as many descendants as the number of stars he saw in the sky. But in the course of history, quite a lot of people must have laughed at this promise of God.

First, the number of stars that can be seen with the naked eye is laughably small compared with the number of descendants that a man can have in roughly four thousand years. Hipparchus (190–120 BC), the founder of Greek astronomy, counted 1,080 stars in the sky. Three hundred years later, around AD 150, the famous astronomer Ptolemy (Ptolemaeus) catalogued 1,056, and Kepler (1571–1630) counted 1,005. Later it was revealed that in the *whole* celestial sphere, that is around the whole of the earth, in ideal conditions you can distinguish a maximum of 9,000 stars with the naked eye. This is an absurdly small number for forty centuries of descendants.

Second, the number of stars you can see with the naked eye is less than the number of grains of sand that fit into *half a teaspoon*! Therefore it is absurd to compare the number of *visible* stars in the sky with the number of grains of sand "on the seashore."

But . . . God knew what was behind the boundaries of human powers of observation. With our modern telescopes, we have discovered that it is completely impossible to count the number of stars in the sky, and that their number is practically infinite, just like the number of grains of sand on the shores of the sea. In our galaxy, there are about 200 to 300 billion stars. It has been calculated that with the largest telescopes, 100–150 billion galaxies can be seen. This means 10^{23} stars. Some astronomers estimate that the number of stars in the universe is another thousand times as many, which means 10^{26}, that is 100,000,000,000,000,000,000,000,000 stars.

In Jeremiah 33:22, it says, "as countless as the stars of the sky and as measureless as the sand of the seashore." A doubly correct statement: (1) The number of stars and the number of large and small grains of sand on the earth, including loam and clay, are more or less in the same order of magnitude; (2) It is impossible to measure them. We can only make an estimate, just as with the number of descendants of Abraham.

In our times, the criticism regarding the number of stars is precisely the opposite of the criticism prior to the invention of the telescope (around 1600). Before that time, there were too few stars, and now there are too many. Far too few Jews have lived to be able to compare their number to the number of stars in the sky. This is true, but consider that Abraham is not only the forefather of the Jews, but also of the "lost" tribes of Israel, who were taken into exile in Assyria by Shalmaneser V in 723 BC and later were scattered among the nations (see 2 Kings 17). Abraham is also the forefather of the Arabs, and likewise of the Edomites, Midianites, and other extinct peoples (see Genesis 25 and 36). Spiritually speaking, Abraham is even the forefather of all Christians (see Galatians 3:29 and Romans 4:16–17). So he has indeed become the forefather of "many nations." In the course of the centuries, these must have been many billions of people.

Infinity of the Universe

Thanks to modern science, we never have to fear that God will abandon the people of Israel, "Only if the heavens above can be measured and the foundations of the earth below be searched out will I reject all the descendants of Israel" (Jeremiah 31:37). Thousands and yet more thousands of scientists have been investigating the universe and the earth. But there is no one who has ever claimed that the universe can be measured or that the inside of the earth can be searched out. We can only examine the universe and the inside of the earth through theories, indirect measurements, and estimates.

The remark by Jeremiah about the infinity of the universe is in line with the picture the Bible gives us of God. He is infinite and almighty. To express it through the words of the prophet, "As the heavens are higher than the earth, so are my ways higher than your ways and my thoughts than your thoughts" (Isaiah 55:9).

THE THEORY OF PROBABILITY

An interesting branch of modern science is probability calculus. If we toss a coin and catch it a thousand times, we can be sure that about five hundred times it will turn up heads and five hundred times tails. If it were a thousand times heads, there would be something unusual going on. If in 1880 somebody had predicted that in 1980 a queen would be crowned in the Netherlands who was called Beatrix, it would be a real miracle when that indeed took place. Especially because until 1890, only kings reigned in the Netherlands. How could anyone know that precisely one hundred years later a *queen* would come to power, much less know her name? If that person turned out to be right, it would not be by chance.

In the Bible, there are dozens of such predictions about the future that in the course of the years have been fulfilled exactly. This is not by chance. God purposely makes use of statements of this kind. He says, "I knew how stubborn you were; the sinews of your neck were iron, your forehead was bronze. Therefore I told you these things long ago; before they happened I announced them to you" (Isaiah 48:4–5; see also 46:10). With such predictions of the future (prophecies), God wants to demonstrate that the Bible is a trustworthy book, and He wants to challenge His followers to trust in Him completely.

The hundreds of prophecies in the Old and New Testaments are not vague and obscure or subject to all sorts of interpretations, as with horoscopes and with ordinary predictors of the future, such as Nostradamus. And they are not short-term predictions, but sometimes made four hundred to fifteen hundred years in advance. This is an amazing fact without equal in world literature. In the Old Testament, there are more than three hundred prophecies about the life of Jesus, which have almost all been fulfilled, and of which the others are still to be fulfilled when Jesus returns to the earth. This cannot be the work of man. Something like this is only possible through inspiration by God Himself.‡‡‡

---

‡‡‡ Many prophecies in the Bible have been fulfilled in such a wonderfully precise way that liberal theologians claim that the books of the Bible in which they occur were only written after the time that the prophecy was fulfilled. This is the case, for example, with Deuteronomy, Daniel, and Zechariah. And also with Mark 13:1, 2, where Jesus prophesies about the destruction of Jerusalem, which was only to take place forty years later. Examples of such disbelief can be found in some Bible translations in the marginal notes or in the introductions to the Bible books.

PROPHECIES ABOUT THE LIFE OF CHRIST

Prophecy	Book in the Old Testament	Year before Christ	Book in the New Testament
Born of a virgin	Isaiah 7:14	730	Matthew 1:18-25
Born in Bethlehem	Micah 5:1	720	Matthew 2:1-6
Murder of infants	Jeremiah 31:15	600	Matthew 2:16-18
Flight to Egypt	Hosea 11:1	730	Matthew 2:15
John in the desert	Isaiah 40:3	710	Matthew 3:3
Forerunner	Malachi 3:1	430	Matthew 11:10
On donkey into Jerusalem	Zechariah 9:9	520	Matthew 21:4-9
Rejected	Psalm 118:22	1000	Matthew 21:42
Betrayed for 30 coins	Zechariah 11:12	520	Matthew 26:15
Money thrown into temple	Zechariah 11:13	520	Matthew 27:5
Money for potter's field	Zechariah 11:13	520	Matthew 27:7-10
Spat on, beaten	Isaiah 50:6	710	Matthew 26:67
Killed by crucifixion*	Psalm 22:1-18	550	Matthew 27:33-50
Vinegar to drink	Psalm 69:22	1000	Matthew 27:34, 48
Exact year of death	Daniel 9:25-26	1000	Luke 19:37-44
Lots cast for clothing	Psalm 22:18	1000	John 19:23, 24
No bone broken	Numbers 9:12	1440	John 19:36

*In Psalm 22:1-18, David describes in detail the suffering of a crucifixion, although this practice was only introduced in Palestine by the Romans a thousand years later.[47]

Some of the hundreds of prophecies about the life of Jesus Christ, of which it is established that they were written hundreds of years before the events in question. The numbers of years are estimates on the basis of the *New Bible Dictionary*.[48]

Probability Calculus

For forty-eight prophecies about the life of Jesus, Professor Stoner has calculated the probability of their being fulfilled by chance.[49] Six hundred students helped him to gather and evaluate all the data and, after that, to calculate the probability that each occurrence should happen by chance. For example, that Jesus should be born in Bethlehem (see Micah 5:2). Jesus might just as well have been born somewhere else on earth. The chance that Jesus would be born in Bethlehem is determined by the number of people who lived in Bethlehem at the time, divided by the number of the entire world population. In all the world, there were probably 300,000 times more people living than the number of people in Bethlehem; so the probability is estimated to be one in 300,000. In this way, Stoner and his students calculated the probability for the fulfillment of forty-eight of the over three hundred prophecies about Jesus. The probability that all these forty-eight prophecies would by chance be fulfilled in the life of Jesus is $1:10^{157}$. *That is a* probability of 1:10,000,000,000,000, 000,000,000,000,000,000,000,000,000,000,000,000,000,000,000,000, 000,000,000,000,000,000,000,000,000,000,000,000,000,000,000,000, 000,000,000,000,000,000,000,000,000,000,000,000,000,000,000,000 (157 zeros).

On pages 166–168, in another context, an explanation is given as to how impossibly small such a probability is. It is immeasurably easier to find a secretly marked electron in ten billion universes (which together contain 10^{90} electrons) than that by chance forty-eight prophecies would be fulfilled in the life of one person. Let alone that three hundred prophecies would be fulfilled in his life!

SOME PROPHECIES IN MORE DETAIL

Tyre

From the eleventh century before Christ, Tyre was one of the largest and most powerful cities to the north of Israel; see map on page 207. It really was an impregnable fortress, partly on the coast and partly on an island, six hundred meters out in the sea. Who during the heyday of this splendid, unassailable town, in 590 BC, would have dared to prophesy, "I am against you, O Tyre, and I will bring many nations against you, like the sea casting up its waves. They will destroy the walls of Tyre and pull down her towers; I will scrape away her rubble and make her a bare rock. Out in the sea she will become a place to spread fishnets. . . . From the north I am going to bring against Tyre Nebuchadnezzar[§§§] king of Babylon. . . . They will break down your walls and demolish your fine houses and throw your stones, timber and rubble into the sea. . . . You will never be rebuilt" (Ezekiel 26:3–5, 7, 12, 14)?

Sixteen years after the prophecy (in 573 BC), Nebuchadnezzar was able to conquer the part of the town on the mainland. But the rich among the inhabitants had fled with their possessions to the island, and he could not reach it. The fortress was impregnable. The siege took Nebuchadnezzar thirteen years, but to no avail. He had to return to his country without reward (see Ezekiel 29:18, 20). The town on the mainland was conquered, but not completely razed to the ground, as had been predicted. This might have been cause for people at the time to laugh at Ezekiel, because the prophecy had not been completely fulfilled after all.

It is remarkable that in the first part of the prophecy (Ezekiel 26:7–11) it is written that Nebuchadnezzar will demolish the towers and will kill the inhabitants on the mainland, but that there is nothing said about many nations, about scraping away rubble, or about bare rock. Note that between verses 11 and 12, the description changes from "he" to "they" (the many nations).

From history books, we know that 240 years later (in 332 BC), Alexander the Great: (1) attacked the town with soldiers from many different countries; (2) destroyed the remnant on the mainland; (3) swept up all the stones, beams, and rubble and threw them into the water to make a causeway to the island; (4) after seven months, took the town on the island and destroyed it so completely that bare rock remained; (5) on which a town was never built again (Ezekiel 26:3–4, 12, 14). On the mainland, there is now a small town in the vicinity of the old Tyre, but on the island

---

[§§§] An explanation as to why a word can be spelled differently, such as Nebuchadnezzar and Nebuchadrezzar, is given on page 220 in chapter 7.

in the sea, after two thousand years there is still bare rock, on which the fishermen dry their nets!

Sidon

Sidon is on the coast of the Mediterranean Sea, thirty-five km to the north of Tyre and forty-five km south of Beirut; see map on page 14. It was one of the oldest and most important cities in the time of the patriarchs. But after the time of King David, it lost its influence, and by the sixth century before Christ, it had become an insignificant little town. A town like this could much more easily be destroyed or depopulated in wars than the strong, unassailable Tyre, which was on an island.

Around 590 BC, Ezekiel also preached judgment on Sidon, "I am against you, O Sidon. . . . I will send a plague upon her and make blood flow in her streets. The slain will fall within her, with the sword against her on every side" (Ezekiel 28:22–23). Despite this severe judgment, God does not say anything about walls being razed to the ground, about only bare rocks being left, about nothing being left but rubble, and about never being rebuilt.

In the course of history, Sidon was indeed the scene of fierce combat and was seized by many different armies. For example: by Nebuchadnezzar (587 BC), Artaxerxes (350 BC), and Alexander the Great (332 BC); three times during the Crusades, also during the wars between the Druze and the Turks, and between the French and Turks. In 1840, it was bombarded by the fleets of three countries. As prophesied, "the sword [was] against her on every side," but the town was never completely destroyed. Sidon still exists and there are now about 200,000 people living there.[50]

It is rather remarkable that such *different* predictions about two towns so close together should have been fulfilled so precisely.

Edom

The Edomites lived in the wilderness to the south of Israel, between the Dead Sea and the Gulf of Aqaba; see map on page 14. Throughout their existence, they lived on a war footing with Israel. There was a bitter hatred between the two peoples. If they had the chance, the Edomites raided Israel and stole everything they could get hold of. God prophesied that He would destroy the land of Edom, "I will stretch out my hand against Edom and kill its men and their animals. I will lay it waste. . . . I will make you desolate for ever; your towns will not be inhabited. . . . All its towns will be in ruins forever" (Ezekiel 25:13; 35:9 and Jeremiah 49:13).

At the time of the above-mentioned prophecies (around 750 and 570 BC, respectively), Edom was a prosperous vassal state of the mighty Assyria. It contained sufficient agricultural land and was situated on important caravan routes, such as the famous King's Highway (see Numbers 20:17–20). The most important towns were Bozrah, Teman, and Sela. Sela in particular was an impregnable fortress, surrounded by a wall of high rocks. Later the town of Petra was built in the same rock formation. (*Petra* is Greek, and *sela* is Hebrew for "rock"; see 2 Kings 14:7.)

Between 500 and 300 BC, Edom fell into the hands of Arabian nomads, the Nabateans, who made Petra their capital. After Petra was captured by the Romans in AD 106, the town started to lose its influence, and the Edomites disappeared as a nation. When in AD 630 Petra was occupied by Muslims, the remaining inhabitants left the town and it became one great ruin.[51] Until today, the land of Edom is one great desert. It is so completely desolate that until 1812, when the first finds of this lost kingdom were made through excavation, critics of the Bible thought that the country and the people of Edom had never existed.

The scholar Wilbur Smith writes, "The Bible . . . is the only volume . . . in which is to be found a large body of prophecies relating to individual nations, . . . to certain cities, and to the coming of . . . the Messiah. . . . Not in the entire gamut of Greek and Latin literature . . . can we find any real specific prophecy of a great historic event to come in the distant future, nor any prophecy of a Savior to arise in the human race. . . . Mohammedanism cannot point to any prophecies of the coming of Mohammed uttered hundreds of years before his birth. Neither can the founders of any cult."[52]

The same can be said of all other predictors of the future, such as the well-known Nostradamus. Even his most famous predictions remain vague. And most of the predictions have not been fulfilled at all.

The information on the prophecies about Tyre, Sidon, Edom, and about the life of the Lord Jesus is taken from the book *Evidence That Demands a Verdict.*[53]

Tombs, hewn out of the rocks near Petra.

SUMMARY

In the field of the natural sciences, there are remarkable facts in the Bible. Noah's ark is shown to be an exceptionally stable and seaworthy design of vessel. It is also large enough to contain all the basic types of birds and terrestrial animals. Although the account of the Flood in the Bible seems very similar to the stories of ancient Babylon, it is not a reworking of these ancient stories. If you study the details of the accounts, it is clear which account of the Flood is the original one and scientifically the most reliable. Only the account in the Bible stands up to scientific scrutiny. In the course of years, the Babylonian version had become considerably distorted through the oral tradition. The same can be said of the hundreds of other accounts of the Flood around the world. Although they are not scientifically well founded, they are indications that there was indeed a *global* flood. Other sources, including the Grand Canyon and the Chinese characters, also reveal that the Flood was a global catastrophe.

In the area of earth sciences, the Bible gives many intriguing facts about the water management of the earth, about the weight of the clouds, about the paths of the sea, and even about the fact that the earth hangs like a ball in empty space. Even the comments about the Orion and the Pleiades and about the number of stars are shown to be amazingly accurate scientifically. All these facts and the accuracy of dozens of prophecies in the Bible lead us to the incontrovertible conclusion that the Bible is a supernaturally inspired book.

Even though we cannot see God or prove His existence, we can still clearly demonstrate from biblical laws and physical indications that God is the Creator of heaven and earth and that He maintains the universe through His influence and power.

Since the creation of the world
God's invisible qualities
—his eternal power and divine nature—
have been clearly seen,
being understood from what has been made.

ROMANS 1:20

6.

CREATION OR EVOLUTION

As long as mankind has existed, men and women have been wondering how the earth and the universe originated and how they themselves came into being. In every tribe and nation around the globe are stories about the origin of the universe and of mankind.

The creation story of the Babylonians, for example, describes gods and goddesses who were involved in a cosmic conflict and were constantly massacring one another, until the god Marduk seized power and murdered the goddess Tiamat, from whom he created the heavens and the earth. In Egypt, there were several creation stories. Every major city had its own story, through which the local priests tried to demonstrate that their god was at the start and therefore was the most important. According to the priests of the city of Heliopolis, the god Atum had spontaneously arisen from the primeval waters. He went to rest on an island, and there he spit out Shu, the god of air, and Tefnut, the goddess of water. From these two primal gods, the other gods originated. The priests of the city of Memphis claimed that their supreme god, Ptah, was the father of Atum, and so existed before Atum! The priests of Thebes claimed that their god Amun was the father of Atum, and so the first.[1]

These and other creation stories around the world are obviously works of man, concoctions of creative minds. The characters of these gods are human through and through, and the worldview is demonstrably wrong. There is a vast difference between all of these battling brutes and the sober account of Creation in the Bible. It truly is a miracle that we do not come across such absurd stories in the Bible.

MODERN SCIENCE

The first people who tried to present a sound and rational worldview were the Greek philosophers, especially Plato and Aristotle. Their notions had a great influence on the way of thinking of scholars, even up to the time of the Middle Ages.

Since the Enlightenment in the eighteenth century, a sharp division developed between faith and science. This division was given a powerful impetus in 1859 through the publication of the book by Charles Darwin *On the Origin of Species*. From that time, the idea spread that life on earth was not created by God but came into being by pure chance and that life subsequently evolved spontaneously from a single-celled organism into the millions of different species of plants and animals we know now. This is what is called the "theory of evolution."

THREE KEY QUESTIONS

At secondary school, I learned that the theory of evolution was the only scientific explanation for the origin of life, and I was inclined to believe it. In general terms, it was not too difficult to believe this theory, but the problems started when I tried to fit the finer *details* of life into it. "How on earth can such a refined and almost supernatural organ like the eye have ever developed by chance?" Totally inexplicable is the eye of the Anableps, a little fish that swims near the surface of water. It has *two* lenses in each eyeball: one to see under water and one to see above water. Could something like this ever have developed by pure chance?

If I ignored all the details and all the problems, I was able to believe in the theory of evolution, but three key questions kept bothering me and no one provided a satisfactory answer to them:

1. How did matter come into being?

2. How did life come into being?

3. How did the human mind (self-awareness) come into being?

If we make a thorough study of nature, these are not the only questions. The problems stack up, and we discover hundreds of facts that are completely at odds with the theory of evolution: petrified trees that stand erect, protruding through ten strata (layers) of coal, primitive Neanderthals who had bigger brains than we do, seventy tons of dinosaur bones in a mass grave at a height of four thousand meters, hundreds of species of plants and animals from *different* eras together in one mass grave, and so forth. In this chapter, we will cite more such examples and demonstrate that these facts fit better into the theory of creation than into the theory of evolution.

MODERN BIOLOGY

INSURMOUNTABLE BOUNDARIES

During his journey around the world between 1831 and 1836, Charles Darwin visited the famed Galápagos Islands in the Pacific Ocean. There he saw that species of plants and animals were not invariable, as biologists of the time taught, but that there was variation within the species. On the basis of this variation within the species, Darwin came upon the idea that every species derived from another—more primitive—form. Darwin *saw* variations within a certain group of plants or animals (we call this microevolution*) and *assumed* a complete evolution of life (we call this macroevolution†).

Such an assumption is extremely premature. After all, no one has ever observed any macroevolution. On the contrary, it appears that variations can only occur within certain boundaries, and these boundaries really are extremely clear-cut. Rose growers can cultivate hundreds of varieties of roses, but a rose is a rose is a rose. And a pig is a pig is a pig. And a dove will certainly not become a crow. Both among plants and animals, the groups are separated by *insurmountable boundaries*.

---

* Microevolution is actually a misleading term, because it has nothing to do with evolution, but only with the variation of characteristics already present.

† When the word "evolution" is used in this book, it always refers to macroevolution and with it the notion that life, and ultimately the whole universe, came into being by itself and evolved further by itself, without interference of God.

According to creationists (people who adhere to the theory of creation), these boundaries clearly correspond with what the Bible says about plants and animals in Genesis 1: "according to their kinds." God did not create a few million separate species, but He created a number of basic types—baramins‡—within which the plants or animals are related to one another and can produce offspring.

Two species of animals belong to the same baramin if their sperm cells can fertilize the egg cells. This is only possible if the distinctive proteins on the surfaces of the egg cell and the sperm cell fit together, like a key in a lock. The chemical processes that are necessary for fertilization are only activated if the key fits in the lock. If the proteins do not fit, nothing happens.

Sometimes the varieties within a species have grown so far apart that in natural circumstances they no longer mate. Then a separate subspecies has developed. If the subspecies grow farther apart, in this way sometimes new *species* develop. In some cases, different species can still (artificially) inseminate one another, but their offspring are infertile. This is, for example, the case with a cross between a horse and a donkey, a sheep and a goat, a rat and a mouse, a duck and a goose. But the formation of new varieties and new species is always restricted within the boundaries of the basic type.

Between the species of *different* basic types, the situation is fundamentally different. Their sperm cells cannot fertilize the egg cells. The distinctive proteins on the surface do not fit together; they are too diverse. The same applies to all other proteins in the cells.

If there had been evolution from one basic type to another, the distinctive proteins on the surface of both the egg *and* sperm cell would have to have changed—by pure chance—at the same time! On top of that, the countless proteins in the egg and sperm cells, too, would have to have changed *all at the same time*.[2]

---

‡ The word is derived from the Hebrew words *bara* (create) and *min* (kind). It is sometimes used by creationists.

Mutations

Variation within a basic type is also possible through the occurrence of mutations. These are changes in the genetic material of an organism.

This genetic material is stored in the nucleus of a cell and determines how an animal or plant should be constructed: its color, the shape of its nose, the length of its limbs, and so forth. This genetic material, also known as DNA (deoxyribonucleic acid), is found in the genes, which together form the chromosomes—small threads in the nucleus of the cell.

Mutations may take place by chance, but also through the action of radioactive radiation or through a chemical substance. Mutations can occur in any cell of the body, but if they occur in a reproductive cell (egg cell or sperm cell) or in a cell that gives rise to a reproductive cell, the mutation may be transmitted to the offspring. Mutations in some bacteria and insects have made the offspring immune to poisons. Color blindness and hemophilia in humans have developed through mutations. It is claimed that mutations provide important evidence for evolution (improvement).

The opposite is true.

Sometimes through mutation, a species may become better adapted to a certain environment, but its *general* adaptability is always reduced in this way. Any specialization means a degeneration in genetic potential. Peter Scheele has written a convincing book about this, with the revealing title *Degeneratie, het einde van de evolutietheorie (Degeneration, the End of the Theory of Evolution).*[3]

The vast majority of all mutations (nearly 100 percent) are neutral, that is, with no effect on the survival of the species. The rest of the mutations that occur generally have a harmful effect. Only in very rare occasions are the mutations positive, i.e., the information in the genetic material is changed in such a way that the species is better adapted to its environment. But it is always a change in the *existing* material. No new genetic material is generated. No *extra* information is added. Existing material can be copied, shuffled, or cut into parts, but *new* information is not added, and this is what it is all about!

You might compare it to a pack of cards. You can shuffle it and damage it in a million ways, but it remains the same pack. Only if a *new* card were added to the pack spontaneously could you speak of evolution. If you can alter the order of the cards or can deface the figures on a card, this does not mean that you can make new cards! (By the way, how did the whole pack of cards originate?)

The problems with mutation are much greater than those with the pack of cards, because if you get the order wrong in your pack of cards, you simply start again. But if useless (or harmful) mutations are passed on to the next generations, they will form an increasingly large ballast of unusable material. The chance of survival in the long run becomes even smaller than for animals in which no mutations have taken place.

Through mutations, a species is able to adapt to a changing environment, but the offspring is never more highly developed than the previous generation. This has been demonstrated, for example, by experiments with the fruit fly (*Drosophila*). The ability to breed countless races and artificial species of this fly is cited as evidence of evolution. But here, too, it is shown that all the mutations are merely the destruction of existing, well-functioning material. Wings are deformed or disappear; pigments are lacking; limbs shrivel up. External features can change, but *new genetic material is never generated. And that is all-important in evolution.*

Actually, the differences between the various fruit flies are so small that one of the most renowned researchers in this field, geneticist Richard Goldschmidt, said of this phenomenon, "If we were able to combine a thousand or more of such mutants in a single individual, this still would have no resemblance whatsoever to any type known as a species in nature," and "It is true that nobody thus far has produced a new species or genus by macro-mutation."[4]

For mutations to be viable, we come up against insurmountable boundaries. The shape of a beak or the color of a feather can indeed *change*, but this does not mean that you can *generate* a completely new beak—or feathers, eyes, a heart, kidneys, or a brain!

Anyway, if—by pure chance—completely new species did evolve because their offspring were better adapted to the environment than their parents, how can a peacock or a bird of paradise have come into being? First, their tails are of such extraordinary beauty and mathematical precision that chance is completely excluded. For details, see the book *Hallmarks of Design*.[5]

Second, their tail feathers get in the way so much that it really is a *disadvantage* for survival. A biologist might say, "Those tails are necessary to attract and impress a female." Well, how does an ordinary house sparrow, then, manage to attract a female with his simple gray-brown plumage? Or how does a penguin or a coot or a goose find a mating partner, even though the males are hardly distinguishable from the females? With geese, the male and female are so similar that even the birds frequently make a mistake—and form a lifelong partnership with a goose of the same sex.

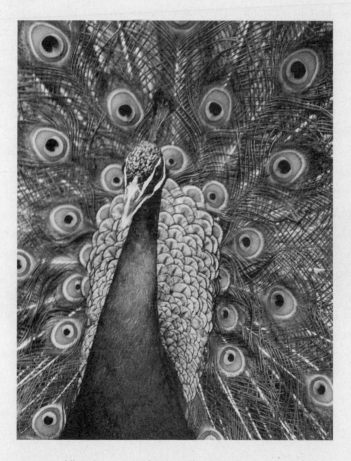

A peacock's tail is so mathematically precisely constructed that chance is excluded.

TRANSITIONAL FORMS BETWEEN BASIC TYPES DO NOT EXIST

It is asserted that life on earth began with a simple, single-celled organism. By chance mutations and natural selection, the offspring evolved into higher and more complex plants and animals. After many stages, a simple fish came into being and later an amphibian, a reptile, a mammal, and, finally, a human. According to the theory of evolution, all plants and animals, and humans, are therefore more or less related to one another, and a clearly ascending line can be seen from primitive organisms to more complex plants and animals. The theory of evolution stands or falls on the proof of whether organisms are related or not, whether there are primitive ancestors between two groups—so-called transitional forms (see also pages 150–56).

Fish or frogs may look "primitive," but whether they really are is the question. They are smaller and built in a different way than mammals, but this does not mean they are primitive ancestors of the mammals. In recent years, remarkable discoveries about this subject have been made, especially in the field of molecular biology. Michael Denton has written a fascinating book about this.[6] Of the many examples he mentions, we will consider one: cytochrome C.

First a brief explanation about proteins. Proteins are molecules out of which plants and animals are built. Muscles, eyes, brains, and also skin, intestines, and blood are made of proteins. These protein molecules are constructed from simple organic compounds, the amino acids. The construction of a protein might be compared to a page full of text. The page may contain five hundred or two thousand letters, but you never have more than twenty-six *different* letters (a–z). In the same way, a protein can be built up from dozens to thousands of amino acids, but in a protein there can never be more than twenty *different* amino acids.

Cytochrome C

We use cytochrome C as an example because it is so commonly present in the living world. It is a protein necessary for breathing, and it occurs in all cells of plants and animals. Cytochrome C is composed of approximately one hundred amino acids, of which scientists know exactly how frequently and where each type of amino acid occurs. In different plants and animals, the sequence of the amino acids in cytochrome C appears to be slightly different. For example, the sequence in the horse and the dog, two mammals, which according to the theory of evolution are closely related to each other, differs by 6 percent. The sequence in the horse and the tortoise, two vertebrates that are less closely related, differs by 11 percent. Between the horse and the fruit fly, two very different animals, the difference is 22 percent. So the difference in the sequence of amino acids in cytochrome C becomes greater as the external difference between the groups of animals become greater. In books about evolution you can read about this, and it is used as a proof of evolution.[7]

But now comes the interesting part—which you do not read in books on evolution!

If we compare the cytochrome C in a primitive bacterium with the cytochrome C of other organisms, we see the following differences:

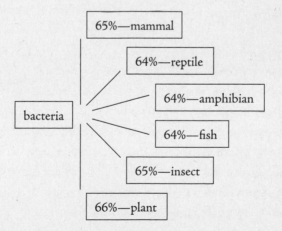

All these differences are of equal value. In other words, the difference between bacteria and ALL other organisms is equally great! In spite of all those tremendous, fantastic differences between the multicellular organisms, there is not one species that can serve as a transition between bacteria and multicellular organisms. You cannot say that a fish or a frog is more primitive—closer to a bacterium—than a mammal. There is no ascending line running from primitive to more developed. There has never been any evolution through a fish, amphibian, or reptile to a human being.

A second example may illustrate this further. If we compare a fish with various vertebrate land animals—such as amphibians, reptiles, birds, marsupials, and mammals—all these animals appear to be equally far away from the fish. There is no transitional form to be found between fishes and vertebrate land animals.

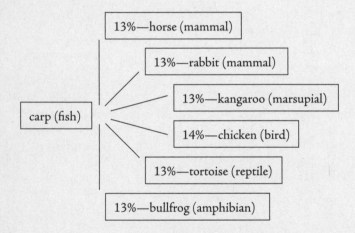

The same applies to the difference between mammals and nonmammals, for example, reptiles. ALL mammals are at an equal distance from ALL reptiles. Nowhere is a transitional form to be found between reptiles and mammals. The same holds true for the smaller groups within the mammals or within the reptiles, and so forth.

In evolution, the speed of propagation is of critical importance, because mutations and other genetic changes can only take effect when they are inherited by the new generation. The faster a species reproduces, the faster it can change. But though a mouse, for example, reproduces about one hundred times faster than an elephant, still both animals are equally far removed from the reptiles.

According to evolutionists, the group of "primitive" lungfish from central Africa has not undergone any evolution whatsoever during the last 350 million years. It has remained at a standstill, while other fish have evolved further. Yet the lungfish and the "modern" fish are at the same distance from all nonfish groups.

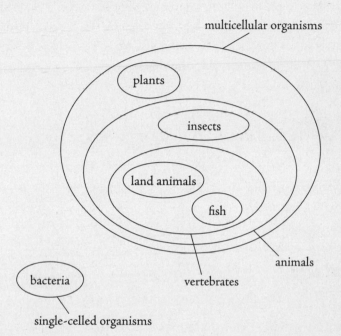

Living beings can be divided into groups that are each completely independent and unique. The two main domains are the "single-celled organisms" and the "multicellular organisms." The multicellular organisms can be divided into plants and animals. The animals are divided into vertebrates, insects, etc. Each and every group is completely independent and unique.

To summarize: the distance between ALL members of a group and ALL members of another group is always (nearly) the same. It is incredible, but true, that a transitional form is nowhere to be found. All plants and animals live *alongside* each other. There is no overlap in any respect whatsoever. Not a single group can be considered as the antecedent of another group. Primitive ancestors do not exist in nature, only in the mind of the evolutionist.

The above findings not only apply to cytochrome C and *all* proteins, but also to the DNA (and RNA) in all plants and animals.[8] This is obvious, because all proteins are made by the DNA (with help of the RNA), so if the sequence within the DNA is changed, then the sequence of the amino acids in the proteins will change in the same way.

It is completely without justification that the sequences in proteins and DNA are used as evidence for transitional forms, as in the books *Scientists Confront Creationism*[9] and *The Language of God*.[10]§ The evolutionist (!) Denton writes, "If this molecular evidence had been available one century ago, . . . the idea of organic evolution might never have been accepted."[11] It is telling that he titles his book *Evolution, a Theory in Crisis*.

IRREDUCIBLY COMPLEX SYSTEMS

Bacteria are the simplest organisms that can live independently. They are between a thousand and a million times smaller than the cells of the human body, and because they are so "primitive," they are seen as the precursors in evolution. Biologists in Darwin's time believed that "a cell was a 'simple little lump of albuminous combination of carbon,' not much different from a piece of microscopic jelly."[12] Darwin knew nothing about the incredibly complex biochemical reactions that take place in the cells and bodies of plants and animals.

For this reason, Darwin could easily claim that through all sorts of small steps, simple parts could grow into the most complicated organs, such as the human eye or the brain. Full of self-confidence, he wrote, "If it could be demonstrated that any complex organ existed, which could not possibly have been formed by numerous, successive, slight modifications, my theory would absolutely break down."[13]

Let us take a look at one such "organ" in the most simple cell that exists, namely the flagellum of a bacterium. With this flagellum, bacteria can move about in water. An evolutionist may airily assert that the bacterium, by a lot of intermittent steps, has gained a "little hair" to move about with,

---

§ The fact that organisms from various groups are constructed in the same way is not proof of evolution, but an indication of a great Architect, who used the same successful building plan (blueprint) for several basic types. With evolution, there ought to be transitional forms between the basic types.

so that it will have a better chance of survival than its kind. But things are not that simple.

A "simple" flagellum is built up of more than fifty *different* types of proteins, which all work together flawlessly. The most amazing thing is that the flagellum does not have any fixed connection with the outer wall of the cell. The driveshaft of the flagellum is *loose* within the wall and is driven by a motor and rotates like the propeller of a ship. Something like this can never have developed by gradual improvement. It must have been perfectly constructed right from the beginning, otherwise it would not be able to work. If even *one* protein of the many thousands in the flagellum were fixed to the cell wall, the flagellum could no longer turn.

The biochemist Michael Behe calls the flagellum an "irreducibly complex system"—that is to say, a system so complicated, of which the parts work together in such an intricate way that it is not possible for any part to be missing. The parts cannot have been made step-by-step but must all have been present *simultaneously* and working together flawlessly in one go.

In living beings, dozens of such irreducibly complex systems exist. For example, the chloroplast in plants, the coagulation of blood, the eye, a bird's feather, and the knee joint.[14] According to Behe there is no single book or scientific article that has ever described the evolution of such complex biological systems in an adequate way, simply because this is scientifically impossible. He writes, "The assertion of Darwinian molecular evolution is merely bluster."[15] We can indeed say that the theory of Darwin has collapsed completely.

In modern biology, there is no proof whatsoever to be found for evolution. Nearly all observations of experiments, mutations, proteins, DNA molecules, complex systems, and so forth, speak in favor of creation. That is, the creation of basic types, within which great adaptations are possible, but which are divided by insurmountable boundaries.

Many researchers are inclined to believe that evidence for evolution especially can be found in the fossil world. The evolutionist Carl Dunbar once said, "Fossils provide the only historical, documentary evidence that life has evolved from simpler to more and more complex forms."[16] Let us have a look at this.

GEOLOGY

Geology is the scientific study that deals with the earth's strata and the fossils that occur in them. In the course of the years, literally billions of fossils have been found and studied. According to evolutionists, the fossils are clear evidence that there has been a gradual development—evolution—from primitive single-celled organisms to modern-plants and animals. The most widely used arguments for this evolution are the fossils of humans, horses, and the so-called transitional forms.

Ape-Men and Dawn Horses

Humans

In secondary school, the evolution of mankind is a favorite topic. Everyone has seen the imaginative drawings of hairy ape-men sitting around a fire with primitive tools in their hands. According to the theory of evolution, these primitive human ancestors evolved over four million years ago from apelike beings.

The most significant representative of this transition from ape to human was the Australopithecus, literally "southern ape," that lived in Africa two to four million years ago. This group includes the Zinjanthropus and "Lucy," a female ape, of which fragments were discovered by D. C. Johanson in 1974.[17]

The most striking characteristics of the Australopithecus are: skull capacity of 450–700 cc (present anthropoid apes 300–700 cc; modern human 950–2000 cc), weight 35 kg, height 120 cm, long arms, short legs, protruding teeth, no large canine teeth, less heavy jaws than most present apes.

The teeth and the jaws of the Australopithecus resemble the teeth of a present species of baboon (*Theropithecus gelada*) in Ethiopia.[18] This is probably because they are both adapted to eat the same type of food. From the shape of the pelvis and the place where the spinal column enters the skull, it is shown that the prehistoric ape walked more erect than present apes, but still on all fours. This is even revealed by the small, semicircular ducts in the inner ear, which are necessary for the sense of balance required when walking upright. Based on the scans of the inner ear, the scientist who investigated the skull of the Australopithecus writes, "Among the fossil hominids, the Australopithecines show great-ape-like proportions."[19]

In brief: the Australopithecus had brains like an ape, teeth like an ape, walked like an ape, and looked like an ape. It is an extinct species of ape. This can also be said of all the modern discoveries, which are constantly reported with much ado in the news, such as *Sahelanthropus tchadensis*, which was described in *Time* magazine on July 22, 2002.

Much can be said about the discoveries of "ape-men." We will suffice with the comments of two (evolutionist) researchers who specialize in the field of fossils of ape-men. The first is Yves Coppens, who, with his staff, reached the conclusion that "Lucy was a typical tree-dweller and did not walk erect at all."[20] Note that this is not said by just any biologist, but by one of the most renowned researchers in France, someone who, with a whole team of people, does nothing else in life except study the bones of "Lucy" and other ape-men!

The second is the top researcher Lord Zuckerman. He wrote, "There is indeed, no question which the Australopithecine skull resembles when placed side by side with specimens of human and living ape skulls. It is the ape—so much so that only detailed and close scrutiny can reveal any differences between them."[21]

What should we think when we read these remarks by experts and a while later read enthused reports in the newspapers about new discoveries of ape-men or other evidence for evolution? Usually I just wait and watch out for the brief announcements in the media, which appear a few months or years later, reporting that on closer inspection, a mistake has been made and that the discoveries do not constitute proof of evolution at all.

The Horse

Another "classic example" of evolution is the development of the horse. According to the theory of evolution, the horse has evolved over 60 million years from a small, primitive, four-toed horse (*Hyracotherium*—the dawn horse) the size of a dog into the modern, single-toed racehorse.

All over the world, over three hundred types of fossil horses have been discovered, especially in North America. The fossils have feet with one, two, three, or four toes. They were not found in strata in one area, but occurred in the most diverse strata, spread all over the continent of North America. A clear, consecutive line of development has never been found anywhere in the world.

Horse fossils have been collected from different regions and artificially ordered in such a way that it seems as if evolution has taken place. But it is obvious that all these fossils are of horses, varying in size from the smallest ponies to the largest racehorses. With regard to the hoofs, they all are only *variations* on the theme of "hoof."

What biology books neglect to mention is that single-toed and three-toed fossils have been discovered in strata of the same age, even according to evolutionists. So "modern" horses lived at the same time as the three-toed dawn horses. The dawn horses are not at all the "primitive precursors" of the modern horse, but probably an extinct basic type, alongside the basic type of horse as we know it. Because the dawn horse belongs to another basic type, a transition has never been found between the dawn horse and the single-toed horses.

What biology books also fail to mention is that prominent evolutionists acknowledge that this whole story is inaccurate. Years ago, the famous professor George Simpson wrote, "The most famous of all equid [horse] trends, 'gradual reduction of the side toes,' is flatly fictitious."[22]

Sometimes mules (an infertile cross between a horse and a donkey) are born with additional toes on each foreleg, complete with hoofs. This is not a proof of evolution, but it shows that the mule is related to the extinct species of horses and that a great variation is possible within the basic type of horse.

TRANSITIONAL FORMS BETWEEN BASIC TYPES HAVE NEVER EXISTED

If there has been macroevolution, changes will have taken place not only *within* a basic type but also from one basic type to another. This is the reason why traditional evolutionists assumed that in the fossil world many animals would be found that are placed between two present basic types. Darwin hoped these missing links between the basic types would be found when more fossils were discovered and knowledge about fossils increased. He wrote, "If my theory be true, numberless intermediate varieties . . . must assuredly have existed."[23]

If a reptile were to evolve into a bird, thousands of transitional forms would be necessary to change the front legs into wings with feathers. A large bird's feather has thousands of barbs on either side of its shaft, which are kept together by over a million little hooks. These are spread across the feather with incredibly precise, mathematical regularity. And this is all supposed to have happened by chance!

The transition from invertebrates to vertebrates should also have produced millions of transitional forms. Invertebrates have soft internal parts and a hard exterior (external skeleton). Vertebrates have hard internal parts and a soft exterior (internal skeleton). Not only must the skeleton have undergone a complete change, but also the muscles that are attached to the skeleton. And what about the nerves, which in invertebrates lie loose in the body and in vertebrates run *through* the backbone? If evolution has taken place, almost the entire fossil world should consist of transitional forms. Even in present nature, there should still be millions of "half-finished" animals and transitional forms running around.

All those billions of transitional forms should have had thousands of descendants before another new transitional form developed. These countless transitional forms surely ought to be found *somewhere* in the earth's strata, shouldn't they?

Hiatuses

Darwin's expectation was never fulfilled. Despite billions (!) of fossils of the strangest types of plants and animals having been discovered, transitional forms have never been found. Sometimes plants and animals are found that seem to be between two groups, but this is because in the fossil world there lived far more species and groups than at present. For that reason many fossils do not fit into the existing groups of our time. But if we study the so-called transitional forms more closely, they appear to be completely independent and fully developed plants and animals.

Prominent evolutionists write in their professional journals, "The fossil record . . . has become almost unmanageably rich. . . . The fossil record nevertheless continues to be composed mainly of gaps."[24] The hiatuses are real and equal to the hiatuses we find in the present world. The famous professor Niles Eldredge acknowledges, "We paleontologists have said that the history of life supports [the principle of gradual transformation of species], all the while really knowing that it does not."[25]

Because many evolutionists acknowledge that the hiatuses are real and that a gradual development of life is not supported by the record, they try to think up all sorts of theories in order to maintain their doctrine. Some decenniums ago some biologists believed in evolution with jumps (saltational evolution). According to them, the offspring of an animal all of a sudden gets complete new features, like a new organ, or sometimes even a new species is born. To put it in an exaggerated form: a *reptile* lays an egg and a *bird* creeps out of it! This absurd idea of "hopeful monsters" is even more impossible than the gradual development Darwin believed in. Moreover, where should this "hopeful monster" find a suitable mate in order to have offspring?

Nowadays many biologists believe that evolution took place with great intervals, long periods of rest, interspersed with short periods with an eruption of evolution. This is known as the theory of the "punctuated equilibrium."[26] According to them, this is the explanation why no transitional forms are found between the basic types and why we do not observe evolution taking place in our time.

As a last resort, more and more people believe that life fell down from space in the form of so-called organic molecules, which sometimes occur in meteorites. This would certainly be a miracle! But if life were to originate on another planet, the same problems of time and chance would have to be overcome as when life were to originate here on earth. So this is not much of a reasonable conclusion either.

Single-Celled Organisms

According to the theory of evolution, all flora and fauna developed from a single-celled being, something like a primitive bacterium. Through cell division, life forms developed with 2, 4, 8, 16, 32, 64, 128, 256, etc., cells.

But in nature today and in the fossil world, there are no independently living species with these numbers of cells.

Between single-celled organisms and those with about five hundred cells, there is a big gap. There are no transitional forms between single-celled and five-hundred-celled organisms. Parasites with fewer than five hundred cells do exist, but they cannot live independently. They have *degenerated* rather than evolved! And there are single-celled organisms (*Volvox*) that cluster together like a ball and cooperate with each other, but they are and remain single-celled organisms!

There is an unbridgeable gap between the cells of bacteria and of other living organisms. Bacteria do not have a cell nucleus; all other organisms do. Moreover, the cells of multicellular organisms are a million times larger and infinitely more complicated than bacteria. Between the two groups, there is no single transition (as is also demonstrated on pages 142–46 under "cytochrome C").

Fully Developed from the Beginning

Another problem in the theory of evolution is that nearly all groups of animals appear *suddenly* and *simultaneously* in the strata of the earth. And not in primitive forms, but *fully developed*. According to the theory of evolution, this was just under 600 million years ago. It is certainly not the case, as most school textbooks would have us believe, that the various groups came into being consecutively and very gradually. According to the doctrine of evolution, no life occurred in 4 billion years from the beginning of the earth, with the exception of a few single-celled organisms. But suddenly we find in strata of 600 million years old representatives of all the larger groups in the animal kingdom, except the insects and vertebrates. Prominent evolutionists write, "Within just a few million years, nearly every major kind of animal anatomy appears in the fossil record for the first time."[27]

Professor Edred Corner (an evolutionist) writes in an article about evolution in plants, "To the unprejudiced, the fossil record of plants is in favor of special creation."[28]

FOSSIL RECORD & EVOLUTIONARY TIME SCALE

Era	Period	Epoch	Years since beginning	Years duration	Conditions and characteristics
Cenozoic	Quaternary	Recent	15,000		moderating climate; glaciers receding
		Pleistocene	1,000,000	1,000,000	warm and cold climates; periodic glaciers
	Tertiary	Pliocene	10,000,000	9,000,000	cold climate; snow building up
		Miocene	25,000,000	15,000,000	temperate climate
		Oligocene	35,000,000	10,000,000	warm climate
		Eocene	55,000,000	20,000,000	very warm climate
		Paleocene	70,000,000	15,000,000	very warm climate
Mesozoic	Cretaceous		120,000,000	50,000,000	warm climate; great swamps dry out; Rocky Mtns. rise
	Jurassic		150,000,000	30,000,000	warm climate; extensive lowlands and continental seas
	Triassic		180,000,000	30,000,000	warm, dry climate; extensive deserts
Paleozoic	Permian		240,000,000	60,000,000	variable climate; increased dryness; mountains rising
	Pennsylvanian (Late Carboniferous)		270,000,000	30,000,000	warm, humid climate; extensive swamps; coal age
	Mississippian (Early Carboniferous)		300,000,000	30,000,000	warm, humid climate, shallow inland seas; early coal age
	Devonian		350,000,000	50,000,000	land rises; shallow seas and marshes; some arid regions
	Silurian		380,000,000	30,000,000	mild climate; great inland seas
	Ordovician		440,000,000	60,000,000	mild climate; warm in Arctic; most land submerged
	Cambrian		500,000,000	60,000,000	mild climate; extensive lowlands and inland seas
Proterozoic (Pre-Cambrian)			1,500,000,000	1,000,000,000	conditions uncertain, first glaciers, first life
Archeozoic (Pre-Cambrian)			3,500,000,000	2,000,000,000	conditions uncertain, earth probably lifeless

Time chart as used in the theory of evolution. Note that even according to evolutionists, all groups of animals appear suddenly at the same time in the Cambrian era.

Bacteria

Protozoans

Fungi

Algae

Mosses

Ferns

Gymno-sperms

Flowering Plants

Sponges

Coelenterates

Segmented Worms

Arthropods

Mollusks

Echinoderms

Chordates

Two Famous Transitional Forms

The *Coelacanth*, a species of fish bearing the scientific name *Latimeria chalumnae*, for a long time was considered to be the best evidence of a transitional form between fish and amphibians. According to the theory of evolution, this fish lived 220–70 million years ago and then became extinct. But in 1938 and in 1952, it was found alive and well in the deep sea near Madagascar. When it was discovered, it was found to be a real fish and definitely not a transitional form. This shows that fossil finds can be assessed quite wrongly, especially if the researcher has a preconceived idea about the origins of life.

From fossil finds it had been concluded that the Coelacanth was a transitional form. When a living Coelacanth was found, it was shown to be an ordinary fish.

The Coelacanth is one of the many examples that make clear the circular reasoning of the doctrine of evolution. For people who believe in evolution, all finds help to "prove" evolution.

The Archaeopteryx is still held as the best evidence of a transitional form between a reptile and a bird. The Archaeopteryx was warm-blooded, about the size of a dove. It had complete plumage with fully developed flight feathers and a large wishbone for the attachment of strong muscles for the downstroke of the wings. These are features of modern birds.

The Archaeopteryx had teeth and a long, bony tail. These features do not occur in birds nowadays, but they did in a few extinct species. Its wings had rather clawlike extremities. To a limited extent, these also occur in the present Turaco in Africa and the Hoatzin in America. The young of the Hoatzin can hold on to branches of trees with these claws. The Turaco and the Hoatzin are, however, 100 percent birds.

The Archaeopteryx, too, was a real bird: both its feathers and its brain were fully developed. It was definitely not a "primitive precursor" of modern birds.[29]

Incidentally, in Texas, a modern-looking bird, the Protoavis, has been found in a stratum that, according to evolutionists, is 75 million years older than the stratum in which the Archaeopteryx was found.[30]

In the present world and in the fossil world, no single transitional form is to be found between basic types, not between apes and men, not among horses, not among fish, and not among birds—nowhere. Is it then strange that Colin Patterson, the leading paleontologist (scientist who studies fossil plants and animals) of the British Museum, admits, "Evolution not only conveys no knowledge but seems somehow to convey anti-knowledge"?[31]

BOMBS UNDER THE THEORY OF EVOLUTION

According to the theory of evolution, "modern" plants and animals (and mankind) originated hundreds of millions of years later than the simpler forms of life. This means that modern fossils could never be found in ancient strata. After all, the modern plants and animals did not exist at the time. A second assertion is that the formation of the entire sequence of strata also took hundreds of millions of years. A relatively thin stratum may develop in a short time because of a local disaster, but for thick layers, or for many layers on top of one another, millions of years are needed.

According to the theory of creation, all plants and animals (and mankind) originated at the same time and many of them were killed and fossilized during the Flood or some other disaster. This means that it is possible for all types of organisms to occur in the same strata. However, it is not surprising that highly developed organisms occur mostly in higher strata. This is because: (a) they lived in more elevated areas, (b) they had greater mobility to escape the violent waters of the Flood, and (c) if they drowned, their bodies would not sink so quickly to the bottom because they have greater buoyancy (see page 191). Let us see which of the two theories is confirmed by facts.

1. In many places in the world, fossilized trees have been found that protrude through two or more layers of coal. For example, in a coal mine near Lancaster in England, a fossilized tree has been found that is over thirty-six feet tall.[32] This is proof that the strata were formed within a very short time, otherwise the tree would have rotted away. Yet geology teachers at school say that coal strata developed in the course of millions of years.

    The same applies to the gigantic fossils of dinosaurs. Even if such a huge animal lies on its side, it is still sixteen feet high. If the layers of earth were to develop millimeter by millimeter, the creature would have rotted away before it was completely covered with sediment.

2. In Scotland, a stratum of sandstone has been discovered with clearly visible fossilized traces of the digging of worms, which lived in the seabed during a great catastrophe (the Flood).

    The worms were trying to escape from the rapid depositing of sand by digging long, straight tunnels upward. The fossilized tunnels are clearly evident and run straight through different layers of 20 cm in thickness. This is proof that the strata were not formed thousands of years after one another—the whole stratum in a few million years—as the evolutionists claim, but that they were deposited in a very short period of time, probably within a few days, because otherwise such a short-lived worm could not crawl through several of these layers.[33]

Such fossilized trees are evidence that the strata formed very quickly.

3. In 1860 in Italy, near the little town of Castenedolo, a human skull was discovered in a stratum ten million years old. In 1880, near the same spot and in the same strata ten million years old, two skeletons of children and later the skeleton of a woman were found. In 1880, articles appeared about a skull in a stratum ten

million years old, close to the little town of Calaveras in California. At the time, a lot was written about these finds, but later they sank into oblivion.

N.B. The above-mentioned finds were made during excavations in (coal) mines and were solidly embedded in the strata. They did not roll or sink into them. A review article with references to literature about more such finds can be found in the journal *Creation Research Society Quarterly* and in *The Illustrated Origins Answer Book*.[34] Two Hindu scientists from America have also written a book about the discovery of a large number of human remains that do not fit into the framework of evolution.[35]

4. Occasionally very old strata are found *on top of* younger strata. In Wyoming, across an area of about 30 x 60 miles (2,000 square miles), a layer 300 million years old was found above a layer 60,000 years old. According to evolutionists, this whole stratum of 2,000 square miles slid over the younger stratum. Another example of an ancient stratum on top of a younger stratum is found on the Matterhorn and the Mythentop in Switzerland. The phenomenon is explained by supposing that the top layer of the Matterhorn, together with other mountains, moved over a distance of about sixty miles to the place where it is now. The Mythentop, according to some evolutionists, even shifted all the way over from Africa.[36]

It really is very strange that only the top stratum of the mountains shifted (how is this possible?) and that these two mountains, which are so close to each other, shifted across such different distances. An additional factor is that there are no traces of such great shifts. In all these cases—and in dozens of others—the strata lie completely evenly on top of one another. The strata are not found deep in the ground, but visible to the naked eye. There is no indication whatsoever that they have shifted across great distances: no fracture areas, no broken-off or pulverized rocks, no scree or grit. Even in the smallest glaciers, you do find the formation of scree, but not here. How is this possible? The forces necessary to move such massive mountains would cause the strata to fold or break apart and would completely pulverize entire rocks.

There is just one way in which the earth's strata could shift over one another without areas of fracture or the formation of scree: only if the strata are still soft when shifting and are covered with water. Soft strata do not leave fractures or scree, while in water the weight is reduced and the fluid acts as a lubricant. This means that the only possibility for strata to shift over one another is a great catastrophe, such as a Flood. Readers who would like to make a detailed study of the course of the Flood will find some interesting theories in books and articles by Dillow, Brown, and Baumgardner.[37]

THE LAWS OF NATURE

From biology and geology, it appears that evolution is impossible. There are dozens of other facts that contradict the theory of evolution and show that, scientifically speaking, evolution is a house of cards, an egg without the chicken. Let us have a look at what the laws of nature do teach us.

THERMODYNAMICS

The First Law of Thermodynamics

This is one of the most fundamental laws of nature. All scientists, both evolutionists and creationists, acknowledge that this law applies to everything that exists. This "law of conservation of energy" says, "*No energy can be created or be destroyed.*"

Energy can exist in many forms, such as light, heat, sound, electricity, mechanical energy, *and so forth*. The energy can be changed from one form to another, but the total amount of energy in the universe always remains the same. In fact, matter itself is also a form of energy—this is the principle behind the atom bomb.

How can the universe have originated out of nothing if the total quantity of energy has never changed, if no energy can ever be added or taken away?

Nowadays evolutionists believe that the universe originated from a small, immensely dense primordial cloud (or even a primordial atom), which exploded with an incredible blast—the so-called Big Bang. But what existed before the Big Bang? Where did that primeval cloud come from? In my opinion, there must be something that stands outside matter and time, that has produced the universe, something immaterial, something eternal . . .

The biblical idea that the universe had a beginning is unique in world history and is in agreement with modern science. (The Koran maintains the same, but is largely based on the Bible and was written much later.) All other religions assume that time and matter always existed. Even the greatest scientists, such as Albert Einstein, could not believe that the universe had a beginning. Einstein tied himself in knots trying to prove that the universe was eternal, but in 1922 he admitted defeat and acknowledged that the universe had a beginning. About his use of a "cosmological constant" to prove an eternal universe, he later admitted, "It was the greatest blunder of my life."[38] Since that time other scientists have again and again tried to prove that the universe is eternal, but their theories are constantly undermined by their fellow experts.

The Second Law of Thermodynamics

This important law of nature is also acknowledged by all scientists. In simple terms, this "law of decay" says, *Every system left to itself decays into chaos.*

In other words, all things in the universe have a tendency to become mixed up and chaotic. All particles in a room have a tendency to spread all jumbled up throughout that room. If you turn on the gas tap, the gas molecules spread through the whole kitchen. If you pour hot and cold water together, the hot and cold water molecules spread throughout the whole mixture, so that warm water is produced. These processes can never be reversed. Gas never goes back into the tap on its own. From warm water, you never spontaneously get hot and cold water, and you can never beat an omelet back into an egg.

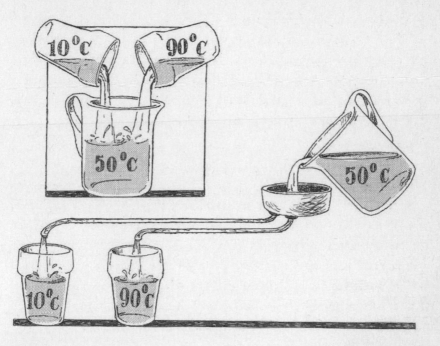

Hot and cold water can be mixed to make warm water, but the warm water can never be divided into hot and cold water.

The second law of thermodynamics says that everything in the world "strives" toward the greatest possible chaos—even in living nature. An organism is constantly busy with making and repairing the complex protein molecules of which it is built. As soon it stops with these "restoration activities," it will die, go moldy, rot away, and decay into humus. The humus decomposes further into a "load of loose molecules," which are carried off by wind and water. Molecules will never automatically join (or stay) together to form a big protein molecule. Protein molecules will never automatically join (or stay) together to form a living cell. Everything in the universe works in precisely the opposite way. There is nothing on earth that can escape this ironclad rule . . .

Yes, there is!

In the whole universe, there is only one possibility to create or to maintain order: namely, through the activity of living beings. *Without life, a complex, highly developed order can never arise or be maintained.*

But how can a complex order of life ever have come into being, if only *life* can create order? There is only one possibility: life was brought forth by something . . . Someone living! The living God created life, the earth, and the whole universe, and straightaway in a perfect form, with the possibility to take in food and reproduce. Otherwise the organisms would die out at once.

Two Objections

Often it is claimed that in special circumstances, order can develop without the help of living beings. The crystals of snowflakes, for example, and the ice crystals on a frozen window have a high degree of order. These examples are cited as proof that in lifeless nature, order can develop on its own and therefore that evolution is possible.

Without using technical formulas, it is difficult to explain why this objection is not valid. According to the second law of thermodynamics, atoms and molecules not only tend to form a chaotic mixture, but also tend to reach the *lowest level of energy*. With many substances, the lowest level of energy is a crystal. For example, if you extract energy from water (by cooling it down), snow or ice crystals form. In other words, when a crystal forms, energy is released. To break a crystal link, you *need* energy.

Exactly the opposite is true of molecules of living organisms. They have a *high* level of energy. If their molecules are broken, energy is *released*. This is why you can warm yourself by a fire of wood, coal, or oil—the remains of living organisms—and why you can gain energy from food.

To summarize: Molecules of crystals can form spontaneously because they have a low level of energy. Molecules of living beings *cannot* form spontaneously because they have a high level of energy. This makes evolution impossible.

The second objection is this: Evolution is possible because the earth is not left to its own devices (it is not a closed system), but is constantly supplied with energy through the rays of the sun. This, too, is not a conclusive argument. Sun rays in themselves do not have a *usable* form of energy. It is not important at all whether there is enough energy available to have a process function, but whether there is enough *usable* energy. If a bomb is dropped on a stack of planks, nails, paint, glass, and bricks, there is enough energy, but this does not mean that a building will be formed. That would be contrary to the second law of thermodynamics. Uncontrolled energy is useless and even harmful, destructive. To construct a building—to create order—you need a building plan, muscle power, and electric machines with all sorts of cables and switches to be able to use the electric energy at the right time, in the right place, and in the right quantity.

In the same way, the energy in the sun's rays is unusable and even destructive unless you are able to *store* it and to use it at the right place, time, and quantity. The only mechanism in nature that can harness and store the energy of the sun—make it usable—is chlorophyll.

Chlorophyll, the Green Motor

Only green plants, and a few bacteria that work according to the same principle, can capture the simple energy of sunlight and transform it into higher, usable forms of energy, such as food and fuel. This process is called photosynthesis. Plants are capable of storing this energy because of the chlorophyll, a green substance in the chlorophyll granules in the cells of green plants. If there were no chlorophyll, sunlight would be unusable and no energy-rich compounds (food) could be made, on which plants, animals, and mankind live. *Without chlorophyll, life on earth would not be possible.*

So even if life on earth originated on its own, it would immediately become extinct if the incredibly complicated chlorophyll hadn't originated simultaneously.℃ At the same time there must also be a mechanism for reproducing chlorophyll granules, otherwise they would still die out. Rather complicated! In order to make this all work well, there must be an exceptionally Intelligent Designer.[39]

℃ Chlorophyll is an "irreducibly complex system," as Michael Behe calls it. It is so complicated and all the parts are so interrelated that not a single part can be missing.

Complexity of the Cell

According to the theory of evolution, life started a few billion years ago in the lifeless chaos of a primeval sea. By chance, the right molecules bumped into one another, and increasingly long and complicated molecules came into being. This continued until a molecule originated that was able to reproduce itself and that developed into the first living being. Evolutionism assumes that the longer a molecule or a living being exists, the greater the chance that it will develop to a higher level. At first sight, this seems reasonable enough. But the more we know about the structures and the chemical processes in the cell, the more we see that life could never have originated on its own. The proteins in a cell are constructed in a very special way, and all these proteins must work together very precisely, otherwise nothing will happen. It is absolutely essential that all proteins do their job at the right time and at the right speed, i.e., that they are properly organized. *Only organization brings a cell to life.*

What are the problems a simple protein must overcome in order to develop through purely random processes? As we have seen with the second law of thermodynamics, all molecules that are once formed will rapidly disintegrate. The more complex a molecule is and the higher the temperature, the quicker it will fall apart. But for the sake of argument, we will assume the following *absurd and impossible situation*: (a) a molecule that once forms in the primeval sea never disintegrates again; and (b) all the necessary elements for the construction of the molecule are available and within reach.

Probability

Protein molecules are made up of a maximum of twenty different types of amino acids. Suppose that a simple protein molecule of one hundred amino acids were to originate spontaneously; then the probability that such a molecule would be formed according to a particular pattern is 1 in 20^{100}. This is about the same as 1 in 10^{130}.

Of course a protein can be built in several ways and still have the same function. If we take that into consideration, then the probability for a spontaneous origin of a good, working protein would be far greater. According to professor Hubert Yockey, a specialist in information theory and biology, for a protein of one hundred amino acids to be formed spontaneously, the chance would still be less than one 1 in 10^{65}. In other words, the probability would be less than 1:100,000,000,000,000,000,00 0,000,000,000,000,000,000,000,000,000,000,000,000,000,000 (65 zeros).[40]

Such figures are too large to comprehend. The following calculation gives an idea how much this is. The ink line in the illustration below is 10 x 1 x 0.001 mm and contains more than 1,000,000,000,000,000,000 (= 10^{18}) electrons. Suppose you are looking for one specific electron, which is heavier than the others, and you examine *one thousand per second*. Then you would need 30 million years to check them all one by one!

———

The ink line (10 x 1 x 0.001 mm) contains more than 1,000,000,000,000,000,000 electrons. If you were to examine one thousand electrons per second, you would need 30 million years before you had checked them all.

But suppose that you needed to find such an electron somewhere in the Rocky Mountains, or maybe in the immense Pacific Ocean . . . or even in the sun, which is more than a million times bigger than the earth! Or suppose that your search encompassed a million suns. That would be a gigantic task indeed. Still it would be easier to find that one special electron in a million suns than it would be for a properly functioning protein of a hundred amino acids to be originated spontaneously. Let alone that such a protein had to originate somewhere in a little primeval sea on earth, containing only a limited number of amino acids, which are not available at the right time and not at the right place. Moreover, when a part of the protein would have been formed, it would be quickly broken down by heat, sunlight, lightning, acids, etc. On top of that, a protein with one hundred amino acids is far too small to be viable.

The probability that one gene—a part of the genetic material (DNA) that ensures the production of a medium-size protein—should come into being spontaneously is as little as 1 in 10^{600} (a 1 with 600 zeros).[41]

The above calculations are really too difficult to comprehend, but they do give an impression of the impossibility that even one small "living molecule" should come into being by chance. And then consider that the simplest living *self-supporting* creature (not a parasite that cannot live independently, and is in fact a degeneration) consists of many tens of thousands of complex molecules.

One single human liver cell contains as many as 53 billion complex protein molecules. A human being consists of more than 50,000,000,000,000 cells, which exhibit vast degrees of variation in function and construction. Do you really think that this all originated spontaneously? Impossible, even if you were to give it 100 billion years!

Sequence

Even if by chance thousands of complex protein molecules happened to be present in a cell along with enough genetic material (DNA) . . . still nothing would happen! The building blocks in the proteins and in the DNA must be in a particular sequence, just like the letters in a word and the words in a book. If the order of the letters or words is incorrect, the book is worthless and no one can gain any information from it. The DNA must contain information, a "script" that tells how to build the proteins and ultimately a complete cell. If the DNA doesn't make up a comprehensible account, nothing will happen.

There is more chance that an ape should by itself copy the whole Bible six hundred times (while another ape is trying to erase every word that has been typed) than that a cell would develop on its own.

Scientists have calculated that the genetic material in a cell contains as much information as two thousand books, each six hundred pages long with five hundred words on a page, with three billion letters. This is about the same as six hundred Bibles. So the probability that a cell were to originate spontaneously is as remote as if an ape were to type the complete Bible six hundred times, while another ape is trying to erase every word that has been typed. (Keep in mind, everything in nature has a tendency to become chaotic and all molecules have a tendency to fall apart.) To put it another way, the probability is the same as if you were to throw three billion separate letters into the air and, spontaneously, two thousand correctly written thick books were to form. In fact, the claim of the evolutionist is like saying that if you were to stand on the Eiffel Tower in Paris and throw the letters down, there is much more chance that the two thousand books would be correctly compiled. After all, the letters then have more time to fall down and to meet one another.

There are many more insurmountable problems in the evolution of life. An example: the "language" of the genetic information in the cell is written in a "four-letter alphabet" (there are four different bases/nucleotides in the DNA) and must be translated into a "twenty-letter alphabet" (there are twenty different amino acids in the protein molecules). For this translation, very special "translation proteins" are needed. But these translation proteins can only be formed with the help of other proteins, which in turn can only be formed with the help of the translation proteins.

100 Percent Levorotary

A remarkable characteristic of proteins in living organisms is that they are made of amino acids that cause light to rotate to the left (levorotary). This means that if you shine light onto a protein in a specific way, the light is turned counterclockwise—to the left. All proteins in all organisms in the whole world are always made of amino acids that cause light to rotate counterclockwise (except for a few rare and highly unusual single-celled organisms). If proteins were to develop through natural processes, as in the theory of evolution, an equal number of amino acids would develop that make light rotate clockwise (dextrorotary) as those that make light rotate counterclockwise. The proportion would be 50:50. But for living beings, even a *single* amino acid that causes light to rotate clockwise makes a protein molecule completely unusable because the molecules cannot make the correct connections with other protein molecules. In all the billions of billions of billions of proteins in the living organisms in the world, there is not one amino acid that causes light to rotate clockwise! In my eyes, this seems like an amusing ploy on the part of the Creator in order to rib the belief that life developed by chance.

Another problem to overcome in building a cell is that the individual elements of the genetic material (ribose, a sugar) and of the proteins (amino acids) are "hostile" to each other. If they are loose in a cell, they destroy each other.

Finally, all the molecules in a cell must be kept together; otherwise the necessary reactions cannot take place. This means that the molecules must be enclosed by a membrane that transports food in and waste matter out but does not let out any molecules of the cell itself. There is indeed such a unique and very complex membrane around every cell. It "knows" exactly which substances must and must not be admitted and which (waste) materials must be removed. This membrane itself is made of protein molecules. But . . . how could this membrane come into being if at the beginning there was no membrane to hold the molecules together?

Viruses

Scientists long thought that viruses formed the missing link between life and death. They are so simple that they cannot be reckoned as living beings: they have no respiratory system and cannot reproduce independently. Most viruses consist of only a piece of genetic material (DNA) surrounded by a protein molecule.

Viruses can only reproduce if they occur in living cells of bacteria, plants, humans, or other animals. So even if a virus had by chance come into being in the "primeval soup" of the earth, still nothing would happen. *A virus can only multiply with the help of very special, complex proteins (enzymes) from living cells.* These enzymes cannot originate on their own, but must be built with the help of other enzymes in the cells of living beings.

On closer inspection, scientists have abandoned the idea that viruses came into being spontaneously. After all, they can only exist when normal cells are present. So the normal, complex cells were already in the world before viruses came into being. It is now assumed that viruses are pieces of dislodged and parasitical genetic material, which is a kind of degeneration.

Every living cell is so complex and constructed on the basis of so many factors that are mutually dependent and must all function completely correctly at the same time that it is *impossible* that cells have ever originated spontaneously. Until thirty years ago, creationists and evolutionists had to admit that there was no real proof of their theories, but only indications by means of which they could defend their theories. But as scientists do now know how utterly intricate a cell is built, and that it is constructed from countless irreducibly complex systems, we can say that life coming into being by chance is impossible, and that creation is the most acceptable alternative.

Intelligent Design

A new method of thinking that has developed is the Intelligent Design Theory. This theory adds many new facts, which convincingly prove that the earth, life, and even the whole universe is constructed according to a special Intelligent Design. This can be seen from "irreducibly complex systems," such as an eye, a bird's feather, or the power of flight of a bird.[42] But also from the fact that all amino acids in all living beings cause light to rotate counterclockwise. And even from the miraculous characteristics of water. For example, water has the smallest volume at 39°F, which means that ice floats on water and the underlying water does not freeze in severe winters, preventing the death of all aquatic animals in cold climates.

Countless scientists (both evolutionists and creationists) agree that it seems as if everything in the universe is carefully designed to make life on earth possible. The evolutionist Paul Davies writes, "Scientists have long been aware that the universe seems strangely suited to life, but they mostly chose to ignore it. It was an embarrassment—it looked too much like the work of a Cosmic Designer." And after Davies gives a number of remarkable facts about the incredible fine-tuning of the universe, he adds, "The cliché that "life is balanced on a knife-edge" is a staggering understatement in this case: no knife in the universe could have an edge *that* fine."[43]

To give a few examples: If the force of gravity in the universe were only 1 in 10^{55} different than it is now, no life would exist. If the forces in the nucleus of an atom were 1 percent more or less, no life would exist.[44] If the distance from the earth to the sun were a little greater or less, we would freeze to death or be burned up, and so forth. Hugh Ross mentions seventy such "coincidences" in physics and astronomy. Michael Denton cites a number from chemistry, geology, and biology. William Dembski gives a philosophical explanation of this theory.[45]

The evidence against evolution is so conclusive and overwhelming that no one can really be an evolutionist on the basis of scientific facts, but only on the basis of philosophical preferences.

Summary

The origination of a living organism through a series of coincidental reactions is absolutely impossible:

1. According to the first law of thermodynamics, in the universe no energy can be created or lost. Therefore the universe cannot have originated spontaneously. It must have been created from outside.

2. According to the second law of thermodynamics, everything in the universe strives for the greatest possible chaos. Complex and energy-rich molecules fall apart, not together. This process speeds up as the temperature increases.

3. The necessary elements for a protein molecule can never all be within reach of that molecule at the same time.

4. Proteins in living beings are made up of 100 percent amino acids that make light rotate counterclockwise. If proteins were to originate by chance, 50 percent of them would consist of amino acids that make light rotate clockwise.

5. In order to bring a cell to life, thousands of different and complex molecules have to originate simultaneously.

6. There must be information—a "script"—present in the cell about how the molecules should be constructed.

7. This information must be: (a) faultlessly written, (b) faultlessly read, and (c) faultlessly transported.

8. The information must also be faultlessly translated into a completely different alphabet at the right moment and at the right speed.

9. Energy is needed for all these reactions. So there must be a mechanism to absorb, digest, store, and use energy (food).

10. There must be a mechanism to remove waste products.

11. To make matters worse, the individual elements of protein molecules and of DNA are each other's "enemies" and will destroy each other when they are loose in the cell.

12. The parts must be held together by a membrane; otherwise the cell does not work and the molecules fall apart. The membrane must know exactly which materials should and should not be absorbed and which should be removed.

13. The first living being must have a mechanism for reproduction, right from the beginning; otherwise it will immediately die out again.

14. All the above-mentioned functions must be perfectly attuned to one another. Only then can a cell continue to live.

Artificial Life?

Hitherto all human efforts to make anything like an "organic protein" have completely failed. The most advanced experiments have only resulted in the formation of a few simple proteins, simple "building blocks." Making a series of building blocks is something quite different from building a cathedral, for which a building plan (intelligence) is needed—let alone the building of an independently *living* cathedral.

Even if man were ever capable of creating life, all the experiments required would only prove that for this *an exceedingly great and concentrated intelligence* is needed, plus perfectly controlled laboratory conditions.

In some experiments, such as the famous experiments by Stanley Miller in 1953, amino acids were formed, from which later simple proteins could be made. These amino acids were immediately removed from the test environment and cooled off, which prevented them from disintegrating. It is completely unjustified to cite such experiments as proof that life has originated on earth spontaneously: (1) such local and controlled cooling is impossible under natural circumstances; (2) over 98 percent of the molecules were composed of poisonous tar and other toxic products; (3) amino acids came into being that make light rotate both clockwise and counterclockwise, while life is constructed of 100 percent amino acids that make light rotate counterclockwise; (4) only fragments of proteins, which could easily be formed, came into being, while life is actually constructed from long and very complex proteins; (5) all proteins that might come into being in nature would very quickly be destroyed again by sun rays, lightning, and heat.

PECULIAR ANIMALS

A great problem for the theory of evolution is the countless number of peculiar plants and animals, possessing the most marvelous organs.

One of the thousands of examples is the bombardier beetle (*Brachinus crepitans*), which is found near rivers and pools all over the world. When the bombardier beetle is attacked by an enemy, it aims two small tubes in its tail at its attacker, a tiny explosion is heard, and a shot goes off. A glowing hot, caustic liquid shoots out and when it hits the enemy, it causes painful burning injuries. If the enemy is not hit, the liquid disintegrates in a bluish smoke. The smoke screen serves to conceal the retreat of the beetle, but also acts as an irritant, which usually causes the enemy to flee.

The beetle has two groups of glands that produce liquids. These liquids together form a very concentrated mixture of 10 percent hydroquinone and 28 percent hydrogen peroxide. The mixture is kept in a reservoir, and when danger arises, it is pushed into an actual combustion chamber. There a catalyst is added to the mixture, and immediately an explosion follows, causing the mixture to be shot out, just like a rocket with liquid fuel. The boiling hot fluid is aimed at the enemy by movable nozzles.

Just suppose that a system like this were to originate through purely accidental changes (mutations) and natural selection. For such a process, the beetle would not only have to develop a complete mechanism of glands, muscles, reservoir, combustion chamber, and tubes, but the whole system would also have to work perfectly, right from the beginning. On top of that it must produce three highly concentrated chemicals: hydroquinone, hydrogen peroxide, and a catalyst. These substances must be produced at the right place, in the right quantities, and at the right time. The beetle must also be able to mix them in the right chamber and at the right time, otherwise it will cost its life. If this entire complicated mechanism were to have developed through a gradual process of evolution, millions of generations of beetles would have been necessary. However, all the intermediate stages of development would be perilous for the survival of the beetle.

Suppose that the beetle has developed all the necessary organs—a miracle in itself—but has not yet prepared the right liquids. If then a hungry enemy comes along, he aims the nozzles at the enemy—but nothing happens because the weapon is not loaded. Gulp—beetle gone. And that goes on for many generations. Then by a miracle, the beetle develops the ability to produce hydroquinone and hydrogen peroxide and mix them in his combustion chamber. There comes a great beetle-catcher and . . . again, gulp, beetle gone. The beetle did have the correct substances, but no catalyst to ignite the mixture in the combustion chamber. But as this beetle is a lucky one, there occur millions of beneficial mutations and finally the catalyst is made and used in the combustion chamber at the right time. Marvelous!

Aha, there comes his archenemy. Everything is working well: the right proportions, the right nerve system, the right place, and the right moment . . . Boom, a dull thud, beetle gone. The nozzles were not big enough and the liquid exploded in the beetle. So it continues again for many generations. And here we must assume that all the exploded or gobbled-up beetles keep multiplying anyway; otherwise the species would die out. . . .

But finally everything seems to be set. The system of organs is there; the two basic ingredients are there; the catalyst is added at the right moment. The process of evolution is now complete. But then the worst thing of all happens. There comes a lovely little lady beetle. The beetle aims his nozzles and shoots. . . . Alas, there goes his only opportunity to start a family. Why on earth would he do that? Well, the most difficult thing has not yet happened: through evolution, the beetle has to develop an *instinct* as well, which causes him to fire his guns at the right moment—to fire at his enemy, not his (girl)friend. Without this instinct, the beetle will be left all alone, being "Nobody's Boy."[46]

The existence of this little beetle and thousands of other such marvelously constructed creatures cannot be explained by any process of evolution, but only by a perfect work of creation by an almighty God.

The scientist I. L. Cohen writes, "Every single concept advanced by the theory of evolution is imaginary as it is not supported by the scientifically established facts. The theory of evolution may be the worst mistake made in science."[47]

EVIDENCE OF A YOUNG EARTH

All publications at school, in the library, and on television broadcasts are presented as if it were *proved* that the earth is 4.5 billion years old. In particular, dating by means of radioactive substances is used for this. However, these "proofs" are not as strong as we might be led to believe. It would be too much to go into this in this book. Reference is made to the books *Scientific Creationism* and *The Illustrated Origins Answer Book*.[48]

For this book, it will suffice to give three examples showing that dating with radioactive substances is unreliable:

With the potassium-argon method, volcanic rock, which was formed near Hawaii in 1801 (about two hundred years ago), was dated as being 160 million to 3 billion years old.[49] Using the same method, lava deposits that were formed near Mount St. Helens in the state of Washington in 1980 were calculated to be between 0.35 and 2.8 million years old, while the rock at the time of the test was less than ten years old.[50]** In strata 250

** With the dating of rock by means of radioactive substances, it is not a question of how long the material has been present in the earth, but when it was formed by volcanism or by sedimentation (depositing by water). From that moment on, the "geologic clock" starts to tick.

million years old (!), fossilized wood was found that contained *radioactive carbon* (^{14}C). But ... the presence of radioactive carbon is proof that a fossil is not older than about 50,000 years.[51]

Many actual *facts* have been discovered that fit better into a theory of a young earth than into the theory of evolution. We have seen this also on pages 156–60, under "Bombs under the Theory of Evolution." But there are dozens of other facts that point to a young earth. We will look at just four.

1. When uranium breaks down into lead, helium is formed. In the course of time, this helium escapes from the rock in which it has formed and enters the atmosphere. But there is so very little helium in the atmosphere that this could be formed in a few thousand years. If the decay of uranium had been going on for five billion years, it is estimated that there should be about one hundred thousand times more helium in the atmosphere. Evolutionists try to get around this problem by pointing out that helium is a very light gas that rises up through the atmosphere and finally escapes into space. But calculations and measurements with rockets show that the atmosphere absorbs much more helium from space than could ever escape.[52]

    Second, it has recently been discovered that crystals of 1.5 billion years old (according to the evolution theory) contain much too much helium. In such a long time the helium should have escaped from the crystals. On top of that, the amount of helium in the crystals is so great that there must have been a time when the radioactive decay was much greater than nowadays. At that time large amounts of helium have developed that had not yet had time to diffuse out of the crystals. According to the reliable helium diffusion method, the crystals and the rocks in which they occur are about 6,000 years old.[53]

2. Rivers transport large quantities of dissolved substances to the sea, such as salt, nickel, lead, and so forth. It is possible to calculate how much of each substance is transported to the sea by all rivers annually. We can also measure how much of each substance

there is in the sea. In this way, we can calculate for how many years the rivers have been flowing, and therefore how old the earth is. With this calculation, we have to bear in mind that there was already a certain quantity of these substances in the sea when it came into being.

Even if you ignore this fact, you still end up with an earth aged somewhere between a few thousand and a few million years. This is a period far too short to make evolution possible. If you look at the quantity of substance transported to the sea, the amount of salt indicates a maximum age of 260 million years—in this we have not taken any account of the large quantities of salt that have entered the sea due to volcanic activity.[54] The amount of copper indicates 50,000 years, nickel 18,000 years, and lead 2,000 years.[55] With all the results taken together, the average age of the earth is about 9,000 years. Research has shown that the substances are not precipitating on the seabed.

An additional problem with the theory of evolution is that the rivers transport so much sand and clay to the sea—about twenty-five billion tons per year—that in three billion years, the continents would have been eroded away about three hundred times, and the oceans would have been filled up twenty times with sand and clay.[56] The theory of evolution cannot solve this problem by assuming a so-called geologic cycle, according to which the continents have constantly risen up and sunk in different places, and where the newly formed mountains have repeatedly been eroded away. Not many evolutionists believe in such a geologic cycle anymore, but even if there were such a geologic cycle, this could only account for the eroding away of the continents two or three times, not one hundred to three hundred times![57]

If the continents had been eroded away several times, no strata on earth would be found that were hundreds of millions of years old. After all, these strata would have been eroded away with the rest of the continent. Yet all over the world, strata are found that, according to the theory of evolution, are hundreds of millions to a few billion years old.

3. The magnetic field of the earth is becoming weaker all the time. For 160 years now, the strength of this magnetic field has been measured. It appears that the strength is reduced by half every 1,400 years. If we calculate back using these facts, ten thousand years ago the magnetic field must have been as strong as that of a "magnetic star." If the earth were even older, the magnetic field must have been extremely strong. And that is impossible, because the atomic reactions that can produce the necessary energy to maintain such a strong magnetic field for a long time are lacking on the earth. Moreover, the earth would have been blown apart by such strong magnetic forces and the accompanying production of heat.[58]

Evolutionists maintain that the magnetic field in our time is not really becoming weaker, but that it is only subject to fluctuations. According to them, the earth works as a dynamo, in which the magnetic field slowly changes direction in the course of (hundreds of) thousands of years. Research reveals that the direction of the magnetic field of the earth has indeed changed many times. But research has also shown that these changes can take place very rapidly.

The physicist D. Russell Humphreys has refined the creationist theory of the decay of the magnetic field. He postulated that many rapid reversals have taken place during the Flood. Humphreys predicted in 1986 that such rapid reversals could be found in volcanic layers of a single eruption (something that is impossible with the dynamo theory). Three years later his theory was confirmed.[59]

In 1989 scientists studied lava flows at the slopes of a volcano in Oregon in the United States. To their utter amazement they discovered that the magnetic field in these flows was changed 45° within fifteen days (the time needed for the lava to solidify).[60] This means that in two months' time, the magnetic field in a stratum can be reversed completely. This is not only evidence that the claim of "millions of years" is not needed, but even that the mechanism of the earth as a "dynamo" does not exist at all. For with a dynamo as large as the earth, the magnetic field could never change that quickly. For more evidence, see the noted references.[61]

4. Even in the universe there is evidence for a young earth, such as short-period comets and interplanetary dust particles floating around in our solar system. In a limited number of years, short-period comets complete an extended (elliptical) orbit around the sun. Every time they pass the sun, they lose a part of their matter due to the powerful sun rays and other influences. This matter forms the beautiful "tail" that can be seen at night if a comet is nearing the sun. Based on the speed of this disintegration, it has been calculated that comets cannot be much older than ten thousand years.

But since most scientists believe in a very old universe, they have formulated all sorts of theories to explain the existence of comets after so many billions of years. Many scientists believe that outside our solar system there is an invisible "Oort cloud," with more than 200 billion comets. Under the influence of the planets or of passing stars, every now and then a comet falls from this cloud in the direction of the sun and loses matter through erosion in the course of ten thousand years. There is no proof of the existence of such a "store of comets." This theory is not needed at all (and according to some, there are serious objections to it), and it is only a way of supporting the view of an old earth.[62]

DUST PARTICLES

The interplanetary dust particles in our solar system also have a short life span. Due to the gravitational force of the earth, moon, planets, and especially the sun, dust particles are continually "swept up" and so there is less and less dust floating around in our solar system. Had the solar system been very old, then all dust particles would have been swept up long ago, and there would be hardly any dust left. The very fact that there is still a considerable quantity of dust in our solar system is an indication of a young universe.[63]

By the way, for the theory of evolution it is inexplicable that the axial rotation of three planets (Venus, Uranus, and the dwarf planet Pluto) is exactly opposite to the axial rotation of all the other planets and the sun. Also, six of the sixty-three moons in our solar system orbit in the opposite direction to that of the planets and the other moons.[64] If the solar system has originated from a rotating nebular cloud, as asserted by the theory of evolution, everything in the cloud should turn in the same direction and it would be impossible that nine planets and moons would rotate (and even orbit) in the opposite direction.

For a detailed treatment of the above-mentioned points and a wealth of references to literature, *The Illustrated Origins Answer Book* by P. S. Taylor is recommended. In this book, there is an overview of more than a hundred studies that point to a young earth and a young universe. Reference is also made to dozens of addresses of organizations in the area of "Scientific Creationism."[65] See also page 254 at the back of this book.

THE CREATION AND FLOOD MODEL

We have seen that scientific facts of biology, geology, and physics do not contradict the assertions of the Bible. This gives us reason enough to accept the accounts of the Creation and the Flood in Genesis 1–8 as reliable. Many problems with the theory of evolution, such as "modern fossils in ancient strata" and the sudden extinction of many organisms can be well explained by the account of the Flood. From a scientific point of view, creationism is a valid theory. The only problem lies with us ourselves. We are all tuned to *experiences*. We tend to believe only what we have experienced ourselves! And because nobody has ever experienced changes in cosmic and global processes, it is hard to believe that six to ten thousand years ago the earth looked very different and that cosmic catastrophes took place.

The following is a fragmentary description of the Flood. My intention is not to treat the subject extensively but only to give a general idea how the course of the Flood might have proceeded. Let it be emphasized that the account below arises from human research. Any mistake in the reasoning does not detract from the authority of the Bible. Elaborations on various

Flood models can be found in the books by Dillow[††] about a large quantity of water vapor above the atmosphere; by Brown about the "springs of the great deep Hydro Plate Model" (Genesis 7:11), and in the articles by Baumgardner about the "Catastrophic Plate Tectonics Model."[66]

Before the Flood

According to Genesis, God created everything in a perfect form—the universe, the earth, and all living beings (see Genesis 1:31). Therefore creation can never be improved. Any real change is always a degeneration. This is particularly evident with mutations. God created living beings "according to their kinds" (Genesis 1:12, 21, 24–25). This means that of every group of plants or animals, God created a basic type, a "baramin." Every baramin had the built-in possibility to adapt to changing circumstances; a sort of "life insurance" to stand up to extreme changes in the environment.

Adam was a "mature" creation, as was the earth. So even in the first week of creation, everything had the appearance of "maturity." Through the Fall of mankind, a curse came over the earth (see Genesis 3:17) and the negative influences of the second law of thermodynamics came into effect: "Everything decays into as great a chaos as possible."

In the beginning, there was a large amount of vapor above the air (see Genesis 1:6–7 and 2:5–6 RSV), which made for an ideal environment. The vapor ensured an evenly warm climate all over the world. Evidence for this can be found in all sorts of strata. At the South Pole, there was a subtropical climate.[‡‡] In Europe, there lived monkeys, elephants, and hippopotamuses. Through the warmth and humidity, vegetation grew

---

[††] Dillow uses the large quantity of water vapor *above* the atmosphere to explain the tremendous rainfall at the beginning of the Flood (Genesis 7:12). Later calculations have shown that this water vapor could account for only forty inches of precipitation. This is much too little to make a significant contribution to the Flood. Brown and Baumgardner have given better explanations (see the following pages). The model of Dillow, however, does give a good explanation of the ideal living conditions that prevailed on earth before the Flood.

[‡‡] Probably the plants and animals found in the strata at the South Pole did not live there, but were swept there during the Flood. Obviously, even if a warm climate existed all over the world, there would still be too little sunlight at the South Pole for large numbers of plants (and animals) to live there. At the poles, it is dark for almost six months of the year, and if there is sunlight, the sun is always extremely low on the horizon.

particularly well, and even more so because there was much more carbon dioxide (CO_2) in the atmosphere than at present. The vapor caused an increased air pressure, which meant that people and other animals could live longer and healthier and even become bigger than at present. It also formed a thick protective layer against destructive cosmic rays and against the harmful ultraviolet light from the sun.

In addition to the vapor canopy, the strong magnetic field of the earth and a thick ozone layer (at an altitude of fifteen miles) ensured extra protection against the harmful cosmic radiation. Because of this three-fold protective layer, hardly any radioactive carbon (^{14}C) was formed, no harmful mutations occurred, and the process of aging was very slow. The organisms lived to a great age (see Genesis 5). Especially the reptiles became very large, because these animals continue to grow all their lives. The various groups of animals, just like now, lived in specific areas, such as swamps and woods. The terrifying giant reptiles (dinosaurs), for example, lived primarily in the "Cretaceous areas," swamps with their typical flora and fauna. These *areas* are mistakenly defined by evolutionists as *eras* (periods in time).

DURING THE FLOOD

All of a sudden, tremendous natural disasters befell the earth—perhaps due to impacts by one or more huge comets.[67] Due to the violent shock waves, major "rifts" came in the earth's crust, which caused volcanic eruptions and earthquakes on a global scale. These rifts became so great that the vast original continent of Pangea broke up and the continents drifted apart. This is called the "continental drift." Because the continents shifted, the strata at the edges of the continents were pushed up and ever higher mountains were being formed. This happened, for example, with the Alps, the Rocky Mountains, and the Himalayas (where India collided into Asia). A huge rift formed all around the globe, running forty thousand miles through the middle of the oceans. Traces of this are still visible (see illustration on the next page).

There is a rift along the oceanbed, 40,000 miles long, which may be a remnant of the "bursting forth of the great deep," as described in Genesis 7:11.

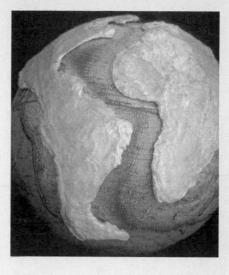

According to the "Hydroplate Model" of Walt Brown,[68] this huge rift in the middle of the oceans released water that had been under tremendous pressure far below the surface of the earth. The water (plus mud and boulders) shot up into the air with incredible force and caused an overwhelming torrent for forty days.

According to the "Catastrophic Plate Tectonics Model" of Baumgardner,[69] the ocean floor broke open at the "great rift" and the pieces (tectonic plates) drifted apart, sometimes as fast as a few meters a second. Because the plates moved apart extremely fast, along the "great rift" a vast quantity of liquid rock burst up, like a kind of volcano, but tens of thousands of miles long. Along the whole length, the sea was explosively brought to a boil and superhot steam shot up into the air, forcing liquid water up with it to the highest reaches of the atmosphere. There the steam and the water cooled down and, during the first forty days of the Flood, fell on the earth in a global torrent.

The "millionfold" volcanic eruptions along the "great rift" and elsewhere on the earth caused vast tidal waves (tsunamis), which ravaged the coastal regions and destroyed all forests. Even a "small" eruption of a single volcano, such as Krakatoa in Indonesia in 1883, caused a tidal wave, initially 120 feet high, that raced over the surface of the ocean at a speed of four hundred miles an hour across a distance of thousands of miles, killing thirty-six thousand people.[§§] Ash and pumice stone were ejected into the air to a height of twenty-five miles, changing the color of the sky all around the world.[70]

---

§§ The force of a tsunami became clear in 2004, when a small earthquake in the Indian Ocean near Indonesia caused a tsunami that inundated the coastlines of the surrounding countries. This tsunami was only a dwarf compared with the Krakatoa tidal wave.

The Devastating Force of Water

With a global Flood, we must not think of water that rose higher and higher due to torrential rain, but of natural disasters that are beyond our imagination. Through the shock waves, volcanic eruptions, landslides, mudflows, hurricanes, and so forth, the waters of the sea raged for weeks and raced in huge tidal waves across the earth.

Only since the 1960s was it discovered how destructive water can be. Steven Austin gives the following overview: (1) Fast-flowing water (faster than twenty miles an hour) can pulverize solid rock. This is due to cavitation, the formation of vacuum cavities around irregularities and rough surfaces. When these bubbles implode, this produces shock waves that hit on the bedrock surface like a hammer, with pressures running from a few hundred to as many as thirty thousand times the atmospheric pressure. The force of these shock waves is many times greater than a rock can withstand. (2) Fast-flowing water pulls on rocks in a very forceful way (hydraulic plucking), which dislodges large blocks of rock from the bed. (3) Fast-flowing water causes whirlpools (kolks) that lift pieces of rock out of the bed as a tornado (whirlwind) does in the air, but much more forcefully.[71] (4) The pieces of rock that are pulled out and swirled around bang like sledgehammers on the rocks over which the water flows. The faster the water flows, the greater the effects are.

Fast-flowing water literally pulverizes rocks and hard strata in a short time and can also carry along a vast quantity of sediment (clay, sand, stone, and rocks). The quantity of material transported increases hugely when the velocity of the water increases. If the water is flowing slowly or at a moderate speed, the quantity of sediment transported is proportional to the fourth or fifth power of the speed of the water. With fast-running, turbulent floods of water, the amount of sediment can even increase to the eighth (!) power of the velocity of the water.[72] In other words, if a large quantity of fast-flowing water starts to flow three times as fast again, it can transport 6,651 (=3^8) times as much sediment. Increasingly larger stones and boulders are swept along.

This knowledge gives a completely new understanding of the destructive effects of the Flood. And it provides a good explanation of the thick and vast strata that developed at that time!

Frozen Mammoths

At the beginning of the Flood, the water poured out of the air, and locally the air pressure plummeted, causing the temperature to fall too. Warm air flowed in from the sides and a gale began, becoming increasingly strong and on an increasingly large scale. In the polar regions the temperature plummeted far below freezing point, and devastating hail and snowstorms arose. The blizzards, plus the freezing water, raged across the land and overtook whole herds of animals, such as the mammoths in Siberia. Thousands of individuals were frozen on the spot and were later buried under tons of mud, which was thrown over them by the tidal waves.

Many mammoths were preserved, some even with their food still in their mouths. They didn't even have time to swallow their last mouthful. Even the food in their stomachs (grass, buttercups, beans, seeds, and young shoots of pine trees) was not digested or decayed. When scientists discovered their carcasses just over a hundred years ago, their meat could even still be eaten by the sled dogs. This means that the mammoths must have been deep-frozen very, very suddenly indeed. They certainly did not fall through the ice of a frozen river, as is often suggested. For in that case, a mammoth would have swallowed or let fall what was in its mouth. What is more important, a frozen river is not cold enough to prevent digesting or rotting of the food in the stomach of such a huge and well-insulated animal. Because of the enormous volume of the body and the thick insulating fur, it would take days before the freezing cold would have reached the stomach. In the meantime, part of the food would already have been digested or gone rotten.

For the same reason, it is impossible that the mammoths fell en masse into a cleft in the earth, as is sometimes asserted. Besides, if the animals had fallen into a cleft in the ground, their bones would be found some distance *under* the bones of other animals that perished. But the bones and corpses of the mammoths are just lying among the bones of the other mammals. It is estimated that along the northern coast of Siberia, millions of mammoths are buried in this way.[73]

With the help of some scientists, the researcher Dillow has calculated that the temperature in the polar regions must suddenly have dropped to negative 175°F.[74] Brown mentions dozens of facts about these deep-frozen mammoths that cannot be explained by the theory of evolution.[75] The only acceptable explanation is a global catastrophe, such as described in the account of the Flood in the Bible.

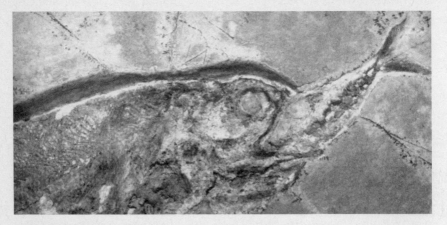

Fossils are only formed if the organism is suddenly buried under a layer of airtight material, such as this fish, which did not have time to finish its meal.

"All the springs of the great deep broke forth" (Genesis 7:11), and the whole world disappeared under water. Noah probably had some (tens of) thousands of animals in the ark—only two of each basic type. Obviously there were no aquatic animals in the ark, while these represent more than 90 percent of all species of animals, if we do not count the insects.

Powerful tidal waves churned up the earth. Whole forests were uprooted and billions of trees floated as driftwood on the water. Near the shores, particularly in enclosed inlets, the wood stacked up and was covered by avalanches and landslides. In other places, giant waves lashed against the continents, depositing sand and clay on top of the wood. With new waves, new wood was carried along, which was again buried under heavy masses of earth. In this way, in many places in the world dozens of coal seams have been deposited on top of one another—each time intersected by a layer of sand and clay. Because of the tremendous pressure, the wood was compressed and coal was formed. (According to laboratory tests, coal can be formed in a matter of hours to weeks.)[76]

Coal deposits can only be formed as described above, not by a gradual accumulation of leaves and the remains of trees in a swamp. Nowhere in the world are there any swamps that are gradually transformed into coal beds—although this is wrongly suggested in popular biology books.

It is utterly impossible that in the same area sixty swamps—all growing in *fresh*water—should be formed after one another, each time flooded by *sea*water for many thousands of years. When the seawater had deposited a thick layer of sand and clay, the swamp should develop again in exactly the same place, the same circumstances, the same climate, and so on. Sixty times![77] It becomes even crazier when fossilized trees are sticking up straight through several strata (see the picture on page 159).

Billions of invertebrate marine animals, such as simple worms and starfish, lived on or near the seabed and were the first to be buried alive by the landslides or by streams of lava and mud. Such mud streams (also called turbidity currents) on the bottom of the sea occur even nowadays, like the one on November 18, 1929, caused by a landslide on the northeast coast of America. The mud stream shot forward with an average speed of more than sixty miles an hour and covered about forty thousand square miles of the oceanbed with three feet of sediment, burying everything on or near the oceanbed. The speed could be measured very accurately because it was known exactly when and where the various telephone cables between America and Europe were broken.[78]

Other simple invertebrates either floated around in the sea or had a limited ability to swim. They could not flee from danger. They also had little resistance to the violence of the churning water and the immense amounts of poisonous chemicals dissolved in the water through volcanic eruptions. Therefore, they were among the first animals to die in the natural disaster. The dead creatures sank to the bottom. The simple forms (round and ellipse) sank faster than the more complex forms with protrusions.

This means that during excavations, we usually find the following situation:

1. The lowest stratum is the seabed or the original dry land and does not contain any fossils.

2. The next strata contain simply structured animals, which lived on or near the seabed.

3. As the strata are more elevated, we find a progression from sim-
    ple to complex forms.

This solves the problem of evolutionists with regard to why fossils are
never found in the lowest stratum and in the following strata they suddenly are found in great abundance. After all, according to the theory of
evolution, this means that for the first four and a half billion years of the
earth's existence, no living beings existed, except a few bacteria, and just
over half a billion years ago, *suddenly* all the major groups of animals developed at the same time.

Mass graves of thousands of animals from different climates and different evolutionary periods can only be explained by the occurrence of a worldwide Flood.

Vertebrate marine animals, such as fish and seals, have a better ability to flee and are therefore not so easily trapped by mudflows or landslides. Their greater resistance to poisonous substances also ensured
that they did not die immediately at the start of the Flood. That is the
reason that their fossils are found in higher strata. Often they are found
in mass graves, because they were washed up together or were collectively

overtaken by a disaster. For example, in California there is a shoal of fish with more than a billion individuals together, spread across an area of four square miles. The terrified, twisted posture in which they are found speaks of violence and death agony.[79] In Belgium, there are tens of thousands of dinosaur bones and whole skeletons stacked up in a layer almost one hundred feet thick.[80] In China, at an altitude of over thirteen thousand feet, seventy tons of dinosaur fossils have been found. Such dinosaur mass graves have been found on every continent. Near Los Angeles tens of thousands of plants and animals from *different* climates and *different* evolutionary periods are found together. Did these all go and lie neatly together and then die a natural death?

The theory of evolution has never been able to give a satisfactory explanation for the dozens of such mass graves. Mass graves with thousands of animals from different climates and different eras can only have been brought about if the animals lived at the same time and were swept together by a great flood.

Only when an organism is suddenly cut off from the air can it become a fossil. Otherwise, the carcass would be destroyed by the influences of erosion, rotting, and weathering before the process of fossilization could start. The very few fossils that are formed nowadays come into being—just as in the past—primarily because flowing water rapidly covers a corpse with compact material. Fossils never form when bodies are gradually cut off from the air or when they are covered with loose material, such as leaves in a wood or sand on a beach—as is often suggested in popular books and films.

Amphibians and reptiles such as frogs, crocodiles, and dinosaurs lived primarily in damp coastal areas. This is why these animals are found in higher strata than the marine plants and animals. Obviously very few fossils of mammals and people are found, and even then only in the uppermost strata. This is because with the rising water, they fled to the nearest hilltop, where they were ultimately drowned. Their corpses rotted away, because they were not suddenly covered with solid material. For the same reason, bird and insect fossils are, of course, extremely rarely found, and also only in the uppermost strata.

By the way, many petrified footprints on hills and mountains run upward, indicating that the animals were indeed fleeing the rising water.

Another reason why fossils of more highly developed animals occur only in higher strata is that their bodies float longer than the bodies of simple creatures. On average, dead amphibians continue to float around for five days, dead reptiles for thirty-two days, dead mammals for fifty-six days, and dead birds for seventy-six days.[81]

Because of the violence of the Flood, at least two thirds of all species of plants and animals were wiped out. And as less than a third of the original species remained, it is obvious that many of the species found in excavations look strange to us. We are apt to think that they are fossils of transitional forms, because they do not fit into any of the existing groups of our time. This is, for example, the case with the Archaeopteryx, the three-toed horse, and the Australopithecus.

AFTER THE FLOOD

Because the continents drifted apart, ever higher mountains and deeper seas were formed, causing the water level to sink and dry land to appear (see Psalm 104:6–8 RSV).

The animals were let out of the ark and spread all over the world. Initially there were only a few animals of each basic type, which formed small, isolated groups that lived in extreme circumstances. According to biologists, such conditions are ideal for the development of many varieties and for the rapid formation of new subspecies within the basic type, the more so since the original basic types are much richer in genetic information than the more adapted and specialized animals that live today (see under mutations on page 139).

After the Flood, there was a relatively cold era, the "ice age." The water in the ocean was still warm because of the contact with the liquid rock during the Flood, causing an exceptionally great evaporation. The air above the continents was cold because the sunbeams were blocked by the volcanic ashes in the atmosphere. Consequently, the cold air became oversaturated with water, and snowfall became excessive, especially in the polar regions.

Many indications that point to earlier ice ages—such as the displacement of large boulders and parallel glacier marks over long distances—can better be explained by landslides under water than by any "ice age."[82]

Powerful earthquakes, storms, and water flows had destroyed all houses and all expressions of human civilization. The descendants of Noah had to start all over again. From sheer necessity, they had to live in caves and tents and make tools of wood and stone by hand—the Stone Age. Only after they had found iron ore were they able to make more refined tools—the Iron Age. The unfamiliar environment, the harsh climate, the damp caves, and the inadequate and monotonous diet made the people stunted and sickly. Of course, this differed per region as with the famous Neanderthals and the early *Homo erectus*, who both lived shortly after the Flood. Only when people had adapted to the environment, could make tools, practice agriculture, and build solid houses did their health improve.

The fact that the Flood was a global catastrophe has been dealt with in chapter 5: there are hundreds of stories of the Flood around the world, three-quarters of the strata were formed by water, the summits of many mountains are covered with marine flora and fauna, shells and marine animals are found on the highest peaks of the Himalayas, the earth layers of the Grand Canyon can only be explained by sedimentation by waters of a gigantic flood, and so forth.

After the Flood, it took hundreds (or thousands?) of years before the earth's crust settled down. During that time there were probably many smaller catastrophes, some still with a worldwide effect. These may have been during the ten plagues in Egypt (see Exodus 7–12), during the battle at Gibeon, in which the earth changed its axial rotation (see Joshua 10:13), and when the sun went back ten steps for Hezekiah (see 2 Kings 20:9–11). Many fossils from later eras, like those of the mammoths in Siberia, may have been formed during these "minor" catastrophes.

The most striking fact in the development of modern geology is the renewed interest in catastrophism. Geologists have come to an understanding that their previous ideas about the slow development of strata—uniformitarianism—were wrong. Almost everything in the strata points to catastrophic formation. In the study of geology, it is now taught that catastrophes indeed played an important role in the forming of strata. This means that geology is coming very close to the biblical model of the Flood; only the timescales are completely different.

Languages

According to biblical history, the different languages on the earth came into being during the building of the tower of Babel (see Genesis 11:1–9). It is remarkable that in linguistics, the older languages can*not* be traced back to one original language. According to the theory of evolution, this indeed ought to be the case. But the languages on the earth can only be traced back to a *number* of language groups, which is in agreement with the account in Genesis 11.

The oldest languages on earth—Sumerian, Akkadian, and Egyptian—are extremely complicated in their verb forms and conjugations.[83] Professor George Simpson of Harvard University says of this, "The oldest language that can reasonably be reconstructed is already modern, sophisticated, complete from an evolutionary point of view."[84] With evolution, we would expect the opposite, namely that the oldest languages would be more primitive than modern languages. Nothing is farther from the truth. According to linguists, the old languages did not evolve, but rather *degenerated* into the modern languages! Many modern languages do contain more words, but they are grammatically poorer than in the past. The languages of "primitive tribes" nowadays, such as the Qetchua Indians of South America, are often much more complicated than modern languages.

Creationist Research

On the creationist side, much research still has to be done to get a better picture of these eventful periods, and in fact more and more scientists are doing just that. An interesting example is the study about the speed of light conducted by the Australian researcher Barry Setterfield. He investigated all available measurements of the speed of light. According to him, dozens of measurements show that this speed has decreased since 1675 from 187,219 miles per second to 186,282 miles per second in 1976. This is a reduction of 937 miles per second in three hundred years. According to scientific calculations, six thousand years ago the speed of light must have been 500 billion times as great as nowadays.[85]

Professor V. S. Troitskii (an evolutionist) of the Radiophysical

Research Institute in Gorky (Russia) claims that the speed of light used to be ten billion times as great as now. According to him, this can well explain many cosmic phenomena, such as the red shift of light from far distant stars (which increases when the distance between a star and the earth increases) and the background radiation in the universe.[86]

A number of astronomers have come up with research results revealing that the red shift has nothing to do with the expansion of the universe. They found that some star clusters that are linked together have completely different red shifts, and moreover, that the red shift often takes place at *regular intervals*. This causes a headache for evolutionists, because this is incompatible with the Big Bang theory.[87]

More and more scientists think that the speed of light was greater in the past than it is now[88] and that there is something essentially wrong with the Big Bang theory.[89] In laboratories scientists have succeeded in making light move much faster than the normal speed of light.[90] If the speed of light was indeed greater than today, then all sorts of atomic processes would have worked faster than today, for example the decay of radioactive substances. The result of this would be that all radioactive dating would indicate far too great an age.

Scientists at the Institute for Creation Research have found evidence that the speed of decay of radioactive substances in the past was indeed greater than nowadays. They have also discovered radioactive carbon (^{14}C) in fossils hundreds of millions of years old, something that is impossible according to the theory of evolution. Moreover, radioactive carbon has been found in diamonds, which according to the theory of evolution must be billions of years old (!) and formed deep in the earth.[91]

Conclusion

Since Darwin published his book in 1859, thousands of scientists have tried to prove evolution. But as our knowledge of nature increases, this appears to be more and more difficult. It is as the molecular biologist Denton writes, "If this molecular evidence had been available one century ago . . . the idea of organic evolution might never have been accepted. *Neither of the two fundamental axioms of Darwin's macro-evolutionary theory . . . have been validated by one single empirical discovery or scientific advance since 1859* [italics mine]."[92]◖◖

The so-called proofs of evolution all refer to *microevolution*, that is to say, variation within an existing group of plants or animals. The two main facts Darwin and his followers *really* discovered are: (1) the process of microevolution and (2) the existence of basic types, which are built according to a standard "building plan" (blueprint) with a built-in possibility of variation. Both discoveries are entirely in agreement with the Bible.

Of course, anyone may have his own view on the origin of life. But if people claim to believe in "naturalism"—the theory that no God exists— on the basis of scientific facts, they are making fools of themselves. Almost all the scientific facts point in the direction of an Intelligent Design. It is a pity that so many scientists so narrow-mindedly oppose the idea that there is a God.

After all, science has to do with finding and explaining real facts, regardless of the outcome. The evolutionist Denton writes on pages 353–54 of his book, "It has always been the anti-evolutionists, not the evolutionists, . . . who have stuck rigidly to the facts and adhered to a more strictly empirical approach."[93]

SUMMARY

The biblical accounts of the Creation and the Flood are the *only* accounts from antiquity that are in agreement with modern science. The facts discovered in science are not in disagreement with, but in strong support of, the Creation: insurmountable barriers between basic types, both in living nature and in the fossil world; no transitional forms between basic types, neither on a molecular level nor on the level of appearance; irreducibly complex systems, of which every part is essential, and in which everything must work together flawlessly, right from the beginning; cells of an organism that are constructed in an extremely complicated way and with which

---

◖◖ Full quote: "Neither of the two fundamental axioms of Darwin's macro-evolutionary theory—the concept of the continuity of nature (that is the idea of a functional continuum of all life forms linking all species together and ultimately leading back to a primeval cell), and the belief that all the adaptive design of life has resulted from a blind random process— have been validated by one single empirical discovery or scientific advance since 1859."

so many mechanisms must be working at the same time that gradual development is completely impossible, and so forth. Furthermore, all processes in nature point toward degeneration, not toward evolution.

In the fossil world, all the major groups of animals appear suddenly, completely developed and simultaneously in the earth's strata. In geology, hundreds of finds are made that can be better explained by the theory of the Flood than by the theory of evolution. From various fields of science, there is increasing criticism of the idea of evolution by pure chance. An increasing number of discoveries indicate that nature and the universe are the result of an Intelligent Design.

If we carefully study God's Word and God's creation and pay attention to the details, they are shown to be in perfect harmony with each other.

My personal reflection:
If the Christian faith were founded on as few facts as the theory of evolution, I would certainly become an atheist.

Now faith [in Christ] is being . . .
certain of what we do not see.

HEBREWS 11:1

7.

THE RELIABILITY
OF THE BIBLE

"Everything we say about the Above comes from below," wrote the famous Dutch theologian Kuitert in 1974, and since then, this idea has been expressed in many words by many different people.[1] By this statement Kuitert meant that the Bible is not a supernaturally inspired book, the Book of God, but a book of man, invented by human beings. Some of his colleagues even claim that the Bible contains more than twenty thousand errors plus an endless number of fallacies and outright mistakes.

According to Kuitert and many other theologians, the "books of Moses" were not written by Moses at all, but by priests from the tenth to sixth centuries before Christ. These critics say that the books of Moses were completed during the exile in Babylon in the sixth century before Christ. In Babylon the priests wanted to give their oppressed compatriots heart, and also secure their own position. Therefore, they committed the "folk stories and myths" to paper, rewrote historical events, and drew up a large number of sacrificial laws.

If what Kuitert and other such critics say is true, it is not surprising that many churches are becoming empty,* and we should do away with the Christian faith as quickly as possible. But is what they claim true?

After the Enlightenment in the eighteenth century, scholars became increasingly disgusted with the idea that the Bible is a supernatural book. The disgust was fed by anti-Christian notions of philosophers such as Kant, Bacon, and Spinoza.[2] According to these thinkers, it is impossible that God revealed Himself to mankind in a supernatural way. It is

---

* It is noticeable that it is only in the rich, Western countries that the churches are becoming empty, in particular the churches where this type of theology is preached.

impossible that God should have informed a man about a kingdom that would only come into being three hundred years later, or about an exile that would only take place eight hundred years later (see Deuteronomy 17:14–20 and 28:36–37).

This disbelief is seen among well-known theologians such as Wilhem de Wette (1780–1849) and Abraham Kuenen (1828–91), who made their views on this plain, and especially with Julius Wellhausen (1844–1918), who openly ridiculed everything about divine revelations and miracles.[3]

The books of these scholars are still used by many theologians in our days. A professor who has taught these books to her students for years wrote, "It is not the examination of Bible texts but the criticism of the clergyman which is the driving force for these scholarly 'advances.' . . . Scholarly theology is a meaningless game . . . which only satisfies the intellect."[4] According to this professor, these theologians study the Bible superficially and with arrogance. The writings of their fellows are diligently studied, but the Bible is not given opportunity to speak for itself.

THE AUTHORITY AND THE INSPIRATION OF THE BIBLE

DIVINE AUTHORITY

During a theological discussion, the Lord Jesus refuted the claims of a group of Sadducees by the fact that *one* specific word in the Bible is not in the past tense, but in the present tense. The Sadducees did not believe in the resurrection of the dead, but Jesus says about this, "Now about the dead rising—have you not read in the book of Moses, in the account of the bush, how God said to him, 'I am the God of Abraham, the God of Isaac, and the God of Jacob'? He is not the God of the dead, but of the living. You are badly mistaken!" (Mark 12:26–27; see also Exodus 3:6). Simply because it says in Exodus "I am" instead of "I was," Jesus claims that the patriarchs in heaven are still alive. For Jesus, the authority of the Bible is so great that one word is enough to bring down the false doctrine of the Sadducees.

The same applies to the apostle Paul. He constructs a complete theology on the fact that one specific word in the Scriptures is not in the plural, but in the singular. Starting with the word "seed," Paul claims that the blessing of Abraham did not come to the Gentiles through the Jewish people, but through one Jewish person, Jesus Christ. "The promises were spoken to Abraham and to his seed. The Scripture does not say 'and to seeds,' meaning many people, but 'and to your seed,' meaning one person, who is Christ" (Galatians 3:16).

The Lord Jesus and the apostles always referred to the Old Testament as the absolute and literal Word of God, "God said . . ." (Matthew 15:4 and Hebrews 7:21).

Jesus warns us not to change anything regarding the words in the Bible, not even the smallest letter, "Until heaven and earth disappear, not the smallest letter, not the least stroke of a pen, will by any means disappear from the Law" (Matthew 5:18). The Hebrew used here, a jot and a tittle, can be compared with the dot on the *i* and the cross of the *t*.

What is important here is not the fact that a letter is correctly written, but that nothing may be left out or added that might change the meaning of a word. Not even the smallest alteration. This is what Jesus is warning us about. According to Him, we are not allowed to introduce even the smallest change in the meaning of a word in the Bible. Every word is perfectly in the right place and indicates exactly what God means.[†]

In the Old Testament, there are over 3,800 direct instances of divine inspiration. In the New Testament, over 250 quotations from the Old Testament are cited, pleading its absolute authority, as in Matthew 19:4 and John 10:35.[5]

---

† Jesus and the apostles often referred to texts from the Septuagint, the Greek translation of the Old Testament, which is not always particularly accurate. The reason that they did not use the original Hebrew text, but a Greek translation, is that Greek was the global language, the only language with which all Jews and all non-Jews could be reached. In New Testament times many Jews lived outside Israel and no longer knew Hebrew. It is comparable to using references to the NIV translation used in this book. For most readers, it is impracticable to be presented with a reference in the original Hebrew. But even in a translation enough of God's meaning shines through in order to speak of God's Word. For a detailed Bible study or a point of contention about the faith, the original Hebrew should be studied.

VERBAL INSPIRATION

The Bible writers claimed that they literally wrote down the words of God: "Moses then wrote down everything the LORD had said. . . . In accordance with these *words* I have made a covenant with you" (Exodus 24:4 and 34:27). The writer of Proverbs gives the warning, "Do not add to his *words*" (Proverbs 30:6), and Jeremiah is given the warning not to omit anything (see Jeremiah 26:2). In the New Testament, we encounter the same divine claims: "Your word is truth" (John 17:17), and "All Scripture is God-breathed" (2 Timothy 3:16).

When we say that the Bible is inspired by God, we do not mean a poetic inspiration, like an ordinary writer who feels inspired to write a great literary work. Neither do we mean that God inspired only the *thoughts* of the Bible writers, after which the writers themselves were allowed to determine how they would put them into words. By biblical inspiration, we mean that God influenced the writers of the Old and New Testaments in such a way that they used precisely the right words to convey God's message. Therefore their writings have divine authority and are entirely trustworthy in every area.

The fact that the Bible was inspired word for word and not just with regard to the "transfer of ideas" is revealed by various facts.

1. *Scientific facts*—Many Bible writers recount facts they certainly could not have known. In the preceding chapters, we have mentioned dozens of such examples—about nutrition, hygiene, circumcision, the ark, the spherical shape of the earth, and so forth.

2. *Details about the life of Jesus*—Dozens of texts from the Old Testament give a detailed description of the person and work of Jesus Christ. Zechariah 11:12–13 describes how Jesus would be betrayed for thirty pieces of silver, that the money would be thrown into the temple, and that the money would be for the potter. The fulfillment of this prophecy is described in Matthew 26:15 and 27:5–10.

   Isaiah 53 and parts of Psalm 22 describe how Jesus would be

put to death. We have mentioned a number of such prophecies in chapter 5. If the Bible writer in question had not written down literally what God told him, he would have made huge mistakes. It was not a question of what the prophets thought about the subject, but about the precise words they wrote down.

3. *The writers did not understand their own words*—Often the writers themselves did not understand what they had written down (see Daniel 12:8–10). Sometimes they did not agree with God (see Jeremiah 20:7–9). Sometimes they wrote about something they could not have known, such as King David, who in Psalm 22:1–18 described the soul's affliction of someone who is being crucified, a form of punishment that was only introduced in Palestine by the Romans shortly before the time of Christ. All the writers meticulously wrote down every word about which they felt an inner compulsion.

How Did God Inspire the Writers?

Did God inspire the Bible writers by holding their pens and forcing them to write down certain words, or by using them like a "typewriter," a secretary who in ecstasy wrote down the divine dictation? This is known as "mechanical inspiration."

Inspiration of this type occurs in spiritism and in other religions, where the prophet writes down divine dictation in ecstasy. This was also the case with the prophet Mohammed, who claimed that an angel grabbed him by the throat three times and forced him under threat of death to speak aloud and tell others what was dictated to him.[6] We do not encounter such compulsion in the Bible.

The God of the Bible did not compel the prophets, but God made everything in the life of the prophet work toward shaping and polishing him. His character and his vocabulary were developed by the specific family he lived in and by the education he received. The same applies to the events that took place in his life and difficulties he encountered, so that he could use the right words in writing down God's message. Sometimes a prophet was selected for this special work even before his birth, as with Jeremiah (1:5), Isaiah (49:1), and Paul (Galatians 1:15), and as also alluded to in Amos 2:11. God did not physically compel His prophets literally to write down what He dictated. He accepted them as they were and used their personalities and their characters. This is referred to as "organic inspiration."

Multicolored

The writers of the Bible reflected the message of God according to a "multicolored" pattern, as a stained-glass window reflects the light of the sun. On the window falls pure white light, which contains all the colors in the world, but the glass reflects it in the form and the color the designer thought of. The same is the case with all the "differences of form and color" in the Bible.

It is not that a writer "colors" the pure light, that is to say, reflects it imperfectly. Rather the opposite is the case: with his personality, he gives an accent, a color to the story, according to a marvelous design of the Great Architect, which means that the message comes across much more clearly and strongly. All these "colors," all these people together give a much better picture of God's greatness, omnipotence, and multicolored wisdom than one person could ever reflect. God is too great for one person to be able to describe His greatness and omnipotence.

THE FIVEFOLD INSPIRATION OF MOSES

Of all the books in the Bible, the inspiration is most clearly evident in the books of Moses (the Torah). The Torah is not a collection of beautiful but incomprehensible stories that came into being in the course of history or were concocted during the exile in Babylon. No, the stories form the framework, the foundation of the Jewish faith and Jewish society. In addition, they give a detailed description of the work of atonement of Christ in the New Testament, as well as a detailed prescription of the Christian faith. When you discover this, a realm of understanding opens up to you! If you do not see this, you get bogged down in a muddle of incomprehensible stories and laws about the tabernacle and sacrifices.

One author of a Bible textbook writes, "It is not possible to find explanations for the detailed instructions of the building of the tabernacle and of the procedures with the offerings."[7] Another writes, "Leviticus does not have much to say in a religious sense. There are Christians who do find Leviticus edifying by applying all sorts of regulations about sacrifices symbolically to Christ; in this they make the great mistake of wanting to see far and far more in the symbolism of Israel's sacrifices than the most dedicated priest or prophet in Israel ever saw in it."[8]

This writer is right when he says that the priests in the Old Testament had no understanding of the deep symbolism of the sacrifices in the book of Leviticus, but this does not mean that this symbolism is not contained in it. The writer himself makes the mistake of thinking that all these laws were simply made up by "ordinary priests," that the Bible is the result of the "work of man." The authors mentioned are missing one of the most important aspects of the Torah and of the whole Old Testament, namely, the foreshadowing of the work of Jesus Christ, as is indicated in Luke 24:27.

The marvelous thing about all the stories in the Torah is they really took place, that they describe actual history—events that the patriarchs and the people of Israel actually experienced—and many give a detailed description of the work of Jesus Christ on earth and of the faith of His followers.

Tabernacle

Eighteen chapters (13 percent, see page 7) of the four books of the Law are dedicated to a detailed description of the tabernacle. In this, Moses describes in great detail the redemptive work of Jesus Christ and what the life of a Christian should be like in God's eyes. Dozens of books have been written about this subject.[9] The construction of the tabernacle is not a collection of strange stories that slowly developed in the course of the centuries, but a divine pattern for the Christian faith, which was devised in heaven (see Exodus 25:9 and Hebrews 8:5).

Festivals and Sacrifices

Twenty-two chapters (16 percent) of the four books of the Law are dedicated to the description of the sacrificial laws and feasts. These laws, too, give a detailed picture of the work of Jesus and of the Christian faith. Two of the three major feasts in Leviticus 23 were literally completed to the *day* in the New Testament, and the third is still to be completed.

Feast of the Passover—The Feast of the Passover, at which a lamb was slaughtered, gives a picture of the death of Jesus (see Exodus 12:5–13 and 1 Corinthians 5:7). The Passover lamb had to be perfect, as Jesus was perfect, without sin.

Feast of Weeks—The Feast of Weeks was, just like Pentecost, celebrated exactly fifty days after Passover. It gives a picture of the outpouring of the Holy Spirit, exactly fifty days after the death of the Lord Jesus (see Leviticus 23:15–16 and Acts 2:1–4).

Feast of Tabernacles—The Feast of Tabernacles at the end of the harvest time gives a picture of the return of Jesus to earth. At that time the "Great Harvest" will be brought in (see Deuteronomy 16:13–15 and Matthew 13:30, 36–43). Many books have been written about the spiritual meaning of the sacrifices and feasts.[10]

Journey through the Desert

Sixty-five chapters (47 percent) of the four books of the Law describe how the Israelites left Egypt and went through the desert to the Promised Land. It was not a random trip through the desert, but an accurate illustration (foreshadowing) of the Christian life of faith. We mention four of the dozens of examples.

Slavery in Egypt	—Mankind is a slave to sin (Exodus 1:14; Romans 6:16–17)
Redeemed by a lamb	—Redeemed by Jesus Christ (Exodus 12:5–13; 1 Corinthians 5:7)
Crossing the Red Sea	—Baptism in water (Exodus 14:27–30; Romans 6:4)
Law on Mount Horeb	—Outpouring of the Holy Spirit (Exodus 19:1, 11; Acts 2:1)

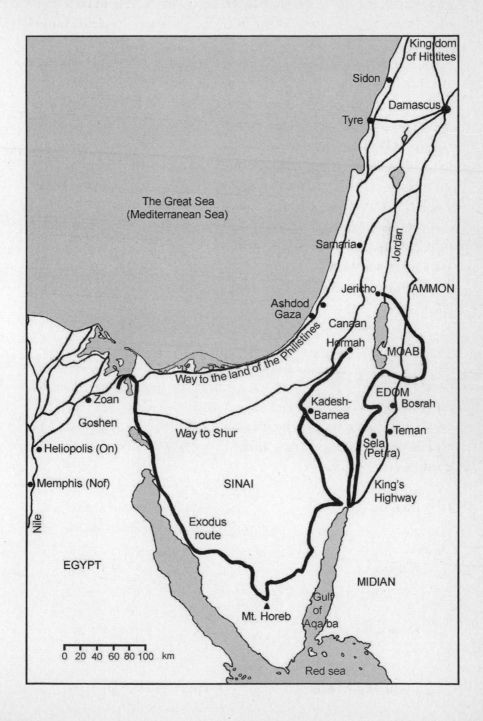

Typology

The persons and events in the Old Testament are often "types" (illustrations) of spiritual truths. For example, Abraham who, just like God, was willing to sacrifice his son, and Isaac who, just like Jesus, was willing to give up his life (see Genesis 22). Joseph who, just like Jesus, was humiliated in the extreme, but who did not harbor feelings of revenge. In the end, he was given inordinately great power and so saved his family from death (see Genesis 45 and 50:20).

There is a continuous thread running throughout the whole Old Testament, which points to the life of Jesus. He Himself reproached His disciples for not having seen this thread and not having believed, "How foolish you are, and how slow of heart to believe all that the prophets have spoken! . . . And beginning with Moses and all the Prophets, he explained to them what was said in all the Scriptures concerning Himself" (Luke 24:25–27).

A Bible scholar writes, "The types in the Old Testament are just as precise as mathematics. This is a miracle which is not encountered anywhere else in the literature of the world. Moreover, it is amazing that the types are part of the history of the Old Testament and not especially written as types, but were actual events. This one fact is proof enough for any unbiased investigator that such a Book could only be written by God."[11]

Scientific Facts

If we study the scientific facts in the previous chapters of this book, we see that most of the facts are coming from the books of Moses (see also the number of text references at the end of this book). These facts testify to an incredibly precise recording of everything God revealed to Moses. Moses could never have thought this up himself.

50,000 MISTAKES IN THE BIBLE?

According to some people, there are so many mistakes in the translations and transcriptions of the Bible that the text has become completely unreliable. The original text has been mutilated to such an extent that you can no longer speak of "the Word of God." Some people claim that there are as many as twenty thousand mistakes in the Bible; others claim there are as many as fifty thousand.[12]

What are the facts? We do not want to discuss all sorts of seeming mistakes in the Bible, because enough books have been written about these.[13] We only want to present a few general rules, by means of which a large part of the so-called mistakes are cleared up and that make the Bible easier to understand.

The alleged mistakes in the Bible can be found on two levels:

1. Mistakes in the Bible itself—in the generally accepted text, as we now have it in our contemporary Bibles.

2. Mistakes in the ancient manuscripts—in the thousands of separate portions of Scripture, transcribed by hand.

MISTAKES IN THE BIBLE ITSELF

Contradictions and Seeming Mistakes

In the Bible, there are many facts incomprehensible to us that seem to contradict one another. This goes without saying, because the Bible was written over a period of 1,500 years by forty people, from the most diverse backgrounds and cultures. Among them were priests, shepherds, farmers, fishermen, professors, generals, and kings, who wrote in exile, prisons, deserts, and palaces. Of course, not all seeming contradictions and mistakes can be solved or explained just like that. However, it appears that almost all the alleged contradictions are solved if account is taken of the following six points:

1. Difficulties of translation

2. Intentional contrasts

3. Differences in recording

4. Eastern feeling for language

5. Difficult to explain is not necessarily wrong

6. An eye for detail

Difficulties of Translation

Many difficulties we have in reading Bible texts are a result of an inadequate translation. This may be because a language does not contain the right words to convey a certain thought. For example, in the English language there is only one word, *love*, for the translation of the Greek words *agape* and *phileo*, which mean something like divine love and human love, respectively (see John 21:15).

The views of the translators also play an important role. For example, in many Bible translations the familiar Lord's Prayer in Matthew 6 says, "deliver us from *the evil one*"—that is, a request to be delivered from a person, delivered from the attacks of the devil. In other translations it says, "deliver us from *evil*"—that is, a request to be delivered from something impersonal, delivered from the evil in the world.

Intentional Contrasts

Numerous Bible texts seem to contradict one another but are intentionally used to throw light on an issue from two sides. This is generally regarded as one of the best methods of teaching. A good example can be found in Proverbs 26:4 and 5. In verse 4 it says, "Do not answer a fool according to his folly." Verse 5 says the opposite, "Answer a fool according to his folly." If these texts were not so close together, this might be thought to be an error. But I think they are rather intended to instill in us a sensitivity to when and how we should reply to a person.

Differences in Recording

With seeming contradictions in the Bible, you have to bear in mind that the Bible was written over the course of 1,500 years by writers from completely different cultures and with different educations, who recorded their observations in different ways. For example, in Mark 15:25 it says that Jesus was crucified at the *third* hour, and in John 19:14 it says that at the *sixth* hour Jesus was still in Pilate's palace. How is this possible? A mistake in the transcription? It is more likely that Mark kept to the Jewish way of timekeeping, which meant that Jesus was crucified at nine o'clock in the morning. John went by the official Roman timekeeping of Asia Minor, where he wrote his book, and said that at six o'clock in the morning Jesus was still in Pilate's palace.

In modern times with good means of communication, in which everything is standardized, we still have the same problem as Mark and John. In America, if you say that it is 37 degrees outside, it is freezing cold, and if you say that in Europe, it is baking hot. Thirty-seven degrees *Fahrenheit* in America is close to freezing point, and thirty-seven degrees *Celsius* in Europe is body temperature, which means sweltering hot.

In churches in Western countries, Christmas is celebrated on December 25 (Gregorian calendar), and in churches in some Eastern countries, on January 7 (Julian calendar). And if a group of doctors look at the *same* skeleton, one says that the skeleton is made up of 204 bones, another says 246, yet another says 208, and his colleague says 240. Yet none of these physicians is wrong. They all have a different view of how many bones there are, for example, in the skull or the pelvis.

Eastern Feeling for Language

The Bible was written in an Eastern society, using typically Eastern expressions, such as, "the trees of the field will clap their hands" (Isaiah 55:12), and people "soar on wings like eagles" (Isaiah 40:31).

Many critics want to deny the Bible any feeling for prose or poetry and would prefer it to be a dull and dry book employing scientific language. Then you would not have so much trouble with all the scientific slips, such as, "Praise him, all you shining stars" (Psalm 148:3), or, "Night to night declares knowledge" (Psalm 19:2 RSV).

Of course, the psalmist knew this too. Stars cannot praise God with their mouths (but perhaps with the beautiful way they shine in the night?). The night cannot declare knowledge to the night. But fortunately there is an explanation for scientific bores in the next two verses: "There is no speech, nor are there words; their voice is not heard; yet their voice goes out through all the earth, and their words to the end of the world" (19:3–4). What a wonderful use of language!

Difficult to Explain Is Not Necessarily Wrong

With "inexplicable texts" it is not justified to claim right away that the writer has made a mistake. Usually on closer examination, the differences are shown to be quite rational, to complement one another, or to throw light on different aspects of the matter. Until 1951, it was very difficult for Bible scholars to make sense of the periods of the reigns of the kings of Judah and northern Israel. Many saw the insurmountable differences as evidence for the unreliability of the Bible. But then E. R. Thiele discovered the ins and outs of the matter and demonstrated that the differences were quite rational: Judah followed the Jewish calendar, and northern Israel, which was strongly influenced by Assyria, followed the Assyrian calendar.[14]

For many theologians, the accounts in the first three Gospels (Matthew, Mark, and Luke) present an insurmountable problem. Some accounts seem to contradict one another or present facts in a different order. There is even a technical term for this: the synoptic problem. Indeed it is difficult to reconcile certain events in the Gospels with one another, but this does not mean that the problem is insurmountable. A professor of theology who for years taught about the "synoptic problem" writes, "A real solution to the problem shall not be found, because there is not a real problem. The synoptic problem is an invented problem, which has been imposed on the Gospels from outside, artificially and forcefully."[15]

The main reason the accounts in question resemble one another so closely and yet are different is that the writers simply recounted the reports of what they or other eyewitnesses had experienced in their dealings with Jesus. They often emphasized a different aspect of the same event. A second reason for the difference is that the writers intentionally described the life of Jesus in different ways: Matthew writes about Jesus as the King of Israel; Mark describes Jesus as the Servant of God; Luke shows Him as the True Man.

An Eye for Detail

It is noticeable that many Bible critics have little eye for the *details* in a Bible story. Texts that seem to contradict one another often appear to be in perfect agreement if you pay attention to the details. For example, the mistake often referred to in Numbers 25:9 and 1 Corinthians 10:8. In Numbers it says that there were twenty-four thousand people who died in a plague, and in 1 Corinthians, it says that there were twenty-three thousand. A clear mistake! But if you pay attention to the details, you see that the first number indicates the *total* number of the dead, and the second figure the number of people who died in *one* day.

A Model Mistake from the Old Testament

Two passages that initially caused me quite a lot of problems are found in 2 Samuel 24 and 1 Chronicles 21. The two chapters describe exactly the same event, where David holds a census. But there are four points of difference, which are often cited as being mistakes.

Subject	2 Samuel 24	1 Chronicles 21
1. Temptation	By God	By Satan
2. Census	800,000 in Israel 500,000 in Judah	1,100,000 in Israel 470,000 in Judah
3. Price	50 shekels of silver	600 shekels of gold
4. Name	Araunah	Ornan

Temptation

Samuel writes, "God incited David against Israel."

Chronicles writes, "Satan incited David to take a census of Israel."

This is a theological question we encounter often in the Bible. Is it God who causes misfortune on the earth or moves man to evil deeds, or is it the devil who does so? A thorough treatment of this question is beyond the scope of this book. But you might say, "If the devil does something, and God in His omnipotence allows it, the *ultimate responsibility* lies with God"—but this does not mean that God actually did it Himself.

This is also the case with David: because of certain circumstances, God permitted the devil to tempt David. The devil did it, but God bears the ultimate responsibility. For various explanations of this and similar texts, see the book by John W. Haley, *Alleged Discrepancies of the Bible*.[16] In this book, almost all "contradictions" in the Bible are dealt with. Much of the information used in this chapter is taken from Haley's book.

Census

Samuel: "In Israel there were eight hundred thousand able-bodied men who could handle a sword, and in Judah five hundred thousand."

Chronicles: "In all Israel there were one million one hundred thousand men who could handle a sword, including four hundred and seventy thousand in Judah."

The choice of words in the two texts is of note.

Samuel: all the *able-bodied* men numbered eight hundred thousand.

Chronicles: In *all* Israel together there were one million one hundred thousand men.

These numbers indicate the difference between the standing army of David, eight hundred thousand men who were in military service, versus all the men who would be able to fight, including three hundred thousand reserves. The same applied to Judah, but the other way around.

Price

Samuel: "David bought the threshing-floor and the oxen and paid fifty shekels of silver for them."

Chronicles: "David paid Araunah six hundred shekels of gold for the site."

Probably David bought the threshing floor itself—a small piece of rammed-down earth—together with the oxen for fifty silver shekels, but later he bought the whole site—Mount Moriah—for six hundred shekels of gold.

Name

Samuel mentions the name Araunah.

Chronicles mentions the name Ornan.

Araunah is the name of a Jebusite who remained in Jerusalem after David had conquered the city (see 2 Samuel 5:6–10). It was a foreign name, which sounded strange to the ears of the Israelites. Samuel wrote the name as it originally sounded (Araunah), but the later writer of Chronicles uses the Hebrew version (Ornan).

A Miraculous Detail Illustrating the Accuracy of God's Word

King David had given the command to hold a census. He wants to know how many people he has under his command, probably to boast about the large number of subjects he has, or to be able to levy more taxes and to take more laborers and soldiers into his service. When David reaches the threshing floor of Araunah, he sees an angel who is about to destroy Jerusalem. David, realizing he has sinned, is conscious-stricken. He asks God to spare the inhabitants of Jerusalem and rather to punish him personally for the sin he has committed. He knows that he is sinful and not one jot better than the hated, despised Jebusites who live in Jerusalem and who were not killed when David conquered the city. Araunah is one of those Jebusites. Now David is standing next to the threshing floor of such a hated man and is remorseful for his deeds. At this moment, we read in 2 Samuel 24:18 a peculiar "slip of the pen" in the word Araunah.

David hears God say that he must build an altar on the threshing floor of *Aranya*!

In verses 16–24 we read eight times about Araunah, a name that has no meaning for the Israelites, the name of a despised Jebusite. But on this one occasion in verse 18, in the original Hebrew text it says Aranya instead of Araunah. This "slip of the pen" has been translated out and written as Araunah in most Bible translations.

Aranya. This word sounds like heavenly music in David's ears. He is to erect an altar to the Lord on the threshing floor of Aranya. That really is a privilege. Aranya means "Joyful shouting of the Lord." The Lord is pleased, is joyful, that David has repented of his pride. And now David is allowed to build an altar on the threshing floor of "the joy of the Lord."

At the same place, Solomon's temple was later built (see 2 Chronicles 3:1). God wanted to dwell among His people on that spot. On a threshing floor where the chaff was separated from the grain. At a spot where people repent of their sins. This is also a picture of the Christian church, which is compared with a temple and is built "on the joy of the Lord." A place where sinners come to repentance and are cleansed from their sins (see 1 Corinthians 3:16; Matthew 3:12).[17]

A Model Mistake in the New Testament

During one of my lectures, someone pointed out to me a fault often referred to in the New Testament.[18] In Matthew 20:30, it says that *two* blind men were sitting by the roadside near Jericho, and in Luke 18:35 it says there was only *one*.

The man in the audience said that we cannot take the Bible literally, because there are too many such mistakes in it. The mistake mentioned was reason for him to voice an underlying idea: with the Bible, we should only take note of the spiritual meaning of a story and not bother whether it actually happened or not.

When we read the accounts carefully, it appears that matters were actually somewhat different than the questioner initially thought. In Luke 18:35 it says, "As Jesus *approached* Jericho, a blind man was sitting by the roadside begging." In Matthew 20:29–30 it says, "As Jesus and His disciples were *leaving* Jericho, a large crowd followed Him. Two blind men were sitting by the roadside, and when they heard that Jesus was going by, they shouted . . ."

The one blind man was healed when Jesus and His followers were going into Jericho, and the other two blind men were healed when the whole procession was going out of Jericho. The Bible is here talking about two different events.

It becomes more interesting if we also read Mark 10:46. There we read another story about a blind man near Jericho: "As Jesus and His disciples, together with a large crowd, were leaving the city [Jericho], a blind man, Bartimaeus . . . was sitting by the roadside begging." What now? On the way out of Jericho, were there two beggars (in accordance with Matthew) or was there only one beggar (in accordance with Mark)?

First. in the two accounts both the words of Jesus and of the beggars appear to be quite different. So there may have been two different events. Jericho was a large city—according to some with one hundred thousand inhabitants—and the number of blind people in the subtropics is relatively high: about 1.4 percent of the population.[19] This means that in Jericho, there would have been at least fourteen hundred blind people who had to earn a living by begging. So it is quite possible that on His last visit to Jericho, Jesus healed four people.

Second, the writer may have known Bartimaeus personally and so mentions his name. The fact that he does not mention the other man's name does not mean that he was not there. Mark does not claim that there were definitely not two beggars when they were leaving Jericho, but simply stated that *Bartimaeus* was there.

MISTAKES IN ANCIENT MANUSCRIPTS

At the beginning of the Christian era, Christianity spread like wildfire in the countries around Israel. The churches in the large towns soon received their own handwritten copies of the Old Testament, the Gospels, and several letters of Paul. These books and letters in their turn were copied for the smaller churches in the area. In this way, in the course of the centuries, many thousands of handwritten Bible books were produced. These are called "manuscripts." The main cities where manuscripts were transcribed were Alexandria in Egypt, Antioch in Syria, Constantinople in Turkey, and Rome in Italy. Despite careful transcription, occasionally mistakes slipped in, and these were reproduced in the following versions. In this way, tens of thousands of manuscripts were produced with large and small differences in their texts.

In the past two hundred years, about 30,000 ancient manuscripts have been discovered with the whole Bible or a portion of the Bible. Of the Old Testament relatively few manuscripts have been preserved: a few thousand Hebrew manuscripts and a number of translations, especially in Greek and in Latin. Of the New Testament, many more manuscripts have been preserved: about 25,000. Of these, about 5,700 manuscripts are in Greek, over 10,000 are translations into Latin, and some 10,000 are in other languages.[20]

Mistakes in Manuscripts of the Old Testament

One of the reasons so few Hebrew manuscripts of the Old Testament have been preserved is that the Jews had such a holy respect for their Bible that they respectfully buried the scrolls when the text was in danger of becoming illegible. Because the scrolls were never simply thrown away and never kept somewhere in a back room, in later times no ancient scrolls were rediscovered, as was the case with the New Testament.

Jewish Bible scholars transcribed the Old Testament with such painstaking accuracy that hardly any mistakes occurred in the text. In particular the Masoretes, rabbis from Tiberias and Babylon, who transcribed the Old Testament in the fifth to tenth centuries after Christ, were exceptionally accurate in their work. As a check, they counted all the words and all the letters in the Hebrew Bible. The Hebrew text of the Torah contains 79,847 words and 304,805 letters. The middle verse in the Torah is Leviticus 8:7. And the middle verse of the whole Hebrew Bible is Jeremiah 6:7. If a scribe made one mistake, sometimes the whole scroll was destroyed.[21]

Of the manuscripts transcribed by the Masoretes, about a thousand have survived. The biblical scholar Kennicott has studied 581 of these manuscripts in the greatest detail and counted all the differences that occur in all these 581 manuscripts. The main differences he discovered were the exchange of the two Hebrew letters v and i, which are very similar. If we do not count these changes, then it appears there is only one slip of the pen, one variant, in every 1,580 letters. That is to say about one variant on each page of the book you are now holding.

Note that these variants are not a matter of actually writing a word completely wrong, but only of variations in the spelling of a word; see also on the next pages. Moreover, most variants only occurred in one manuscript, or sometimes in a few. Only a few variants occurred in a greater number of manuscripts at the same time.

This is so extremely few that a critical biblical scholar has remarked, "To achieve this result, time, talent, and knowledge have been foolishly wasted."[22] Christians think differently about this and are indeed extremely keen about this incredible accuracy in the Old Testament.

Dead Sea Scrolls Confirm the Reliability of the Old Testament

In 1947 a shepherd boy near the town of Qumran by the Dead Sea found a number of jars in a cave. Later in other caves more carefully sealed jars were found. In them were the remains of 870 scrolls, of which 220 were of texts from the Bible. The scrolls include the complete book of Isaiah and large parts of Psalms, plus parts of all the other books in the Old Testament, except the book of Esther. The books were written between 225 BC and AD 68, the year in which Roman soldiers put an end to the community in Qumran.

When the texts were checked, they were shown to be an astounding testimony to the great reliability of our present Bible. Fewer than 1 percent of the texts differed from "our" Bible. The differences were mainly related to slips of the pen and changes in spelling, which occurred in the course of the centuries. The most interesting thing was that the texts on the Qumran scrolls often provided an answer to the questions linguists had been pondering for years.[23] For example, the translators of the English Revised Standard Version only had to make thirteen small adjustments in the book of Isaiah, of which eight were already known from other manuscripts. Only five adjustments were more or less important.[24]

Hills and caves near Qumran, where the Dead Sea scrolls were found.

Mistakes in Manuscripts of the New Testament

Of the New Testament many more manuscripts have survived, and these contain considerably more mistakes than the Hebrew Old Testament. Some scholars refer to thousands; others even tens of thousands. By the way, it is better not to refer to "mistakes" but to variants. After all, you do not know which variant is correct and which is incorrect. The maximum number of variants in all the Greek manuscripts together is 200,000. With 200,000 variants, is it still possible to know what the original text was?

It is important to realize that these 200,000 Greek variants do not occur in the generally accepted Bible text—that is, not in the Bible as we know it—but they occur in the whole collection of all the 5,700 Greek manuscripts. If one single word in 3,000 different manuscripts is spelled differently from the rest, it is counted as 3,000 variants.[25] In this way, you easily get 50,000 to 200,000 variants. But to then conclude that there are 50,000 mistakes in the Bible[26] is completely misleading.

Precisely this abundance of ancient manuscripts means that the general Bible text is exceptionally reliable. By comparing these thousands of manuscripts with one another, you can deduce what the original text must have been like. Of the "History" of the Greek writer Thucydides (460–400 BC), there are only eight ancient manuscripts in the world, of which the oldest dates from around AD 900. The same applies to the "Histories" of Herodotus (480–425 BC). With such a small number of manuscripts, it is difficult to check whether mistakes have been made in the transcription. Moreover, the time between the original text and the oldest manuscripts we have of these Greek writers is about 1,300 years. With the New Testament, this time is less than one hundred years, and there are 25,000 manuscripts that can be checked. This means the New Testament is far more reliable than any other book from antiquity.

MORE THAN 99.95 PERCENT CERTAINTY

Two hundred thousand mistakes?—Of the 200,000 variants, 95 percent can immediately be put aside: they occur in so few and in such unimportant manuscripts that not a single researcher regards them as competing readings. Most variants are clearly recognizable as mistakes due to a lack of attention or tiredness of the scribes, who had a full-time job making transcriptions. They are mainly mistakes of the eye (omissions, doubling, reversal of letters or words), mistakes of the ear (while the text was being dictated to a group of scribes, consider for example the words in English "to," "too," and "two," which all sound the same), and reading mistakes, because the text of an old, damaged original was no longer clearly legible. Most of the mistakes involve the transcription of numbers and dates, because figures cannot be checked from the context.

Ten thousand mistakes?—Of the ten thousand variants that deserve serious investigation, it appears that 96 percent do not have any influence on the text. They are unimportant differences in spelling, grammar, word order, and numbers. Most variants occur because the spelling changed in the course of the centuries. Just like the development of American with regard to English, for example, centre, colour, honour (English) and center, color, honor (American).

Four hundred mistakes?—A maximum of four hundred variants are of any significance for the text of any specific Bible passage. But they are only of significance for that *one* passage, never for the Bible as a whole. According to the well-known Bible researcher Hort, only two hundred variants are of any significance.[27] Because of the abundance of different manuscripts, in almost all cases it is possible to reconstruct the correct text with a great measure of certainty. The principal variants about which opinions differ are the numbers.[28]

Fifty mistakes?—These are differences that are important in one way or another, texts that in many translations are omitted or put between square brackets or printed in italics to indicate doubt, such as in Mark 16:9–20 and 1 John 5:7–8. However, the differences are never about core issues of the faith or about important commandments in the Bible. Most of these differences occur because in some manuscripts, portions of text were added from other Bible passages. This means that they are not random additions of human ideas, but of matters that are taught elsewhere in the Bible.

Matthew 6:13	[For yours . . . glory forever. Amen.]
Matthew 12:47	[Someone told him . . . speak to you.]
Matthew 16:2,3	[When evening . . . signs of the times.]
Matthew 17:21	[But this kind . . . prayer and fasting.]
Matthew 18:11	[The Son of Man . . . what was lost.]
Matthew 21:44	[He who falls . . . will be crushed.]
Matthew 23:14	[Woe to you . . . more severely.]
Mark 7:16	[If anyone has ears . . . let him hear.]
Mark 9:44,46	[Where their worm . . . not quenched.]
Mark 11:26	[But if you do . . . forgive your sins.]
Mark 15:28	[And the scripture . . . lawless ones.]
Mark 16:9-20	[When Jesus rose . . . accompanied it.]
Luke 9:55,56	[And he said . . . but to save them.]
Luke 10:1,17	[Seventy-two]
Luke 17:36	[Two men will . . . and the other left.]
Luke 23:17	[Now he was obliged . . . at the Feast.]
Luke 24:12	[Peter, however . . . had happened.]
Luke 24:40	[When he had . . . hands and feet.]
John 5:3,4	[And they waited . . . disease he had.]
John 7:53–8:11	[Then each went . . . your life of sin.]
Acts 8:37	[Philip said . . . is the Son of God.]
Acts 15:34	[But Silas decided to remain there.]
Acts 24:6–8	[And wanted . . . come before you.]

These are the most important texts about which scholars are in doubt whether they belong in the original Bible text or not. In many translations they are omitted or mentioned in footnotes or put between "brackets of doubt." More such texts exist, but they are less important and mostly consist only of one, two, or three words.

No mistakes?—There is no doubt whatsoever about the fundamental issues of the Christian faith. The best Greek text of the New Testament (the Nestle-Aland text), the ancient Greek *Textus Receptus* from the sixteenth century, and the oldest Greek manuscripts from the fourth century, such as the *Codex Vaticanus* and the *Sinaiticus*, teach exactly the same Christianity. A more detailed explanation of the points above can be found in the book by René Pache, *The Inspiration and Authority of Scripture*.[29]

If someone does not want to believe in the Bible, that is his or her free choice. But if someone tries to justify this choice by asserting that the Bible is unreliable and that there are thousands of mistakes in it, this is an utter misrepresentation. There are certainly passages in our present Bible that are difficult to explain, and perhaps even a few mistakes, but none of these mistakes whatsoever touches on the core of the Christian faith.

THE MOST IMPORTANT ANCIENT MANUSCRIPTS OF THE BIBLE

Vulgate (Latin)—translation of the whole Bible, by Jerome, made between AD 386 and 405. Jerome went to live in Bethlehem and based his translation on the oldest and best-known Hebrew manuscripts he could find in Israel. The Vulgate is still the official Bible of the Roman Catholic Church. The original does not exist anymore, but ancient copies are kept in the Vatican.

Codex Vaticanus (Greek)—the oldest almost complete Bible, written between AD 325 and 350. Kept in the Vatican.

Codex Sinaiticus (Greek)—almost complete Bible, compiled around AD 350. The largest part is kept in the British Museum in London, and smaller parts in other cities.

Codex Alexandrinus (Greek)—almost complete Bible, compiled around AD 450. Kept in the British Museum in London.

Chester Beatty papyri (Greek)—contains large portions of the Bible, compiled around AD 200. Largely kept in the Chester Beatty Library in Dublin.

King James Version and the *Textus Receptus*

The celebrated English King James Version (KJV) was first published in 1611 and had a great influence on the development of the English language. The Old Testament was translated from a number of Hebrew and Latin Bibles, and the New Testament mainly from the Greek New Testament that was compiled by Desiderius Erasmus.

The Dutch scholar Erasmus (1469–1536) examined the best

manuscripts of his time and compiled the New Testament in the Greek language. This Greek New Testament was first published in 1516 in Basel, and Luther used the greatly improved second edition for his German Bible of 1534. Around 1550, there was a standard Greek text available, which ranked as *the* authority on the New Testament for over three hundred years. This *Textus Receptus* (received text) was the basis for the New Testament of the King James Version (1611) and of the Dutch Statenvertaling (1637).

The Poorest Original Text of the New Testament?

Until 1900 the *Textus Receptus* was ranked as the best rendering of the New Testament. Because of new discoveries, improvements were constantly made, and according to many modern Bible researchers, the best rendering at the present is the Greek New Testament of Nestle and Aland.[30] In the introduction to this Greek New Testament, on the first page it says, "The scholarship of the nineteenth century had conclusively demonstrated the *Textus Receptus* to be the poorest form of the New Testament text."

Thanks to the above remark by *the* authority in the area of text research, Kurt Aland, even as laypersons, we can investigate how reliable our Bible translations are without knowing Greek.

1. Suppose the *Textus Receptus* is indeed the poorest original Greek text of the New Testament; then all other forms of text are better and more reliable than the *Textus Receptus*.

2. The King James Version is based on the *Textus Receptus*, and the New International Version (like other modern translations) is based on the best original Greek text known today. So we can examine all the differences between the best and the poorest Greek text by comparing the King James Version with the New International Version.

Incredibly Accurate

In the Dutch language I have compared the old Statenvertaling (similar to the KJV) and the modern translations word for word. In addition I have investigated more than a thousand places where there is any sort of discussion about the text.[31] I am highly impressed by the incredibly great accuracy with which the Bible has been translated. Where there are differences between the best and the "poorest" translation, these complement one another so wonderfully that one understands the original meaning of the writer much better! Even where there are big differences between the two texts, such as in the table below, theologically the two texts are still 100 percent justified.

Scripture	New International Version	King James Version
Matthew 11:12	Forcefully advancing	Suffers Violence
Matthew 24:36	Nor the Son	
Matthew 26:41	Pray so that you will not	Pray, that ye enter not
Mark 9:23	If you [Jesus] can	If thou [man] canst
Luke 4:44	Preaching . . . in Judea	Preached . . . in Galilee
Luke 23:15	He sent him back to us	I sent you to him
John 13:2	Meal was being served	And supper being ended
Acts 3:19	Turn to God . . . that times	Be converted . . . when times
Acts 13:20	About 450 years.	After that . . . about 450 years
Acts 18:5	After this Paul devoted himself	Paul was pressed in the spirit
2 Cor. 3:18	Reflect the Lord's glory	Beholding the glory . . . Lord
Col. 2:17	Reality is found in Christ	But the body is of Christ
1 Tim. 3:16	He appeared in a body	God . . . manifest in the flesh
Rev. 21:24	The nations will walk	Which are saved shall walk

These texts are—apart from the texts about which the scholars have some doubt (see page 221)—a few of the most striking differences between the New International Version and the King James Version.

For further study, reference is made to the book *A Textual Commentary on the Greek New Testament* by Bruce Metzger and to the Greek New

Testament of the United Bible Societies, in which a detailed list of nearly four hundred important manuscripts is incorporated, including a hundred papyri.[32] A thorough study of all the manuscripts reveals that the Bible is so incredibly accurately transcribed that we can still refer to it as the precise Word of God.

> *If the original Bible books were still to be among the ancient manuscripts, they would differ so little from our present Bible books that they would not even attract attention.*

ARCHAEOLOGY AND THE BOOKS OF MOSES

Many attacks on the Bible are directed at the books of Moses. That is not surprising, because it is precisely these that are the most amazing books that have ever been written in the history of mankind, and precisely these form the written foundation of true faith in God. Claims are made in the school of "higher criticism" that the Torah was not written until the time of exile in Babylon or was compiled at that time from older documents. This means that according to these theologians, the books of Moses are not the *foundation* of the Jewish faith, but the "roof"—the rounding off of a religious evolution.

The best-known proponent of this "religious evolution" was the German theologian Wellhausen (1844–1918). In his day, some scholars suggested that the ancient society in the Middle East was very primitive, that Moses was not able to write, and that Israel still believed in numerous gods (polytheism). The whole idea of one omnipotent Creator God (monotheism) would only develop later. Therefore, for various reasons the Torah had to have been written many years after Moses. According to this view of "higher criticism," the book of Genesis was composed of documents by various priests. One priest (J), who always used the word *Jahweh* in his text (in many translations rendered as "The LORD"), and two other priests (P and E), who always used the word *Elohim* (translated as "God"). See for example the difference between Genesis 1:1–2:3 and Genesis 2:4–4:26.

We will not go into this form of "higher criticism" because this has been adequately refuted by a large number of theologians.[33] Equally, the idea of a "religious evolution" in and around Israel is shown to be completely untenable.[34] Moreover, it is revealed in travel reports by missionaries and explorers that about all of the oldest and most primitive tribes on the earth believe in an omnipotent Creator God.[35] It is true that it is in a distorted form, because of all sorts of human influences, and with a belief in many subordinate gods, but still always with the idea of one supreme Creator God. Wilhelm Schmidt has compiled an overwhelming amount of these stories in a multivolume book totaling four thousand pages![36] Among almost all the peoples on earth, monotheism *precedes* polytheism. There has not been an evolution in religion, but a degeneration!

Our point is that everything indicates that Moses is the writer of the Torah and that in this respect, too, the Bible is completely reliable. Every time some archaeological discovery is made regarding the history of Israel, it is shown to be in agreement with what is claimed in the Bible. The following are a few of the hundreds of examples.

Archaeology Confirms the Bible

"Moses could not write"—According to certain scholars in the nineteenth century, the art of writing was only developed in the Middle East at the time of King David, about a thousand years before Christ, or four hundred years after Moses. But when in 1902 the "black stela" of Hammurabi was discovered in the ruins of the city of Susa, it was shown that the art of writing was already known at the time of Abraham, four hundred years before Moses. Later it was revealed that people had mastered the art of writing in the Middle East and in Egypt around 3,200 years before Christ and 1,300 years before Abraham![37]

"The Hittites never existed"—According to some scholars in the nineteenth century, the Hittites, Edomites, and many other people in the Bible never existed (see Genesis 23:3, 10; 36:9). Outside the Bible, there is no record of these people and no archaeological finds were ever made. From this, scholars drew the conclusion that the Bible was hopelessly wrong. But at the end of the nineteenth century, Hittite relics were found, and in

1906 even the capital, Hattusa, was discovered, two hundred kilometers to the east of the Turkish city of Ankara. Hattusa appeared to be a large city with walls fifty meters thick and ten to twenty meters high. The city had great palaces, parks, and libraries. There were even dictionaries found in six languages.[38] It was revealed that the Hittite Empire was a great and powerful nation, which had its heyday between 1500 and 1200 BC.

"The kingdoms of David and Solomon never existed"—A large number of scholars, including Voltaire (1694–1778), claimed that the mighty kingdom of Solomon, with such vast wealth, could never have existed in the barren desert of Palestine as they knew it. Thanks to excavations, we know that these kingdoms really did exist and that the riches in 1 Kings and 2 Chronicles are described accurately.[39]

"The periods of the reigns of the Kings of Israel do not tally"—Until 1951 no one was able to reconcile the lists of the kings of Judah and northern Israel. This was seen as proof that the Bible was a book of fairy tales as far as history was concerned. When knowledge about the history of Israel increased, the periods of reign were shown to be completely correct. It was discovered that the tribe of Judah followed the Jewish calendar. They recorded the periods of the reigns of the kings as had always been customary among the original people of Israel. But the Israelites in the northern kingdom were influenced by the Assyrians to such an extent that they followed the Assyrian calendar and their system of recording. If we take these facts into consideration, the dates prove to be in precise agreement.[40]

Dr. Nelson Glueck, one of the most renowned archaeologists to have worked in Israel, writes, "The Bible is definitely not primarily a chronicle of history . . . however, it may be stated categorically that no archaeological discovery has ever controverted a Biblical reference. Scores of archaeological findings have been made which confirm in clear outline or in exact detail historical statements in the Bible. And . . . proper evaluation of Biblical descriptions has often led to amazing discoveries. They form tesserae [little tiles] in the vast mosaic of the Bible's almost incredible correct historical memory."[41]

Another renowned archaeologist, W. F. Albright, writes about the Pentateuch, "New discoveries continue to confirm the historical accuracy or the literary antiquity of detail after detail in it."[42]

Limitations of Archaeology

Time and again we read articles in newspapers and magazines that claim that many stories in the Bible are not correct because they are not confirmed by archaeological facts.[43] The researchers in question base their "proof" on what they have *not* found. According to the historian and archaeologist Yamauchi, this is a big mistake in the thinking of researchers. After all, in archaeology, only a fraction of a fraction of everything that has ever taken place in history is uncovered.

First, only a very small portion of everything that has ever been made or written survives the ravages of time. The vast majority is lost in the course of the centuries through erosion and rotting, or through plundering by people.

Second, excavations have only been undertaken in a very small number of all possible sites.

Third, at any site only a small part of the surface is excavated.

Fourth, only a small proportion of the objects found are actually examined and described in publications. Yamauchi calculates that of all the pieces of archaeological evidence that might be available, fewer than six in a hundred thousand (6:100,000), are actually known. And according to him this number might be far less.[44]

EVIDENCE THAT MOSES WROTE THE TORAH

Although the liberal interpretation of the Bible in the media gains the most attention, there is an abundance of evidence that the Torah was actually written by *Moses* and not thought up some eight hundred years later by a number of priests. But in order to discover this, you must study the Bible seriously and without prejudice and pay good attention to the details.

We indicate twelve points that reveal the Torah was written at the beginning of the history of Israel and by someone who was entirely familiar with life in Egypt and in the desert. There is only one man in the whole history of Israel who has satisfied the necessary criteria: Moses. Various books have demonstrated this in a convincing way, in particular the very extensive work of Abraham Yahuda, from which the following points are drawn.[45]

Use of Words in the Torah

1. *Egyptian loanwords*—In the Torah, a large number of *words* occur that are literal translations of Egyptian words (so-called loanwords) and that do not occur in the rest of the Bible, such as the special word "ark" (of Noah). Moreover, in Genesis and Exodus dozens of *expressions* are used that again are literal translations of Egyptian expressions, such as "in the beginning," "living soul," "behold, it was very good," "armed for battle" (Exodus 13:18). Some expressions in the Torah are so unusual that modern commentators who do not take into account the Egyptian origins even regard them as mutilations of the text.

2. *Babylonian words*—It is noticeable that in the first eleven chapters of Genesis, ancient Babylonian words occur that do not occur anywhere else in the Torah. This only makes sense if we consider that for these chapters, Moses used texts from ancient clay tablets from the time of the patriarchs, such as Abraham.

It is even more remarkable that "modern" Babylonian words in common usage at the time of the exile in Babylon are lacking from the Torah, such as the words for earth, fish, birds, creatures that crawl on the ground, snake, nose, head. Such words would certainly have been used if the Torah were based on Babylonian stories, which the Jews were said to have heard in exile in the sixth century before Christ. The books of Daniel and Ezekiel, which were written during the exile, do contain such words. But in the books of Moses, they are completely absent.

3. *Archaic Hebrew words*—In Genesis and Exodus, numerous archaic (outdated) Hebrew words and spellings occur that do not occur elsewhere in the Bible and so indicate an early date. For example, the Hebrew word for "delivery stool" (Exodus 1:16) is written as "the two stones"—a literal translation of an ancient Egyptian word. Research has shown that: (1) the delivery stool was a typically Egyptian piece of equipment that was

not known in any other country, (2) the phrase "the two stones" does not occur anywhere else in the Bible, (3) at the time of Moses (around 1500 BC) the word was written in the plural, "the two stones." At later times, the stool was constructed of a larger number of stones, which formed one whole. Subsequently the word was written in the singular, "the stone." These facts reveal that the writer had lived in ancient Egypt and was personally acquainted with this piece of equipment.

A wooden birthing chair from the time after Moses.

Knowledge of Egypt

4. *Secret Egyptian customs*—In Genesis and Exodus, numerous Egyptian customs are described that would be completely unknown to an outsider, for example, with regard to the secret life at the court of the Pharaoh; the titles of the government officials; and the honorary titles of Joseph, such as "Zaphenath-Paneah" (Feeder of the land; see Genesis 41:45). After dozens of pages of evidence of this kind, Professor J. Garrow Duncan writes, "Thus we cannot but admit that the writer of these two narratives [i.e., of

Joseph and of the Exodus] . . . was thoroughly well acquainted with the Egyptian language, customs, belief, court life, etiquette, and officialdom; and not only so, but the readers must have been just as familiar with things Egyptian."[46]

5. *Egyptian plants and animals*—The writer possessed a detailed knowledge of the flora and fauna of Egypt. For example, the acacia, from which the ark of the covenant, the table, and the tabernacle were made, is a desert tree found only in Egypt, the Sinai desert, and the extremely hot area around the Dead Sea (see Exodus 25:10, 23). The sea cows (dugongs), from which the tent covering for the tabernacle was made, were only found in the Gulf of Aqaba, near Egypt (see Exodus 26:14, Numbers 4:6–14).[47] The order of the harvest in Exodus 9:31–32 was typically Egyptian, and so forth.

6. *Egyptian place names and personal names*—The writer knew exactly where Egyptian towns were situated, such as Migdol and Pi Hahiroth (see Exodus 14:2). He knew when the Egyptian town of Zoan was built (see Numbers 13:22). He knew many Egyptian personal names, such as Potiphera and Asenath (see Genesis 41:45).

Knowledge of the Desert

7. *Details of the journey*—Exodus, Leviticus, and Numbers clearly breathe the atmosphere of a journey through the desert. The writer notes all sorts of particulars about the journey, such as the arrangement of the camp and the marching orders (see Numbers 2 and 10), the sanitary instructions for life in the desert (see Deuteronomy 23:12–13), the sending out of the scapegoat into the desert (see Leviticus 16:10), and the number of springs and palms at an oasis (see Exodus 15:27). These are details that are important for a people moving through the desert, but completely uninteresting for a later writer living in exile in a strange country.

8. *No knowledge of Canaan*—It is striking that the writer was unfamiliar with the circumstances in Canaan. Only in the account of the patriarchs

do we read about places and circumstances in Canaan. This was because the patriarchs wrote down their experiences on clay tablets and passed them on from father to son, until Moses recorded these accounts (see also point 2). If the writer of the Torah wanted to explain something about Canaan, reference was made to examples that were known to his fellow people, namely those of Egypt.

In this way, the Jordan valley is compared with the land of Egypt (see Genesis 13:10), the building of Hebron is compared with the building of the Egyptian town of Zoan (see Numbers 13:22). It is striking that nowhere is the city of Jerusalem mentioned, which nevertheless played an extremely important role for later Israelites. These are all points that would be completely inexplicable if the Torah were written between the reign of Solomon and the Babylonian exile.

9. *Knowledge of the climate*—The writer had a detailed knowledge of the climate and the geography of the desert (see Numbers 33, Deuteronomy 1 and 2).

Historical Evidence

10. *Samaritan Pentateuch*—The Samaritans lived in northern Israel, which split away from Judah around 930 BC. After the separation, the Samaritans did not want to have anything more to do with the temple in Jerusalem (see 1 Kings 12:25–32). The loathing between the Judeans (Jews) and Samaritans became even worse when in 722 BC the Assyrian king carried off the Israelites into exile and ordered pagan people to go and live in northern Israel (see 2 King 17:24–28). The mutual hatred was so great that the Jews did not want to have anything to do with the Samaritans, and the Samaritans never recognized any texts written by Jewish priests in Jerusalem (or Babylon).

The only parts of the Bible the Samaritans did accept were the books of Moses and the book of Joshua. This is evidence that these books were not written just before or during the Babylonian exile, but long before that, before the division in 930 BC. The fact that the Samaritan and Jewish Pentateuchs are very similar is additional evidence that these books did not slowly develop, but already existed as a *complete* book long before the exile. These books were so important for both parties that nothing was to be changed in them and they were regarded as the *foundation* of the faith. The six thousand small differences between the two books mainly concern differences in spelling.[48]

11. *Falashas*—In Ethiopia, there lived the Falashas, black Jews who, according to their traditions, had lived there since the time of King Solomon, around 1000 BC. Between 1984 and 1991, almost all the Falashas immigrated to Israel. Besides their own religious literature, the Falashas only recognized the books of Moses, and not the Jewish Scriptures, which were written after the time of Solomon. This is again evidence that the books of Moses were already complete at the time of Solomon and formed the foundation of the faith of the Israelites who moved to Ethiopia.[49]

Internal Evidence

12. *References in other books of the Bible*—In almost all books of the Bible, reference is made to the "books of Moses." This happens for example in the Old Testament in 1 Kings 2:3, Daniel 9:11, Malachi 4:4, and in the New Testament in Luke 24:44. Jesus Himself also referred to Moses as the author of the Torah, in John 5:46. Would all these writers have consciously and purposely misled the believing masses, and that without any reason or necessity?

The Bible Confirmed Time and Again

As stated before, W. F. Albright, the most renowned archaeologist ever to have worked in Israel, writes, "New discoveries continue to confirm the historical accuracy or the literary antiquity of detail after detail in it. . . . It is sheer hypercriticism to deny the substantially Mosaic character of the Pentateuchal tradition."[50]

There have been endless numbers of claims that scholars have had to retract regarding so-called mistakes in the Bible. According to Lüscher, since 1850 Bible critics have developed over seven hundred theories, of which in his time already more than six hundred were superseded.[51] The same conclusion was reached by a certain Mendenhall, who compiled 747 such theories.[52]

SUMMARY

In the New Testament, so much authority and accuracy are accredited to the Old Testament that the Lord Jesus and the apostle Paul could base their teachings on the fact that one particular word is in the past tense or the present tense, or that a word is in the singular or the plural. Both the Bible itself and the Christians in the New Testament assume that every word in the Bible is inspired by God and is in exactly the right place, as God intended. This literal inspiration is most salient in the books of Moses.

According to critics of the Bible, there are thousands of mistakes and outright blunders in the Bible, but a thorough study reveals that this is grossly exaggerated. It appears that there are only fifty more or less important differences among the major manuscripts. This means that 99.95 percent of the text of the Bible is completely reliable. But there is no doubt whatsoever about the important doctrines in the Bible.

Still there seem to be incomprehensible texts and apparent mistakes in our Bible. However, most of these problems can be solved by taking into account a number of points, including difficulties of translation, differences in recording, the Eastern feeling for language, and intentional contradictions. Moreover, in studying the Bible, it is extremely important to pay attention to the *details*—just as when studying nature.

In this book it has been manifestly proven that the first five books in the Bible were written by Moses. This can be inferred from the influence of the ancient Egyptian language and the knowledge of Egypt and the secret Egyptian court life.

That Moses indeed wrote the Torah under divine inspiration is revealed by the prophecies that have been fulfilled, by the scientifically sound facts about medicine, hygiene, nutrition, physics, biology, linguistics, and so forth. And also by the profound symbolism in the tabernacle, in the festivals, in the sacrifices, and in the typology. There is shown to be a continuous thread running through the whole Torah that points to the life of Jesus Christ and His church.

They have Moses and the Prophets;
let them listen to them. . . .
If they do not listen to Moses and the Prophets,
they will not be convinced,
even if someone rises from the dead.

LUKE 16:29, 31

8.

A FEW MORE FACTS

In the previous chapters, we have read about dozens of facts in the areas of medicine, nutrition, physics, biology, and theology. This list could be extended to dozens more scientifically based facts. But we will confine ourselves to a few remarks in the fields of agriculture and social rules, plus a few final conclusions.

AGRICULTURE AND THE ENVIRONMENT

AGRICULTURE

When the Israelites conquered Canaan, they had little agricultural land available. They could not live in the fertile plains along the coast, because these were dominated by the mighty Canaanites with their iron chariots[1] (see Joshua 17:15–16; Judges 1:19). The Israelites had to content themselves with the hill country between the Mediterranean Sea and the Jordan. Only a small portion of this was cultivated and suitable for agriculture. In order to have as great a yield as possible, the scarce agricultural land had to be intensively worked. Later more arable land became available, but through the considerable population growth, there was constantly a shortage of good farmland.

In view of the shortage of farmland, the laws from Exodus are quite amazing: "On the seventh year you shall let it rest and lie fallow" (Exodus 23:11 NASB). That is strange. Why should Moses (God) say this? He knew there was a shortage of farmland in Canaan, and still He ordered that every seventh year the land must lie fallow for a whole year. It seems unwise to waste 15 percent of what the farm produces in this way, especially with such a shortage of farmland. Only in later times was it discovered that this law is of vital importance to keep the yields healthy and at a high level of production.

First, it is not wise to cultivate the same crops on the same piece of land year in, year out. If you do, all sorts of pests will develop. We see this happen in our times with crops such as potatoes and sugar beet, where small parasitic worms (nematodes) in the ground are given the opportunity to multiply year after year. The same happens with stem and bulb nematodes, which occur in more than four hundred types of crops.[2] By rotating crops or allowing the land to lie fallow, the nematodes will starve and will no longer procreate. This means that leaving the land to lie fallow is an important means of keeping the crops parasite-free.

The fields near Bethlehem where King David watched over flocks in his youth. In the far distance are the hills surrounding the Dead Sea.

Second, the land becomes exhausted of nutrients if the same crops are grown on it every year. In modern days, this can be overcome by the use of artificial fertilizers. But in antiquity, this was only possible through the use of ordinary manure (and that was scarce) and by allowing the land to rest from time to time. Wild plants that may come up on uncultivated land act as an additional fertilizer, such as lupines (*Lupinus*) and alfalfa (*Medicago sativa*) and also some types of clover (*Trifolium*), which absorb nitrogen from the air and store it in their roots. When these plants rot down, these elements are released into the soil.

Third, the structure of the soil will deteriorate if the land is never allowed to rest, that is, if year in, year out, the crop is harvested and no plant waste (humus) is formed. Humus improves the structure of the soil, giving it a looser texture. This results in better availability of nutrients and better retention of water. Especially in (semi)arid regions like Israel, this retention of water is of vital importance.

The following table shows the beneficial effect of the agricultural regulations of Moses. About AD 200 in Israel, for every 100 pounds of seed grain 600 pounds could be harvested. In the early Middle Ages (AD 850) the yield was only around 150 pounds, due to ignorance and a lack of regulations by the government.

With the institution of the "three-field system" the harvest increased to 400 pounds for every 100 pounds of seed. (With this three-field system of land rotation, the land was cultivated for two years and the next year was allowed to lie fallow.) During the rest of the Middle Ages the harvest usually was between 200 and 600 pounds. Only in fertile areas and in modern times with artificial fertilizers did the yield exceed the 600 pounds of the Bible times.[3]

Place	Date (AD)	Seed in Pounds	Yield in Pounds
1. Nitzana, Negev	c. 200	100	600
2. Carolingian Empire	c. 850	100	150
3. Central Europe	c. 1750	100	400
4. Avdat, Negev (with artificial fertilizers)	1960–65	100	600–1,200

Average yield of grain in ancient Israel and in Europe (Hüttermann[4]).

ENVIRONMENT

Protection of the environment was an important issue in ancient Israel. This is evident from Bible passages such as the laws regarding warfare. For example, it says, "When you lay siege to a city for a long time, fighting against it to capture it, do not destroy its trees by putting an axe to them, because you can eat their fruit" (Deuteronomy 20:19).

You should not make light of this "insignificant" environmental measure.

First, at the time, it was a unique rule that did not occur anywhere else in the world. Second, nuts and fruit from trees are important for public health, particularly in difficult times during or after a war. Third, fruit trees grow very slowly, in contrast to pine trees. In the barren climate of Canaan, the chopping down of fruit trees could not easily be put right again. It took at least ten years for a tree to grow large enough to produce a good crop of fruit. Fourth, through this and other environmental regulations, the whole society of Israel was permeated with respect for nature.

This was quite different among other peoples, such as the ancient Greeks. For them it was customary during a siege first to destroy all the orchards and fields near a town. This was so common that the risk of destruction during a siege was covered in tenancy agreements.[5] "Scorched-earth policy" was a favorite weapon of many peoples. For the Israelites, this was strictly forbidden.

SOCIAL RULES

SABBATH AND STRESS

In general, Jews, conservative Christians, and Seventh-Day Adventists are rather strict in the observation of a weekly day of rest. There are Jews who will not light the gas stove or switch on the electric light on the Sabbath (Saturday). After all, this seems like work, and you cause other people to have to work on that day (at the gas company or the power station). For the same reason, some Christians will not buy an ice cream on Sunday or travel on public transport then.

Exaggerated?

Perhaps.

But the fact that men and women may rest for one day a week is really a gift of God. People feel so much better and healthier for the simple fact that, for one day a week, they do not have to labor. With one day of complete rest, they can do more work in the other six days of the week than they would in seven. I know people who—after a nervous breakdown—have clearly experienced this.

God especially appointed the seventh day of the week, the Sabbath, in order to rest from all work and to enjoy life. "For six days, work is to be done, but the seventh day is a Sabbath of rest. . . . The Israelites are to observe the Sabbath . . . for in six days the LORD made the heavens and the earth, and on the seventh day he abstained from work and rested" (Exodus 31:15–17).

Overzealous believers have repeatedly made this "day of rest" into an iron law, a day on which nothing was allowed and from which there was no enjoyment left to be had. But this was never God's intention. In a dispute with an extremely legalistic Jew, Jesus said, "The Sabbath was made for man, not man for the Sabbath" (Mark 2:27). God gave this day of rest to mankind for men and women to feel better spiritually and physically and in order to make time for social contacts.

In our "24/7 economy," a general day of rest is valued less and less. More and more people are superactive seven days a week. It is not surprising that there are more complaints about stress, depression, and burnout than ever before. As a reaction to this, there are all sorts of magazines and books full of tips about how to relax. In almost every newspaper, there are advertisements for relaxation courses and yoga lessons, which can be followed at great expense. And the solution is so simple and cheap!

Let the (stressed) reader keep for two months to the biblical rule about rest, and it is guaranteed that he or she will notice the difference and calm down. And not spending money on expensive courses . . . there will be a nice bit of pocket money left to do something enjoyable with the children or with friends—an important reason why the day of rest must be observed.

C A R E F O R W O R K E R S A N D F O R E I G N E R S

The weekly day of rest in Israel was not only intended to be enjoyed just for oneself. It was also intended to grant workers and slaves one day's rest a week. Among almost all other peoples in the world, it was usual to keep the workers' and slaves' noses to the grindstone seven days a week. But in Israel, all workers and slaves had one day off a week (see Exodus 20:10; 23:12). Unusually progressive.

The laws of Moses were unique with regard to the weak and deprived in society. There is no other book in antiquity that demonstrates so much concern for foreign workers as the Bible: "When an alien lives with you in your land, do not mistreat him. The alien living with you must be treated as one of your native-born. Love him as yourself" (Leviticus 19:33–34). This is quite different from what Western legislators did to guest workers (and still do) when they first came to their countries and were not familiar with the language or culture.

There are dozens of other examples that could be mentioned of humanity in the laws of ancient Israel that really cannot be found anywhere else in the world.

D I F F E R E N C E S B E T W E E N M O S E S A N D H A M M U R A B I

Some scholars claim that the laws of Moses were adopted from older law books of surrounding peoples. This could be the case, for example, with the laws of the great King Hammurabi, who ruled in Babylon about 1800 BC, over three hundred years before Moses.* During excavations in Iran in 1901, a column over two meters tall was found, on which Hammurabi had had his laws carved. Some sentences from the law correspond literally with the Law of Moses, for example, "eye for eye, tooth for tooth" (Deuteronomy 19:21).

It is quite possible that Moses made use of Hammurabi's laws or of other ancient law books. This is certainly not strange, because among all people, views and regulations exist that are in agreement with God's

---

* Some archaeologists think that Hammurabi was a contemporary of Abraham and perhaps the Amraphel referred to in Genesis 14:1.

will. All peoples are descended from Noah and therefore have a rudimentary knowledge about God. In the course of the centuries, this knowledge has become increasingly distorted by human influences and fabrications, but the ancient peoples certainly had a basic knowledge of what is right and wrong. Moreover, every person has a conscience, created by God, which encourages him to do good and to turn from evil (see Romans 2:14–16).

But this does not mean that Moses simply used and adapted the laws of Hammurabi or another king. The laws of Moses are completely independent of any other laws.

The black stela with the law book of Hammurabi.

1. In no other law book in antiquity were the rights of the poor and weak in society, and even of slaves, so strongly guaranteed as in the laws of Moses (see Deuteronomy 24:17–21 and 23:15–16). This was completely unique at the time.

2. In no other law book in antiquity were the social laws so closely linked with the religious laws as in Moses'. In the Old Testament, dealings with one's fellow man cannot be seen independently of dealings with God. The social and religious laws cannot be

separated in the Bible—not even in our time. The Bible demands a high standard of morality and a holy way of life in every aspect of life, including in dealings with one's fellow man.

3. In the Bible the social laws are not only about legal security, as in all other law books in the world, but especially about mercy and neighborly love. "Love your neighbor as yourself" (Leviticus 19:18; Matthew 22:39–40). According to the Lord Jesus, this attitude is the *core* of the Law of Moses (Matthew 7:12).

4. Perhaps the most important difference from all other laws is that in the laws of Moses there is a clear foreshadowing of the life and work of Jesus Christ. I have written in brief about this in chapter 7. Precisely these *details* make the laws of Moses so unique in the history of the world.

The Bible, a Unique Book in World History

If we compare the Bible with other ancient religious books, it becomes apparent how unique the Bible is. Only in the Bible are we able to cite *hundreds* of concrete and weighty facts, besides the dozens that have already been mentioned. Many religious books contain vast amounts of mythology, others contradict science. As we have shown in this book, the Bible continues to be supported by modern medicine, physics, astronomy, and archaeology.

THE EXISTENCE OF GOD NOT PROVABLE

It is understandable that many people have difficulty with believing in God. After all, you cannot *prove* the existence of God in a scientific way, neither from His creation nor from His Word. Furthermore, it is difficult to imagine that the earth and the universe were suddenly created ex nihilo (out of nothing) by a supernatural Power.

Still there are tens of millions of people in the world who have a firm and definite belief in God. There are people who experience God so powerfully in their lives that they are willing to die for their faith. Not only uneducated people or woolly types, but even great scientists, such as Newton and Pascal. Even nowadays, there are numerous scientists and professors who have a rock-solid faith in God. In the United States, there is even a large association of academics, of which one can only become a member if one has graduated from university and is a Christian who believes in the authority of the Scriptures, as well as being a creationist (someone who believes in the creation of heaven and earth as written in Genesis).

Besides this, there are numerous foundations that defend the belief in the Bible and the belief in the theory of creation. So it is absurd if it is claimed in scientific papers or on television that "science has proved that God does not exist," or "evolution is the only scientific explanation for life." Perhaps the majority of scientists believe this, but there are tens of thousands of scientists who think differently, both Christians and non-Christians.

Only "Complete Proof" Is Valid

Based on his profession, the English lawyer Norman Anderson indicates an important rule about providing good evidence. He shows how important it is that the evidence be given in its *entirety*. "If part can be explained on rationalistic grounds, this is unconvincing to the lawyer, at least unless the explanation fits *all* the evidence."[6] In other words, if a certain theory can be used to furnish a part of the proof but does not fit into the larger picture, this theory can never offer an alternative to a theory that does fit in the whole.

This is why, for example, the scientific basis for the theory of evolution is so weak. With a superficial examination of nature, this theory seems reasonably acceptable, but if we start to study the *details*, the theory collapses pitifully. Only the alternative of a Creator God is able to withstand the test of criticism and explain both the smallest details and the larger whole of life.

The existence of God cannot be proved, but the Bible says, "Since the creation of the world, God's invisible qualities—his eternal power and divine nature—have been clearly seen, being understood from what has been made" (Romans 1:20).

Or as Rosetti puts it so beautifully,

> Who has seen the wind?
> Neither you nor I,
> But when the trees
> Bow down their heads,
> The wind is passing by.

FINALLY

The key message in the Bible is not about scientific accuracy or about historical reliability. These are things that go together with it but are only the packaging. However, if even the packaging is scientifically so well founded and so important for our well-being, how important must be the essential spiritual message.

The *core* of the Bible message is that Jesus Christ came to the earth to restore the relationship between God and humanity. This is what the Bible is about. How this works precisely cannot be understood by humans, in the same way the trees in the field sometimes standing with "their heads bowed" cannot be understood by someone who has never been outside and felt the wind.

If someone really wants to know God, the best thing he or she can do is read the four Gospels in the New Testament and without prejudice ask God what it all entails and how the relationship with Him can be restored. The fact that this is really possible is something that I have experienced personally.

A Personal Experience

I grew up in a simple and balanced Christian family. At secondary school, I was involved in the church, but during my studies in Amsterdam, I felt as if there was something missing in my life. I went in search of the truth and the meaning of existence. For years, I immersed myself in Zen Buddhism and yoga. I still remember how, on a remote beach on a Dutch island, I tried to stand on my head in a yoga position to watch the sunset and be one with nature.

When doing military service, I met a chaplain who spoke about God as if he knew Him personally. He said that you can have a living relationship with God and that you can talk to God during daily activities, even at the wheel of a jeep. I thought he was crazy, but still his remarks caused me to think.

Through this man, I came into contact with Open Doors, a missionary organization that helps Christians in countries where persecution is commonplace. I was invited to an introductory weekend to volunteer to smuggle Bibles to Christians in Eastern Europe. It struck me that the people at that weekend spoke about God as if they had a personal relationship with Him. This was quite different from what I was used to in church.

Although I felt like the odd man out, their faith attracted me and I longed for a personal faith such as they had. They talked about miracles that happened at the borders and during dangerous trips through "closed" countries. At the end of the weekend, I asked the leader how I could have a faith like that.

"Very simply," he said, "let us pray together. Tell God that you repent of your sins and ask Him to forgive those sins. Say that you want to place your life in God's hand and that you want to follow Jesus. Ask Him to come into your life, into your heart."† No sooner said than done.

---

† Some Bible texts that explain this from God's side are: Romans 3:23–24; 1 John 2:1–2; Revelation 3:20; Luke 15:11–24; John 3:1–8.

Changed

When we had finished our prayer, I didn't notice anything special. It was simply a conscious decision to follow God, a moment of conversion. Two weeks later, at an Evangelical church, the preacher asked who wanted to make a conscious and public decision for Jesus. Anyone who did was to go out to the front. And before I knew it, I was in front of the stage. Then something happened in me. For the first time since childhood, I wept, and I became a new person. In John 3:1–8, the Bible calls this being born again.

Of course, I retained my own character (with good and bad traits), but a dimension had been added to my life. The Bible came alive for me. I felt like a dried-up sponge, and in the evenings I read the Bible for hours. I had come into contact with God. I had attained the goal for which mankind is created: to associate with God as with a father, a friend.

From that time on, my life dramatically changed. Now I see that it is indeed normal to talk to God in your car, during a walk in the woods, or while doing the dishes, or whatever. You can tell God about everything that concerns you, and you will experience that He listens and answers your prayers in His time.

After that specific afternoon in February 1971, the contact with Open Doors remained, and I have taken Bibles to Eastern Europe and China on dozens of occasions. I have experienced various miracles at heavily guarded borders and in the countries themselves. I have seen how God helps Christians in the most extreme circumstances, how weak people persevere under persecution and torture. I have seen that faith in God is not based on rational grounds, but that it is deeper than the intellect, anchored in the deepest being of men and women. Ridicule, abuse, and even torture cannot do anything to change this. I have met Christians who have been in prison camps for over twenty years and who have come out of them with a rock-solid trust in God and with a faith that is just as real and certain as nature around us.

Intellect and science cannot bring about such things, but only the power of God. Through this creative power and through faith in Jesus Christ, you can receive eternal life, as is written in John 3:15–16, 36.

Eternal life does not only mean "to live eternally after death," but it is also an indication of quality: living forever together with God as a father, as your best friend. This quality life begins at the moment that Jesus comes into your life.

This faith in Jesus Christ not only brings about a change in one's personal life, but also a change in the whole of society. Numerous books describe how societies have been changed by the Christian faith; prisons and brothels have had hardly any customers anymore; policemen have had hardly any work to do anymore. Some of these books are about the lives of John Wesley (1703–91) in England and Charles Finney (1792–1875) in the United States.

Regarding this faith in Jesus Christ, in conclusion I would like to quote from Abraham Kuyper (1837–1920), the founder of the university where I studied, who, after a life of work and study, said during an official address:

> This, this is why, with the artlessness of a little child, kneeling in quiet faith before this Scripture, I rejoice in my soul and thank God. As my Savior believed in Moses and the Prophets, so and not otherwise do I, too, wish to believe in this Scripture.[7]

This is eternal life: that they may know you,
the only true God, and Jesus Christ,
whom you have sent.

JOHN 17:3

RECOMMENDED RESOURCES

BOOKS

Chapters 2 and 3

S. I. McMillen. *None of These Diseases* (London: Marshall Morgan & Scott, 1984). On circumcision, health, and hygiene.

Chapter 4

R. Russell. *What the Bible Says about Healthy Living* (London: Angus Hudson, 1999). On healthy food according to the Bible.

Chapter 5

H. H. Morris. *Many Infallible Proofs*, (El Cajon, CA: Master Books, 1988). On physics and creation / evolution.

J. Woodmorappe. *Noah's Ark: A Feasibility Study* (El Cajon, CA: Institute for Creation Research, 1996). On solutions for physical and biological problems with the ark of Noah.

Chapter 6

M. J. Behe. *Darwin's Black Box* (New York: Free Press, 1996). On irreducibly complex systems.

W. T. Brown. *In the Beginning* (Phoenix, AZ: Center for Scientific Creation, 2008). On the Flood.

S. Burgess. *Hallmarks of Design* (Leominster: DayOne, 2000). On irreducibly complex systems.

M. Denton. *Evolution: A Theory in Crisis* (London: Burnett, 1985). On the impossibility of evolution.

H. M. Morris. *The Biblical Basis for Modern Science* (Grand Rapids: Baker, 1987). On creation / evolution.

———. *Scientific Creationism*, 2nd ed. (El Cajon, CA: Master Books, 1985). On creation / evolution.

P. S. Taylor. *The Illustrated Origins Answer Book* (Mesa, AZ: Eden Productions, 1995). On creation / evolution.

Chapter 7

J. W. Haley. *An Examination of the Alleged Discrepancies of the Bible* (Grand Rapids: Baker, 1977). On solutions to "mistakes" in the Bible.

J. McDowell. *Evidence that Demands a Verdict* (Amersham-on-the-Hill: Scripture Press, 1990). On probability calculus.

———. *The New Evidence That Demands a Verdict* (Nashville: Nelson, 1999). On the reliability of the Bible.

B. M. Metzger. *A Textual Commentary on the Greek New Testament* (Stuttgart: United Bible Societies, 1975). On variations in Bible texts.

R. Pache. *The Inspiration and Authority of Scripture* (Chicago: Moody, 1980). On the authority and reliability of the Bible.

ADDRESSES, WEB SITES, AND MAGAZINES

Access Research Network—PO Box 38069, Colorado Springs, CO, 80937, USA, www.arn.org.

Answersingenesis—PO Box 510, Hebron, KY 41048, USA, www.answersingenesis.org—*Answers*.

Biblical Creation Society—PO Box 22, Rugby, Warwickshire, CV 22 7SY, England, www.biblicalcreation.org—*Origins*.

Center for Scientific Creation—5612 North 20th Place, Phoenix, AZ 85016, USA, www.creationscience.com.

Creation Ministries International—PO Box 4545, Eight Mile Plains, Qld 4113, Australia, www.creation.com—*Creation*.

Creation Research Society—PO Box 8263, St. Joseph, MO 64508, USA, www.creationresearch.org—*Creation Research Society Quarterly*.

Creation Science Fellowship—PO Box 99303, Pittsburgh, PA 15233, USA, www.csfpittsburgh.org.

Creation Science Movement—PO Box 888, Portsmouth, PO6 2YD, England, www.creationsciencemovement.com—*Creation*.

Institute for Creation Research—PO Box 59029, Dallas, TX 75229, USA, www.icr.org—*Acts & Facts*.

Wort und Wissen—Rosenbergweg 29, D-72270 Baiersbronn, Deutschland, www.wort-und-wissen.de—*Wort und Wissen-Info*.

NOTES

Chapter 1: Modern Science in the Bible?

1. W. J. Ouweneel, "De herkauwende haas," *Bijbel en Wetenschap* 2 (December 1975): 24.
2. S. I. McMillen, *None of These Diseases* (London: Marshall Morgan & Scott, 1984), 87–96.
3. H. M. Morris, *The Biblical Basis for Modern Science* (Grand Rapids: Baker, 1987), 290–96.
4. H. T. Frank, *In het voetspoor van de Bijbel* (Amsterdam: Reader's Digest, 1983), 54–55.
5. C. P. Bryan, *Ancient Egyptian Medicine: The Papyrus Ebers* (Chicago: Ares, 1930), 68–73.
6. Bryan, *Ancient Egyptian Medicine*, 73.
7. McMillen, *None of These Diseases*, 19.
8. Bryan, *Ancient Egyptian Medicine*, 155.
9. Homer, *Odyssey*, IV, lines 229–31.
10. H. Rosenstock, *Arizona Medicine* 25 (April 1968): 403.
11. D. T. Atkinson, *Magic, Myth and Medicine* (New York: World Publishing, 1956), 65.
12. W. Penfield, "Ur of the Chaldees and the Influence of Abraham on the History of Medicine," *Bulletin of the History of Medicine* 19 (1946): 140.
13. R. Cavendish, ed. *Mythology: An Illustrated Encyclopedia*, Dutch edition (London: Orbis, 1980), 97.
14. H. Rimmer, *The Harmony of Science and Scripture* (Grand Rapids: Eerdmans, 1945), 64–65.
15. P. H. Peli, *Torah Today: A Renewed Encounter with Scripture*, Dutch edition (Washington, DC: B'nai B'rith Books, 1987), 95.

Chapter 2: Countering Epidemics

1. R. Dolezal, *ABC's of the Bible*, Dutch edition (Pleasantville, NY: Reader's Digest Association, 1991), 139–40.
2. E. Strouhal, *Life in Ancient Egypt*, Dutch edition (Cambridge: Cambridge University Press, 1992), 254–56.
3. Strouhal, *Life in Ancient Egypt*, 248.

4. J. A. Thompson, *The Bible and Archaeology* (Exeter, U.K.: Paternoster, 1973), 82–85, 91.

5. J. D. Douglas, ed. *New Bible Dictionary*, 2nd ed. (Leicester, U.K.: Universities and Colleges Christian Fellowship, 1982).

6. M. F. Unger, *Archeology and the Old Testament* (Grand Rapids: Zondervan, 1974), 174–75.

7. W. F. Albright, *Archaeology and the Religion of Israel* (Baltimore: Johns Hopkins University Press, 1956), 73.

8. E. Neufeld, *The Hittite Laws* (London: Luzac, 1951), 188.

9. A. R. Whitney Green, *The Role of Human Sacrifice in the Ancient Near East* (Missoula, MT: Scholars Press, 1975), 62, 64, 202; N. Glueck, *Rivers in the Desert: A History of the Negev* (New York: Farrar, Straus & Cudahy, 1959), 61.

10. A. S. Benenson, *Control of Communicable Diseases in Man*, 15th ed. (New York: American Public Health Association, 1990), 188.

11. B. Sember, "Silent STDs," www.conceiveonline.com; L. Weström et al., "Pelvic Inflammatory Disease and Fertility," *Sexual Transmitted Diseases* 19, no. 4 (1992): 185–92; B. F. Polk, "PID: How to Track Down Its Cause," *Patient Care* 17 (1983): 81.

12. Nederlands Interdisciplinair Demografisch Instituut: *Het recht om te kiezen*, DEMOS, vol. 13 (July 1997), 4, www.nidi.nl.

13. M. Stoddard Holmes, *Fictions of Affliction: Physical Disability in Victorian Culture* (Ann Arbor: University of Michigan Press, 2004), 64; Atkinson, *Magic, Myth and Medicine*, 263.

14. World Health Organization, *World Health Report* (1998), 45, www.who.int/whr/1998.

15. Centers for Disease Control and Prevention, www.cdc.gov/mmwr/preview/mmwrhtml/mm5254a1.htm, table 8, 9, 10.

16. J. W. Curran, "Economic Consequences of Pelvic Inflammatory Disease in the United States," *American Journal of Obstetrics and Gynecology* 138 (1980): 848; Centers for Disease Control and Prevention, www.cdc.gov/mmwr/preview/mmwrhtml/00035381.htm, figure 20 and table 3, 4.

17. R. S. Morton, *Venereal Diseases* (Baltimore: Penguin, 1972), 36.

18. J. Voorhoeve, *Homoeopathie in de praktijk* (Kampen: La Rivière & Voorhoeve, 1988), 438.

19. J. D. Fawver and R. L. Overstreet, "Moses and Preventive Medicine," *Bibliotheca Sacra*, July–September 1990, 280.

20. A. C. Steere and G. F. Mallison, "Handwashing Practices," *Annals of Internal Medicine* 83 (1975): 684.

21. Commissie Ziekenhuisinfecties, *Voorkom infecties* ('s-Gravenhage: Staatsuitgeverij, 1968), 10.

22. World Health Organization, "WHO Guidelines on Hand Hygiene in Health Care" (Advanced Draft), April 2006, 14, 51, 93.

23. Atkinson, *Magic, Myth and Medicine*, 74.

24. Benenson, *Communicable Diseases*, 244.
25. G. Rosen, *A History of Public Health* (New York: MD Publications, 1958), 62.
26. McMillen, *None of These Diseases*, 21.
27. Rosen, *History of Public Health*, 63–65.
28. A. Castiglioni, *A History of Medicine* (New York: Aronson, 1969), 71.
29. Th. M. Vogelsang, "Leprosy in Norway," *Medical History* 9 (1965): 31–35.
30. Benenson, *Communicable Diseases*, 244–45.
31. J. C. Pedley, "Summary of the Results of a Search of the Skin Surface for *Mycobacterium leprae*," *Leprosy Review* 41 (1970): 168.
32. K. Sudhoff, *Essays in the History of Medicine* (New York: Medical Life, 1926), 146.
33. B. Grzimek, ed., *Animal Life Encyclopedia*, vol. 2, Dutch edition (New York: Van Nostrand Reinhold, 1972–75), 501.
34. R. S. Gottfried, *The Black Death* (New York: Macmillan, 1983), 34–47; R. Margotta, *The Hamlyn History of Medicine*, ed. P. Lewis, Dutch edition (London: Reed International, 1996), 61.
35. H. Bronsema, *Bevolking van toen*, www.nidi.nl/public/demos/dm99033.html, maart 1999, 2; R. Stark, *For the Glory of God* (Princeton, NJ: Princeton University Press, 2003), 60.
36. F. H. Garrison, *An Introduction to the History of Medicine* (Philadelphia: Saunders, 1960), 188.
37. M. N. Chomel, *Huishoudelijk woordboek*, vol. 2 (Leiden: Luchtmans, 1743), 784.
38. Gottfried, *Black Death*, 110–11.
39. Atkinson, *Magic, Myth and Medicine*, 71–77; R. R. Wlodyga, *Health Secrets from the Bible* (Altadena, CA: Triumph, 1979), 2.
40. *The Jewish Encyclopedia* (New York: Funk & Wagnalls, 1906–1910), 233.
41. Gottfried, *Black Death*, 74.
42. Atkinson, *Magic, Myth and Medicine*, 80–81, 84.
43. World Health Organization, www.who.int/wer/2008/wer8333.pdf; Grzimek, *Animal Life Encyclopedia*, vol. 11, 401.
44. D. Riesman, *The Story of Medicine in the Middle Ages* (New York: Hoeber, 1935), 260.
45. McMillen, *None of These Diseases*, 23.
46. R. Dubos, *Health and Disease* (New York: Time, 1965), 53.
47. Margotta, *Hamlyn History of Medicine*, 156.
48. Dubos, *Health and Disease*, 54.
49. United Nations, www.un.org/News/Press/docs/1998/19980202.EVDV461.html; Waterbedrijf Gelderland, "Drinkwater en gezondheid," *de Waterkrant* 2 (April 1999): 2.
50. H. Doornbos, "Meeste poep op straten van India is van mensen," *BN De Stem*, March 18, 2003.
51. Grzimek, *Animal Life Encyclopedia*, vol. 1, 333, 389–91; www.wateryear2003.org.

52. Castiglioni, *History of Medicine*, 70.
53. Atkinson, *Magic, Myth and Medicine*, 30–31.

Chapter 3: Hygiene

1. A. P. M. van der Meij-de Leur, *Van olie en wijn, Geschiedenis van verpleeg-kunde, geneeskunde en sociale zorg* (Utrecht: Bohn, Scheltema & Holkema, 1987), 68.

2. McMillen, *None of These Diseases*, 26; Fawver and Overstreet, "Moses and Preventive Medicine," 278.

3. R. Park, *An Epitome of the History of Medicine*, 2nd ed. (Philadelphia: Davis, 1903), 326.

4. McMillen, *None of These Diseases*, 24–25; Fawver and Overstreet, "Moses and Preventive Medicine," 278–80.

5. Fawver and Overstreet, "Moses and Preventive Medicine," 280.

6. Steere and Mallison, "Handwashing Practices," 684.

7. L. M. Dembry, M. J. Zervos, and W. J. Hierholzer Jr., "Nosocomial Bacterial Infections," in *Bacterial Infections of Humans: Epidemiology and Control*, eds. A. S. Evans and H. A. Feldman, 383 (New York: Plenum, 1982).

8. National Audit Office, *The Management and Control of Hospital Acquired Infection in Acute NHS Trusts in England*, news release (London, 2000), 81.

9. World Health Organization, "WHO Guidelines on Hand Hygiene," 61; www.handhygiene.net.

10. Commissie Ziekenhuisinfecties, *Voorkom infecties* ('s-Gravenhage: Staatsuitgeverij, 1968), 8–10.

11. Strouhal, *Life in Ancient Egypt*, 224–26.

12. Grzimek, *Animal Life Encyclopedia*, vol. 2, 63, 190.

13. P. A. Kager, *Hoe blijf ik gezond in de tropen?* (Amsterdam: Koninklijk Instituut voor de Tropen, 1998), 88.

14. Steere and Mallison, "Handwashing Practices," 684.

15. Steere and Mallison, "Handwashing Practices," 684.

16. G. Singleton, *Impacts of Rodents on Rice Production in Asia*, 2003, 8, 17, www.irri.org. (See also ch. 4, n. 46); D. Cao, D. Pimentel, and K. Hart, "Postharvest Crop Losses (Insects and Mites)," and "Postharvest Food Losses (Vertebrates)," in *Encyclopedia of Pest Management*, vol. 1, ed. D. Pimentel, 645–50 (New York: M. Dekker, 2002).

17. Gelderland, "Drinkwater," 2.

18. Grzimek, *Animal Life Encyclopedia*, vol. 11, 227, 401.

19. Grzimek, *Animal Life Encyclopedia*, vol. 2, 468.

20. E. Warner and E. Strashin, "Benefits and Risks of Circumcision," *Canadian Medical Association Journal* 125 (1981): 969.

21. Warner and Strashin, "Benefits and Risks of Circumcision," 968; "Circumcision in Europe," www.circumcisioninformation.com—General Information—Circumcision Practices around the World; D. Bollinger, "Normal Versus

Circumcised: U.S. Neonatal Male Genital Ratio (2003)," www.cirp.org/library /statistics/bollinger2003.

22. A. L. Wolbarst, "Circumcision and Penile Cancer," *Lancet* 1, no. 5655 (1932): 152–53; Warner and Strashin, "Benefits and Risks of Circumcision," 971; "What Are the Key Statistics about Penile Cancer?" (2008), www.cancer.org; G. W. Kaplan, "Circumcision: An Overview," *Current Problems in Pediatrics* 7, no. 10 (1977), quoted in McMillen, *None of These Diseases*, 90.

23. Fawver and Overstreet, "Moses and Preventive Medicine," 276.

24. R. L. Spittel, *British Medical Journal* 2 (1923): 632, quoted in Wolbarst, "Circumcision and Penile Cancer," 152–53.

25. Wolbarst, "Circumcision and Penile Cancer," 150–53; J. C. Paymaster and P. Gangadharan, "Cancer of the Penis in India," *Journal of Urology* 97 (1967): 110–13; E. Leiter and A.M. Lefkovits, "Circumcision and the Penile Carcinoma," *New York State Journal of Medicine* 75 (1975): 1520.

26. "Key Statistics About Penile Cancer?" (2008), www.cancer.org.

27. E. J. Schoen, "Neonatal Circumcision and Penile Cancer," *British Medical Journal* 313 (1996): 46.

28. E. J. Schoen, "Benefits of Newborn Circumcision: Is Europe Ignoring Medical Evidence?," *Archives of Disease in Childhood* 77 (1997): 258–60; T. E. Wiswell and J. K. Lattimer lecture: "Prepuce Presence Portends Prevalence of Potentially Perilous Periurethral Pathogens," *Journal of Urology* 148 (August 1992): 739–42.

29. B. G. Williams, "The Potential Impact of Male Circumcision on HIV in Sub-Saharan Africa," *PLoS Medicine* 3, no. 7 (2006), http:// medicine.plosjournals.org.

30. www.who.int/mediacentre/news/releases/ 2007/pr10/en.

31. L. E. Holt and R. McIntosh, *Holt's Pediatrics*, 12th ed. (New York: Appleton-Century-Crofts, 1953), 125–26.

32. Fawver and Overstreet, "Moses and Preventive Medicine," 277; J. B. Wyngaarden and L. H. Smith Jr., eds., *Cecil Textbook of Medicine* (Philadelphia: Saunders, 1982), 1003.

33. J. Katz, "The Question of Circumcision," *International Surgery* 62 (1977): 491.

34. J. Katz, "The Question of Circumcision."

35. Castiglioni, *History of Medicine*, 79.

Chapter 4: Nutrition

1. A. S. Yahuda, *The Language of the Pentateuch in Its Relationship to Egyptian* (London: Oxford University Press, 1933), 244; Strouhal, *Life in Ancient Egypt*, 111–12, 130–31, 225; W. F. Albright, *Yahweh and the Gods of Canaan* (New York: Doubleday, 1968), 177–78.

2. P. H. Peli, *Torah Today: A Renewed Encounter with Scripture*, Dutch edition (Washington, DC: B'nai Brith Books, 1987), 103.

3. S. Davidson, *Introduction to the Old Testament* (Edinburgh: Williams & Norgate, 1862), 258; K. A. Dächsel, *Bijbelverklaring*, vol. 1 (Utrecht: Den

Hertog, 1979), 509; W. Zuidema, *God's Partner* (Baarn: Ten Have, 1979), 172–75.

4. *The Jewish Encyclopedia*, 599; D. J. Baarslag, *Baäls en burchten* (Baarn: Bosch & Keuning, z.j.), 52.

5. C. F. Keil and F. Delitzsch, *Commentary on the Old Testament* (Grand Rapids: Eerdmans, 1976), 357.

6. E. Munk, *The Call of the Torah (Leviticus)*, ed. Y. Kirzner, trans. E. S. Mazor (Brooklyn: Mesorah, 1994), 101–2.

7. Zuidema, *God's Partner*,172–75; "Dietary Laws," *Encyclopedia Judaica*, vol. 6 (Jerusalem: Keter, 1972), 42–45.

8. M. Harris, *Good to Eat* (Prospect Heights, IL: Waveland, 1998), 72–73, 81.

9. Strouhal, *Life in Ancient Egypt*, 117.

10. F. Versteeg, "Ruim miljoen mensen lopen thuis voedselinfectie op," *Voeding en Voorlichting* 12 (1997), 's-Gravenhage: Voorlichtingsbureau voor de Voeding, 6–8; Consumentengids, *Zijn wij het schoonmaken verleerd?* (August 1998), 's-Gravenhage: Consumentenbond, 42.

11. Versteeg, "Ruim miljoen mensen lopen thuis voedselinfectie op," 6–8.

12. H. J. Sinell,"Eigenschaften des Fleisches," in *Handbuch der Lebensmittelchemie*, ed. J. Schormüller, 1068 (Berlin: Springer-Verlag, 1965).

13. Grzimek, *Animal Life Encyclopedia*, vol. 13, 562.

14. R. Von Ostertag and F. Schönberg, *Lehrbuch der Schlachttier-und Fleischuntersuchung* (Stuttgart: Enke Verlag, 1955), 403.

15. Von Ostertag and Schönberg, *Lehrbuch der Schlachttier-und Fleischuntersuchung*, 403.

16. Von Ostertag and Schönberg, *Lehrbuch der Schlachttier-und Fleischuntersuchung*, 403, 414, 491.

17. Von Ostertag and Schönberg, *Lehrbuch der Schlachttier-und Fleischuntersuchung*, 68–69, 462; Benenson, *Communicable Diseases*, 447; W. Bommer et al, *Trichinellose-Aufbruch in einem Jugendheim* (Berlin: Weltkongreß 291 Lebensmittelinfektionen und-intoxikationen, 29.6–3.7.1980), 441.

18. Von Ostertag and Schönberg, *Lehrbuch der Schlachttier-und Fleischuntersuchung*, 462–63.

19. Grzimek, *Animal Life Encyclopedia*, vol. 12, 32, 35.

20. Strouhal, *Life in Ancient Egypt*, 130.

21. Albright, *Yahweh and the Gods of Canaan*, 177–78.

22. Grzimek, *Animal Life Encyclopedia*, vol. 1, 337; Kager, *Hoe blijf ik gezond in de tropen?*, 82–83.

23. M. A. IJsseling and A. Scheygrond, *Hoofdzaken der biologie*, vol. 1A (Zutphen: Thieme & Cie, 1963), 61–62; Grzimek, *Animal Life Encyclopedia*, vol. 1, 391–93.

24. Harris, *Good to Eat*, 120.

25. Grzimek, *Animal Life Encyclopedia*, vol. 1, 392.

26. E. A. Josephson, *God's Key to Health and Happiness* (Grand Rapids, MI: Baker, 1976), 59, 63.

27. Grzimek, *Animal Life Encyclopedia*, vol. 1, 329–30; Von Ostertag and Schönberg, *Lehrbuch der Schlachttier-und Fleischuntersuchung*, 419–25.

28. Grzimek, *Animal Life Encyclopedia*, vol. 2, 501.

29. E. Hayes, S. Marshall, and D. Dennis, "Tularemia, United States 1990–2000," www.cdc.gov/mmwr/preview/mmwrhtml/mm5109a1.htm.

30. H. L. Barnett, ed. with A. H. Einhorn, *Pediatrics*, 14th ed. (New York: Appleton-Century-Crofts, 1968), 671–72.

31. E. Croddy, *Tularemia, Biological Warfare and the Battle for Stalingrad (1942–1943)*, www.cns.miis.edu.

32. J. S. Watson, *Proceedings of the Zoological Society of London* 124 (1954): 615–24; E. P. Walker, *Mammals of the World*, vol. 2 (Baltimore: Johns Hopkins University Press, 1968), 647.

33. Grzimek, *Animal Life Encyclopedia*, vol. 12, 491.

34. Grzimek, *Animal Life Encyclopedia*, vol. 12, 486.

35. Grzimek, *Animal Life Encyclopedia*, vol. 12, 600–601, 603.

36. Grzimek, *Animal Life Encyclopedia*, vol. 13, 135, 562.

37. Von Ostertag and Schönberg, *Lehrbuch der Schlachttier-und Fleischuntersuchung*, 462–63.

38. A. Hüttermann, "Die ökologische Botschaft der Tora," *Naturwissenschaften* 80 (1993): 147–56.

39. Grzimek, *Animal Life Encyclopedia*, vol. 7, 382.

40. Grzimek, *Animal Life Encyclopedia*, vol. 7, 373, 379.

41. Grzimek, *Animal Life Encyclopedia*, vol. 7, 243; G. Mauersberger, *Urania Tierreich, Vögel*, vol. 6 (Leipzich-Jena-Berlin: Urania Verlach, 1972).

42. *Spectrum Natuurencyclopedie* (Utrecht: Het Spectrum, 1978–1982), 1124.

43. D. L. Proctor, ed., "The Economic Importance of Rodent Pests," in *Grain Storage Techniques: Evolution and Trends in Developing Countries* (Rome: Food and Agricultural Organization of the United Nations, 1994), www.fao.org/docrep/t1838e/T1838E1j.htm#The%20economic%20importance%20of%20rodent%20pests.

44. D. Pimentel et al., "Environmental and Economic Costs Associated with Nonindigenous Species in the United States," *Bioscience* 50, no. 1 (1999): 53–65.

45. Singleton, *Impacts of Rodents*, 8, 17; Cao, Pimentel, and Hart, "Postharvest Crop Losses," in Pimentel, *Encyclopedia of Pest Management*, 645–50.

46. Singleton, *Impacts of Rodents*, 1, 5. For calculations, see also: http://faostat.fao.org, under: Production-Crops-Country-World-Cereals-Production Quantity-2007.

47. Grzimek, *Animal Life Encyclopedia*, vol. 11, 227, 401.

48. D. B. Sauer, ed., *Storage of Cereal Grains and Their Products*, 4th ed. (St. Paul: American Association of Cereal Chemists, 1992), 393; H. Zinsser, *Rats, Lice and History* (Boston: Little, Brown, 1963), 202.

49. Grzimek, *Animal Life Encyclopedia*, vol. 2, 122–23; IJsseling and Scheygrond, *Hoofdzaken der biologie*, vol. 1A, 41.

50. S. Rajendran, "Postharvest Pest Losses," in Pimentel, *Encyclopedia of Pest Management*, 654–56.

51. Cao, Pimentel, and Hart, "Postharvest Crop Losses," in Pimentel, *Enclyclopedia of Pest Management*, 645–47.

52. IJsseling and Scheygrond, *Hoofdzaken der biologie*, vol. 3, 104.

53. J. Herbig, *Nährung für die Götter* (Munich: Hansler Verlag, 1988).

54. IJsseling and Scheygrond, *Hoofdzaken der biologie*, vol. 3, 111.

55. K. V. F. Jubb, P. C. Kennedy, and N. Palmer, *Pathology of Domestic Animals* (New York: Academic Press, 1993), 254.

56. P. F. Meyer-Waarden: *Krebstiere und Weichtiere*, in J. Schormüller, ed., *Handbuch der Lebensmittelchemie*, vol. 3 (Berlin: Springer-Verlag, 1968), 1585.

57. The Council of the European Communities: "Council Directive of 22 July 1991 laying down the Health Conditions for the Production and the Placing on the Market of Fishery Products" (91/493/EEC), Article 3 and Annex Chapter 1, 4, 8.

58. P. F. Meyer-Waarden: *Krebstiere und Weichtiere*, in J. Schormüller, ed., *Handbuch der Lebensmittelchemie*, vol. 3 (Berlin: Springer-Verlag, 1968), 1585.

59. Kager, *Hoe blijf ik gezond in de tropen?*, 77.

60. Grzimek, *Animal Life Encyclopedia*, vol. 3, 195–96.

61. *Top Santé*, April 2001.

62. G. S. Tessler, *The Genesis Diet*, Dutch edition (Raleigh, NC: Be Well, 1996), 54.

63. R. L. Darwin, "Heart Disease and Stroke: The Nation's Leading Killers," www.cdc.gov/nccdphp/publications/AAG/dhdsp.htm.

64. Consumentengids, *Hart- en vaatziekten* ('s-Gravenhage: Consumentenbond, April 2003), 71, www.consumentenbond.nl.

65. J. de Vries, "Eet meer vis," *Natuur & Techniek* 65, no. 12 (1997): 23–31; M. Buikema, "Visconsumptie," *Health* 3 (2003): 36, www.achmeahealth.nl.

66. W. J. Gerritsen, "Voor gezondheidsclaims olijfolie voldoende onderbouwing," *Voeding* 58, no. 6 (1997): 18.

67. M. P. Heron and B. L. Smith, "Deaths: Leading Causes for 2003," *National Vital Statistics Reports* 55, no. 10 (2007): 7, www.cdc.gov.

68. Over Leven, "Voeding en kanker," *Wachtkamertijdschrift van de Nederlandse Kankerbestrijding* 9, no. 4 (2000): 18.

69. R. Russell, *What the Bible Says About Healthy Living*, Dutch edition (London: Angus Hudson, 1999), 25.

70. Nederlandse Kankerbestrijding, *Geef kanker minder kans, eet volop groente en fruit* (najaar 2000); Russell, *What the Bible Says About Healthy Living*, 25.

71. Russell, *What the Bible Says About Healthy Living*, 16–19.

Chapter 5: Natural Sciences

1. F. M. Th. de Liagre Böhl, *Het Gilgamesj Epos* (Amsterdam: Paris N.V., 1958), 87–95; A. Millard, *Discoveries from Bible Times* (Oxford: Lion, 1997), 42–43.

2. B. Landström, *Zeilschepen in woord en beeld* (Amsterdam: Elsevier, 1970), 42–43, 103.
3. Landström, *Zeilschepen in woord en beeld*.
4. Het Fluitschip van Liorne, www.hoorn.nl.
5. Morris, *Biblical Basis for Modern Science*, 290–96.
6. S. P. De Boer and J. A. Schaap, *Zeemanschap voor de grote handelsvaart* (Amsterdam: Duwaer & Zonen, 1959), 306, 325.
7. J. Lever, *Creatie en evolutie* (Wageningen: Zomer & Keuning, 1958), 12.
8. Morris, *Biblical Basis for Modern Science*, 291.
9. IJsseling and Scheygrond, *Hoofdzaken der biologie*, vol. 3, 1–2.
10. J. Woodmorappe, *Noah's Ark: A Feasibility Study* (El Cajon, CA: Institute for Creation Research, 1996), 13.
11. Woodmorappe, *Noah's Ark*
12. Grzimek, *Animal Life Encyclopedia*, vol. 7, 19.
13. C. L. Woolley, *Ur of the Chaldees* (New York: Norton, 1965), 29.
14. H. F. Vos, *Genesis and Archaeology*, Dutch edition (Grand Rapids: Zondervan, 1985), 28–29.
15. W. Ryan and W. Pitman, *Noah's Flood* (New York: Simon & Schuster, 1998).
16. *The 1989 Information Please Almanac* (Boston: Houghton Mifflin, 1989), 544.
17. S. A. Austin, *Grand Canyon: Monument to Catastrophe* (Santee, CA: Institute for Creation Research, 1994); W. Brown, *In the Beginning* (Phoenix: Center for Scientific Creation, 2008), 182–219.
18. A. P. van der Wolf en T. Zoutewelle, *De paleontologische en geologische aspekten van het kreationisme* (Utrecht: Doctoraalverslag, Laboratorium voor Paleontologie en Palynologie, 1985).
19. S. A. Austin and J. D. Morris, *Tight Folds and Clastic Dikes as Evidence for Rapid Deposition*, vol. 2 (Pittsburgh: Creation Science Fellowship, Proceedings of the First International Conference on Creationism, 1986), 3–15.
20. L. W. Alvarez et al., "Extraterrestrial Cause for the Cretaceous-Tertiary Extinction," *Science* 208 (1980): 1095–1108; W. Alvarez, *T. rex and the Crater of Doom* (Princeton, NJ: Princeton University Press, 1997).
21. A. Tollmann and E. Tollmann-Kristan, *De zondvloed: van mythe tot historische werkelijkheid* (Baarn: Tirion, 1993), 241–44; Vos, *Genesis and Archaeology*, 29.
22. B. C. Nelson, *The Deluge Story in Stone* (Minneapolis: Augsburg, 1958), 169; G. W. Bromiley, ed., *The International Standard Bible Encyclopedia*, vol. 2 (Grand Rapids, MI: Eerdmans, 1982), 319.
23. Tollmann and Tollmann-Kristan, *De zondvloed*.
24. C. H. Kang and E. R. Nelson, *The Discovery of Genesis* (St. Louis: Concordia, 1979); E. R. Nelson and R. E. Broadberry, *Genesis and the Mystery Confucius Couldn't Solve* (St. Louis: Concordia, 1994).
25. Yahuda, *Language of the Pentateuch*, 107–15.
26. Grzimek, *Animal Life Encyclopedia*, vol. "Ecology," 569.

27. J. S. Morton, *Science in the Bible*, Dutch edition (Chicago: Moody, 1978), 51–53.

28. C. C. Plummer and D. F. R. McGeary, *Physical Geology: Earth Revealed*, Dutch edition (Dubuque, IA: Brown, 1992), 10.

29. P. Lafferty, *Weather*, Dutch edition (New York: Crescent, 1992), 63.

30. A. B. C. Whipple, *Storm (Planet Earth,)* Dutch edition (Alexandria, VA: Time-Life, 1982), 6.

31. Ibid., 164.

32. J. D. Fast, *Energie uit atoomkernen* (Maastricht: Natuur en Techniek, 1980), 120.

33. C. L. Lewis, *Matthew Fontaine Maury: The Pathfinder of the Seas* (Annapolis, MD: U.S. Naval Institute, 1927), 252.

34. R. W. Fairbridge, *Encyclopedia of Oceanography*, Stroudsburg, PA: Dowden, Hutchinson & Ross,1966), 612, quoted in Morton, *Science in the Bible*, 118.

35. Lewis, *Matthew Fontaine Maury*, 240–b.

36. M. Franssen, *Archimedes in bad* (Amsterdam: Prometheus, 1990), 21–27.

37. A. D. White, *A History of the Warfare of Science with Theology in Christendom*, 2 vols. (New York: Dover, 1896 and 1960).

38. L. R. Godfrey, ed., *Scientists Confront Creationism* (New York: Norton, 1983), 283–99.

39. C. de Pater, *The Flat Earth: Columbus and Modern Historians* (New York: Praeger, 1991), 264–67; J. B. Russell, *Inventing the Flat Earth: Columbus and Modern Historians* (New York: Praeger, 1991); Stark, *For the Glory of God*, 120–23.

40. G. de Santillana, *The Crime of Galileo* (London: Heineman, 1958), xii.

41. P. J. Sampson, *Six Modern Myths About Christianity and Western Civilization* (Downers Grove, IL: InterVarsity, 2001); Stark, *For the Glory of God*, 163–66; Franssen, *Archimedes in bad*, 57–62.

42. Stark, *For the Glory of God*, 147–57.

43. Stark, *For the Glory of God*, 197, 376.

44. W. J. O. Ouweneel, "Geen natuurwetenschap dan christelijke?," *Bijbel en Wetenschap* 199 (1997): 202–4.

45. Winkler Prins, *Encyclopedie van de astronomie* (Amsterdam: Elsevier, 1986), 244.

46. E. W. Maunder, *The Astronomy of the Bible* (London: Hodder and Stoughton, 1909), 226–29.

47. R. Pache, *The Inspiration and Authority of Scripture* (Chicago: Moody Press, 1980), Dutch edition, 50.

48. Douglas, *New Bible Dictionary* (Fellowship, 1982), 997.

49. P. W. Stoner and R. C. Newman, *Science Speaks* (Chicago: Moody, 1976), 101–12.

50. J. McDowell, *Evidence That Demands a Verdict* (Amersham-on-the-Hill: Scripture Press, 1990), 280–81.

51. J. D. Douglas, ed., *New Bible Dictionary*, 2nd ed. (Leicester: Universities and Colleges Christian Fellowship, 1982), 298–99, 1084.

52. W. M. Smith, *The Incomparable Book* (Minneapolis: Beacon, 1961), 9–10.
53. J. McDowell, *Evidence That Demands a Verdict*, 141–77, 274–93.

Chapter 6: Creation or Evolution

1. Cavendish, *Mythology, An Illustrated Encyclopedia*, 87, 97.
2. P. M. Scheele, *Degeneratie, het einde van de evolutietheorie* (Amsterdam: Buijten en Schipperheijn, 1997), 198.
3. Scheele, *Degeneratie*.
4. R. B. Goldschmidt, "Evolution, as Viewed by One Geneticist," *American Scientist* 40 (1952): 94.
5. S. Burgess, *Hallmarks of Design*, Dutch edition (Leominster: DayOne, 2000), 69–86.
6. M. Denton, *Evolution: A Theory in Crisis* (London: Burnett Books, 1985).
7. Godfrey, *Scientists Confront Creationism*, 117–38; E. Fluyt, "Praktikum in evolutie-lessen," *Bulletin voor het Onderwijs in de Biologie* 61 (1979): 376–77.
8. Denton, *Evolution*, 287.
9. Godfrey, *Scientists Confront Creationism*, 117–38.
10. F. S. Collins, *The Language of God* (New York: Free Press, 2006), 124–30.
11. Denton, *Evolution*, 291.
12. M. J. Behe, *Darwin's Black Box* (New York: Free Press, 1996), 24.
13. C. Darwin, *On the Origin of Species* (Cambridge: Harvard University Press, 1964), 189.
14. Burgess, *Hallmarks of Design*.
15. Behe, *Darwin's Black Box*, 179, 186.
16. C. O. Dunbar, *Historical Geology* (New York: Wiley, 1960), 47.
17. D. C. Johanson, "Lucy, en het begin van de mensheid," *Het Beste—Reader's Digest* (November 1981), 174–24.
18. H. M. Morris, *Scientific Creationism*, 2nd ed. (El Cajon, CA: Master Books, 1985), 173–74.
19. F. Spoor et al., "Implications of Early Hominid Labyrinthine Morphology for Evolution of Human Bipedal Locomotion," *Nature* 369 (1994): 645–48.
20. L. Hellemans, "Resten met een gouden randje," *Intermediair* 30, no. 47 (1994): 27, 29.
21. S. Zuckerman, "Correlation of Change in the Evolution of Higher Primates," in *Evolution as a Process*, eds. J. Huxley, A. C. Hardy, and E. B. Ford, 307 (London: Allen & Unwin, 1958), 307.
22. G. G. Simpson, *The Major Features of Evolution* (New York: Colombia University Press, 1953), 263.
23. Darwin, *Origin of Species*, 179.
24. T. Neville George, "Fossils in Evolutionary Perspective," *Science Progress* 48 (1960): 1, 3.
25. N. Eldredge, *Time Frames* (New York: Simon & Schuster, 1986), 145.

26. N. Eldredge and S. J. Gould, "Punctuated Equilibrium: An Alternative to Phyletic Gradualism," in *Models in Paleobiology*, ed. T. J. M. Schopf (San Francisco: Freeman, Cooper, 1972), 82–115.

27. S. J. Gould, "An Asteroid to Die For," *Discover*, October 1989, 65; Behe, *Darwin's Black Box*, 27; Simpson, *Major Features of Evolution*, 360.

28. E. J. H. Corner, "Evolution," in *Contemporary Botanical Thought*, eds. A. M. MacLeod and L. S. Cobley, 97 (Chicago: Quadrangle, 1961).

29. Denton, *Evolution*, 175–78, 205.

30. "Early Bird Born Late," *Nature* 351 (1991): 677–78.

31. C. Patterson, Address at the American Museum of National History, November 5, 1981, quoted in Brown, *In the Beginning*, 74.

32. Morris, *Scientific Creationism*, 107–8.

33. M. Garton, "The Scottish Piperock—Evidence of Rapid Deposition in the Cambrian," The Sixth European Creationist Congress, August 1995, in *Bijbel en Wetenschap* 182 (October 1995): 187–88.

34. E. A. von Fange, "Time Upside Down," *Creation Research Society Quarterly* 11 (1974): 13–27; P. S. Taylor, *The Illustrated Origins Answer Book* (Mesa, AZ: Eden Productions, 1995), 98–99.

35. M. A. Cremo and R. L. Thompson, *Forbidden Archeology* (San Diego: Bhaktivedanta Institute, 1993), 797–814.

36. *Het Beste—Reader's Digest*, March 1978, 26.

37. J. C. Dillow, *The Waters Above* (Chicago: Moody, 1981); Brown, *In the Beginning*, 103–313; J. R. Baumgardner et al., "Catastrophic Plate Tectonics: A Global Flood Model of Earth History" (Pittsburgh: Proceedings of the Third International Conference on Creationism, Creation Science Fellowship, 1994), 609–21.

38. F. Heeren, *Show Me God* (Wheeling, IL: Searchlight, 1995), 109.

39. R. H. Utt, ed., *Creation: Nature's Designs and Designer* (Mountain View, CA: Pacific Press, 1971).

40. H. P. Yockey, "A Calculation of the Probability of Spontaneous Biogenesis by Information Theory," *Journal of Theoretical Biology* 67 (1977): 337–98.

41. F. B. Salisbury, "Doubts about the Modern Synthetic Theory of Evolution," *American Biology Teacher*, September 1971, 336.

42. Behe, *Darwin's Black Box*; Burgess, *Hallmarks of Design*.

43. P. Davies, *Cosmic Jackpot: Why Our Universe Is Just Right for Life* (Boston: Houghton Mifflin, 2007), 149, 151.

44. J. Leslie, *Universes* (London: Routledge, 1989), 3–4, quoted in J. Byl, *God and Cosmos* (Edinburgh: Banner of Truth Trust, 2001), 98.

45. H. Ross, "The Big Bang Model Refined by Fire," in *Mere Creation: Science, Faith & Intelligent Design*, ed. W. A. Dembski (Downers Grove, IL: InterVarsity, 1998); M. Denton, *Nature's Destiny: How the Laws of Biology Reveal Purpose in the Universe* (New York: Free Press, 1998); W. A. Dembski, *Intelligent Design* (Downers Grove, IL: InterVarsity, 1999).

46. Original source unknown.

47. I. L. Cohen, *Darwin Was Wrong—A Study in Probabilities* (Greenvale, NY: New Research, 1984), 209–10.

48. Morris, *Scientific Creationism*; Taylor, *Illustrated Origins Answer Book.*

49. J. G. Funkhouser and J. J. Naughton, "Radiogenic Helium and Argon in Ultramafic Inclusions from Hawaii," *Journal of Geophysical Research* 73, no. 14 (1968): 4606.

50. S. A. Austin, "Excess Argon within Mineral Concentrates from the New Dacite Lava Dome at Mount St Helens Volcano," *Creation Ex Nihilo Technical Journal* 10, no. 3 (1996): 335–43.

51. A. A. Snelling, "Stumping Old-Age Dogma," *Creation* 20, no. 4 (1998): 48–50.

52. M. A. Cook, "Where Is the Earth's Radiogenic Helium?" *Nature* 179 (1957): 213; J. D. Morris, *The Young Earth* (Green Forest, AR: Master Books, 2001), 83–85.

53. D. DeYoung: *Thousands . . . Not Billions* (Dallas: Institute for Creation Research, 2005), 66–78.

54. S. A. Austin and D. R. Humphreys, "The Sea's Missing Salt: A Dilemma for Evolutionists" (Pittsburgh: Proceedings of the Second International Conference on Creationism, Creation Science Fellowship, 1990), 2:17–33.

55. J. P. Riley and G. Skirrow, eds., *Chemical Oceanography*, vol. 1 (London: Academic Press, 1965), 164.

56. A. Roth, *Origins: Linking Science and Scripture*, Dutch edition (Hagerstown, MD: Review and Herald, 1998), 274; A. Roth, "Some Questions about Geochronology," *Origins* 13, no. 2 (1986): 64–85.

57. S. E. Nevins, "Evolution, the Ocean Says No!," Institute for Creation Research Impact Series, *Acts & Facts* 2, no. 8 (October 1973).

58. T. G. Barnes, *Origin and Destiny of the Earth's Magnetic Field*, 2nd ed. (El Cajon, CA: Institute for Creation Research, 1983); T. G. Barnes, "Earth's Young Magnetic Age: An Answer to Dalrymple," *Creation Research Society Quarterly* 21, no. 3 (1984): 109–13.

59. D. R. Humphreys, "Reversals of the Earth's Magnetic Field during the Genesis Flood" (Pittsburgh: Proceedings of the First International Conference on Creationism, Creation Science Fellowship, 1986), 2:113–26. "The Earth's Magnetic Field Is Still Losing Energy," *Creation Research Society Quarterly* 39, no. 1 (2002): 1–11.

60. R. S. Coe and M. Prévot, "Evidence Suggesting Extremely Rapid Field Variation During a Geomagnetic Reversal," *Earth and Planetary Science Letters* 92 (1989): 292–98.

61. R. S. Coe, M. Prévot, and P. Camps, "New Evidence for Extraordinarily Rapid Change of the Geomagnetic Field During a Reversal," *Nature* 374 (April 20, 1995), 687–92; Morris, *Young Earth*, 74–83; A. A. Snelling, "The Earth's Magnetic Field and the Age of the Earth," *Creation Ex Nihilo* 13, no. 4 (1991): 44–48.

62. R. A. Lyttleton, "The Non-Existence of the Oort Cometary Shell," *Astrophysics and Space Science* 31 (1974): 385–401; P. M. Steidl, "Comets and Creation," *Creation Research Society Quarterly* 23 (March 1987): 153–60.

63. P. M. Steidl, *The Earth, the Stars, and the Bible* (Grand Rapids, MI: Baker, 1979), 60.

64. *The Astronomical Almanac for the Year 1989* (Washington, DC: U.S. Government Printing Office, 1989), E88; J. A. van Delden, "De taal van de hemel," *Bijbel en Wetenschap* 24 (1979): 22–23.

65. Taylor, *Illustrated Origins Answer Book.*

66. Dillow, *Waters Above*; Brown, *In the Beginning*, 103–313; Baumgardner et al., "Catastrophic Plate Tectonics," 609–21; L. Vardiman and K. Bousselot, "Sensitivity Studies on Vapor Canopy Temperature Profiles" (Pittsburgh: Proceedings of the Fourth International Conference on Creationism, Creation Science Fellowship, 1998), 607–18.

67. Tollmann and Tollmann-Kristan, *De zondvloed.*

68. Brown, *In the Beginning*, 103–67.

69. Baumgardner et al, "Catastrophic Plate Tectonics," 609–21; A. A. Snelling, "Can Catastrophic Plate Tectonics Explain Flood Geology?" (November 8, 2007), www.answersingenesis.org/articles/nab/catastrophic-plate-tectonics.

70. E. Ola d'Aulaire and P. Ola d'Aulaire, "Krakatau na 95 jaar," *Het Beste—Reader's Digest*, February 1979, 68–73.

71. Austin, *Grand Canyon*, 104–7.

72. D. B. Simons and F. Sentürk, *Sediment Transport Technology* (Littleton, CO: Water Resources, 1992), 630; T. J. Trout, "Sediment Transport in Irrigation Furrows," in D. E. Stott, R. H. Mohtar, and G. C. Steinhardt, eds., *Sustaining the Global Farm* (West Lafayette. IN: Purdue University, 2001), 711.

73. M. Oard, "Frozen Mammoth Carcasses in Siberia," 2004, www.answersingenesis.org.

74. Dillow, *Waters Above*, 387–90, 414.

75. Brown, *In the Beginning*, 228–61.

76. S. W. Nevins, "The Origin of Coal," Impact Series 41 (San Diego: Institute for Creation Research), 1–4; R. Hayatsu et al., "Artificial Coalification Study: Preparation and Characterization of Synthetic Materials," *Organic Geochemistry* 6 (1984): 463–71.

77. Morris, *Scientific Creationism*, 109.

78. Roth, *Origins*, 225–26.

79. H. S. Ladd, "Ecology, Paleontology, and Stratigraphy," *Science* 129 (1959): 72.

80. E. Colbert, *Men and Dinosaurs* (New York: Dutton, 1968), 58.

81. Roth, *Origins*, 175.

82. E. van der Heide, "Creationisme en geologie: Een kwestie van tijd?," *Bijbel en Wetenschap* 214 (1999): 166.

83. R. Liebi, *Der Mensch—Ein Sprechender Affe? Sprachwissenschaft contra Evolution* (Berneck: Schwengeler Verlag, 1991).

84. G. G. Simpson, "The Biological Nature of Man," *Science* 152 (1966): 477.

85. B. Setterfield and T. G. Norman, *The Atomic Constants, Light, and Time* (Adelaide, Australia: Creation Science Association, 1990).

86. V. S. Troitskii, "Physical Constants and the Evolution of the Universe," *Astrophysics and Space Science* 139, no. 2 (1987): 389–411; S. Adams, "The Speed of Light," *New Scientist* 2326 (January 19, 2002).

87. H. M. Arp, *Quasars, Redshifts, and Controversies* (Berkeley, CA: Interstellar Media, 1987); W. G. Tifft, "Properties of the Redshift," *Astrophysical Journal* 382 (1991): 396–415; Byl, *God and Cosmos,* 49, 52, 65, 72–74, 189–91.

88. F. Guterl, "Crazy Speed Demon," *Newsweek,* March 10, 2003, 42.

89. E. Lerner, "Bucking the Big Bang," *New Scientist* 2448 (May 22, 2004); see also www.cosmologystatement.org.

90. J. Glandz: "Faster Than Light, Maybe, but Not Back to the Future," *New York Times,* May 30, 2000; P. T. Pappas and A. G. Obolensky, "Thirty-six Nanoseconds Faster Than Light," *Electronics and Wireless World* (1988): 1162–65.

91. D. DeYoung: *Thousands . . . Not Billions* (Dallas: Institute for Creation Research, 2005), 48–62.

92. Denton, *Evolution,* 291, 345.

93. Denton, *Evolution,* 353–54.

Chapter 7: The Reliability of the Bible

1. H. M. Kuitert, *Jezus, nalatenschap van het christendom* (Baarn: Ten Have, 1998), 176.

2. E. Linnemann, *Hoe wetenschappelijk is de wetenschappelijke theologie?* (Ridderkerk: Vereniging tot opbouw en bewaring van het gereformeerde leven, 1986), 2.

3. M. J. Paul, *Het Archimedisch punt van de pentateuchkritiek* ('s-Gravenhage: Boekencentrum, 1988), 224, 231; A. Kuenen, *De godsdienst van Israël,* vol. 1 (Haarlem: Kruseman, 1869–1870), 111; J. Wellhausen, *Israelitische und Jüdische Geschichte* (Berlin: Reimer, 1894, 1959), 12.

4. Linnemann, *Hoe wetenschappelijk is de wetenschappelijke theologie?,* 9, 13.

5. Pache, *Inspiration and Authority of Scripture,* 34, 74, 90; F. J. Dake, *Dake's Annotated Reference Bible* (Lawrenceville, GA: Dake Bible Sales, 1982), O.T. 513; N.T. 241.

6. J. H. Kramers, *De Koran* (Amsterdam: De Arbeiderspers, 1992), 7.

7. M. Batchelor, *De Bijbel gaat open* (Amsterdam: Vereniging tot Verspreiding der Heilige Schrift, 1998), 28.

8. D. J. Baarslag, *De Bijbelse geschiedenis,* vol. 1 (Baarn: Bosch & Keuning, 1947), 376.

9. H. Binnendijk, *De tabernakel* (Hilversum: Evangelische Omroep, 1981); R. P. Daniel, *Gods tent in de woestijn* (Apeldoorn: Medema, 1981); B. R. Hicks, *Precious Gem in the Tabernacle* (Jefferson, IN: Christ Gospel Press, 1972).

10. E. van der Poll, *De feesten van Israël* (Putten: Shalom Books, 2002); W. J. Ouweneel, *Hoogtijden voor Hem* (Vaassen: Medema, 2001); H. G. Koekoek, *De geheimen van de offers* (Alphen aan de Rijn: Het Licht des Levens, 1986).

11. F. J. Meldau, *57 Reasons Why We Know That the Bible Is the Word of God,* Dutch edition (Denver: Christian Victory, 1956), 62.

12. A. Deedat, *50.000 Errors in the Bible?* (Durban, South Africa: Islamic Propagation Centre).

13. J. W. Haley, *An Examination of the Alleged Discrepancies of the Bible* (Grand Rapids, MI: Baker, 1977); G. L. Archer, *Encyclopedia of Bible Difficulties* (Grand Rapids, MI: Zondervan, 1982); N. L. Geisler, *Inerrancy* (Grand Rapids, MI: Zondervan, 1980).

14. E. R. Thiele, *The Mysterious Numbers of the Hebrew Kings* (Grand Rapids, MI: Zondervan, 1983).

15. Linnemann, *Hoe wetenschappelijk is de wetenschappelijke theologie?* 15; E. Linnemann, *Is There a Synoptic Problem?* (Grand Rapids, MI: Baker, 1992).

16. Haley, *Alleged Discrepancies of the Bible.*

17. H. F. Kohlbrugge, "De Engel des Heeren boven den dorschvloer van Arauna den Jebusiet," *Standvastig,* September 1986, 13–14.

18. T. Baarda, *De betrouwbaarheid van de Evangeliën* (Kampen: Kok, 1967), 29; W. H. Burr, *Self Contradictions of the Bible* (Buffalo, NY: Prometheus, 1860, 1987).

19. B. Thylefors, et al., *Global Data on Blindness, Bulletin of the World Health Organization,* 1995, 73–81, 115–121. See also www.who.int/blindness/data_maps/blindness.jpg.

20. J. McDowell, *The New Evidence That Demands a Verdict* (Nashville: Nelson, 1999), 34, 72–73, 90; H. H. Morris, *Many Infallible Proofs* (El Cajon, CA: Master Books, 1988), 40.

21. N. R. Lightfoot, *How We Got the Bible* (Grand Rapids, MI: Baker, 1965), 71; Pache, *Inspiration and Authority of Scripture,* 174.

22. Pache, *Inspiration and Authority of Scripture,* 177.

23. K. D. Miller, "The War of the Scrolls," *Christianity Today,* October 6, 1997, 39–45.

24. McDowell, *New Evidence,* 90.

25. N. L. Geisler and W. E. Nix, *A General Introduction to the Bible* (Chicago: Moody, 1968).

26. Deedat, *50.000 Errors in the Bible?*

27. B. F. Westcott and J. F. A. Hort, *The New Testament in the Original Greek* (New York: Harper, 1882), 2.

28. Haley, *Alleged Discrepancies of the Bible.*

29. Pache, *Inspiration and Authority of Scripture,* 178–80. 43.

30. E. Nestle and K. Aland, eds., *Novum Testamentum Graece* (Stuttgart: Deutsche Bibelgesellschaft, 1979).

31. Haley, *Alleged Discrepancies of the Bible*; B. M. Metzger, *A Textual Commentary on the Greek New Testament* (Stuttgart: United Bible Societies, 1975).

32. Nestle and Aland, *Novum Testamentum Graece*; Metzger, *Textual Commentary on the Greek New Testament.*

33. A. G. Knevel, M. J. Paul, and J. Broekhuis, eds., *Verkenningen in Genesis* (Kampen: Kok, 1986); G. L. Archer, *A Survey of Old Testament Introduction* (Chicago: Moody, 1980).

34. C. Marston, *The Bible Is True* (London: Eyre & Spottiswoode, 1934), 58–61, with quotations from S. H. Langdon, "Semitic Mythology," in *The Mythology of All Races,* vol. 5 (Boston: Archaeological Institute of America, Marshall Jones Co., 1931).

35. D. Richardson, *Eternity in Their Hearts* (Ventura, CA: Regal, 1984); R. R. De Ridder, *Discipling the Nations* (Grand Rapids, MI: Baker, 1975), 390–403.

36. W. Schmidt, *The Origin and Growth of Religion* (New York: Dial Press, 1931); De Ridder, *Discipling the Nations.*

37. M. F. Unger, *Unger's Bible Dictionary* (Chicago: Moody, 1971), 1174; Millard, *Discoveries from Bible Times,* 81.

38. Millard, *Discoveries from Bible Times,* 61–62; A. E. Wilder Smith, *The Reliability of the Bible* (San Diego: Master Books, 1983), 45.

39. Frank, *In het voetspoor van de Bijbel.*

40. Thiele, *Mysterious Numbers of the Hebrew Kings.*

41. Glueck, *Rivers in the Desert,* 31.

42. W. J. Albright, *The Archaeology of Palestine* (Baltimore: Penguin Books, 1949), 225.

43. "Geen spoor van Exodus of Davids koninkrijk," *Dagblad Trouw,* October 29, 1999, 17.

44. E. Yamauchi, *The Stones and the Scripture* (Grand Rapids, MI: Baker, 1972), 146–57.

45. Yahuda, *Language of the Pentateuch;* M. H. A. van der Valk, *Mozes' boeken in Egyptisch licht* (Kampen: Kok, 1930); W. J. J. Glashouwer and W. J. Ouweneel, *Het ontstaan van de Bijbel* (Hilversum: Evangelische Omroep, 1998), 145; Archer, *Survey of Old Testament,* 111–14.

46. J. G. Duncan, *New Light on Hebrew Origins* (London: Macmillan, 1936), 176.

47. Douglas, *New Bible Dictionary,* 43.

48. McDowell, *New Evidence,* 90.

49. www.falasha.org and similar sites.

50. Albright, *The Archaeology of Palestine,* 224, 225.

51. A. Lüscher, *Wenn das Wort nicht mehr soll gelten,* 16, quoted in Pache, *Inspiration and Authority of Scripture,* 119.

52. J. Kits, *Kunnen wij de Bijbel vertrouwen?* (Zeist: Morgenster-Stichting,1974), 73.

Chapter 8: A Few More Facts

1. A. Malamat, "Origins and the Formative Period," in *A History of the Jewish People,* ed. H. H. Ben-Sasson, 61 (Cambridge: Harvard University Press, 1976).

2. Grzimek, *Animal Life Encyclopedia,* vol. 3, 385–86.

3. A. Hüttermann, "Die ökologische Botschaft der Tora," *Naturwissenschaften* 80 (1993): 153; A. Aarsbergen, *Kroniek van Nederland* (Amsterdam: Elsevier, 1987), 114.

4. K. W. Weeber, *Smog über Attika* (Zürich-München: Artemis, 1990), 45.

5. J. N. D. Anderson, "A Dialogue on Christ's Resurrection," *Christianity Today,* April 12, 1968, 12.

6. A. Kuyper, "De verflauwing der grenzen," address on the transference of the vice-chancellorship of the VU.

INDEX